An Inventory of State and Local Income Transfer Programs

Fiscal Year 1977

An Inventory
of
State and Local
Income Transfer Programs

Fiscal Year 1977

William J. Lawrence

and

Stephen Leeds

With a Foreword by
Leonard M. Greene
President, The Institute for Socioeconomic Studies

THE INSTITUTE FOR SOCIOECONOMIC STUDIES
White Plains   New York

CONTENTS

FOREWORD

In conjunction with its interest in welfare reform, The Institute for Socioeconomic Studies has sponsored a comprehensive inventory of government income transfer programs. It is hoped that increased understanding of the transfer system now in place will provide a basis for constructive proposals for change. The project has been directed by Dr. William J. Lawrence, director of the Institute for Economic Research, Pace University Graduate School of Business.

The first phase of the investigation resulted in the publication of *An Inventory of Federal Income Transfer Programs.* This volume compiled data on 182 programs for fiscal year 1977 with total Federal expenditures of $248 billion. It comprised the first altogether comprehensive review of the Federal government's efforts to maintain personal income and "fight poverty." The current volume, *An Inventory of State and Local Income Transfer Programs,* completes the study.

While there were many difficulties in compiling the Federal inventory, the state and local inventory proved far more troublesome. The complexities of dealing with 50 states, plus hundreds of local governments, are obvious. For this reason there has been little prior work in the area.

As compared to $248 billion of Federal income transfers in 1977, state and local transfers amounted to $50 billion in 1977. Some of this is state and local spending on federally mandated programs. Actually, less than ten percent of the nation's income transfers are initiated by state and local governments.

Although state and local responsibility in the sphere of income transfers is dwarfed by that of the Federal government, it is important to recognize what is being done by state and local echelons. To that end, this volume provides data on 633 different programs.

It is hoped that the comprehensive inventories of Federal, state and local income transfer programs will contribute significantly to the understanding of our present transfer system. With this knowledge we can begin to consider alternatives that could improve coordination of programs and provide greater equity and efficiency.

Leonard M. Greene
President
The Institute for Socioeconomic Studies

White Plains, N.Y.
July 1980

ACKNOWLEDGMENTS

This report, on state and locally originated programs, represents the second phase of a study in the development of a national inventory of those public income transfer programs that provide individuals with cash and other benefits to support their current standard of living.

Our research has been supported by grants from The Institute for Socioeconomic Studies, White Plains, New York. We are particularly grateful to Dr. Leonard M. Greene, president of The Institute, for his support, counsel and guidance.

We are also indebted to the members of the Department of Economics of Pace University's Graduate School of Business and to the following research assistants who participated in the collection of state and local government program data: Richard Cohn, Lucille Douglas, Robin Gellis, Lilly Karabaic and Richard Serrins. Mr. Serrins derived many of the program outlay estimates.

This report would not have been possible were it not for the scores of state and local government officials who took the time to explain the funding and operation of various programs. We hope that this compilation of programs may prove to be a helpful reference document to those officials as well as to those concerned with rationalizing and simplifying the nation's income security system.

William J. Lawrence
Director
Institute for Economic Research

Stephen Leeds
Policy Analyst

Pace University Graduate School of Business
New York, New York
July 1980

INTRODUCTION

Very little has been accomplished during recent years in the way of simplifying and rationalizing the nation's welfare and other income security programs, even given an early expressed interest in precisely this goal by the Carter Administration. The recent trend, if anything, seems to be in the opposite direction, toward a proliferation of public programs providing cash and other benefits to support individuals' current standard of living.

It is difficult to envision how an effective strategy for national "welfare reform" can even be conceptualized without first taking into account the myriad other programs which, while not strictly known as welfare or public assistance, also distribute essential benefits to various segments of the population. Although many of these programs are aimed at the lower-income stratum in general, other programs benefit middle-and upper-income persons as well. This often occurs because a program's target group is defined by a demographic characteristic, like age, rather than by individual income. Typically, the target group is deliberately structured to include non-poor persons in the hope of broadening the program's appeal and, therefore, its base of support.

A better understanding of the programs currently in place is essential to any long-term improvement in the social welfare system.

This report identifies and describes 633 income transfer programs, originating and primarily funded at the state and local levels of government. Thus, this report follows up our previous work, *An Inventory of Federal Income Transfer Programs, Fiscal Year 1977*, in which 182 different programs originating and primarily funded at the Federal level of government are described.

We estimate that $50 billion was spent on income transfers in fiscal year 1977 by state and local governments, concurrent with the $248 billion of Federal expenditures. Many of the 182 federally enabled programs are designed to operate at the state and local levels by means of a system of intergovernmental grants and administrative agreements. The most important of these are: Aid to

Families with Dependent Children, Social Services and Medicaid. Those three programs represent approximately 75% of all state and local dollars spent on federally enabled programs.

Although the state and locally operated versions of such federally enabled programs are not described in detail in this report, it is important to realize that they account for an estimated $16 billion or approximately a third of all state and local expenditures for income transfer purposes (see Table A).

TABLE A

Estimated State and Local Outlays
for Income Transfer Programs, FY 77
($ in billions)

	Outlay
All states, federally initiated programs...	
To match Federal intergovernmental aid	$16
To parallel Federal income tax provisions	3
25 larger states...	
State-initiated programs	19
Locally initiated programs	7
25 smaller states...	
State-initiated programs	3
Locally initiated programs	2
Total state and local outlays	$50

The program descriptions included in this report, as in the preceding Federal report, are not meant to be exhaustive or definitive. Their purpose is to impart a general understanding of each program's objectives, cost and impact during fiscal year 1977, thus enabling the reader to gain an overall impression of the variety of approaches currently in use by state and local governments. More detailed information about any particular program should be obtained from its administering agency.

Project Approach

In the preceding Federal inventory, we defined public income transfer benefits as government-funded and -regulated assistance which serves to maintain or to supplement the current standard of living of individuals whose personal incomes and resources are inadequate, or who have suffered either a substantial reduction in in-

Introduction

come or increase in expenses, or who are at risk of any of the above. Generally, such benefits are provided to, or on behalf of, individuals from whom the government does not require a product, service or asset in return. And, generally, these individuals must prove their need (e.g., through insufficient income and assets) and/or demonstrate certain qualifying characteristics (e.g., old age, disability) categorically associated with need.

Public income transfer programs provide benefits to individuals in various forms:

1. in direct cash payments, with or without restrictions on their use;
2. in indirect cash payments, by means of decreased personal tax liabilities resulting from property and income tax credits and from reductions in taxable property and income due to exclusions, exemptions and deductions;
3. in kind, through the direct provision, or indirect purchase, of essential goods and services (i.e., food, clothing, shelter, medical care) not otherwise available, or at lower prices or fees than in the private sector;
4. in credit, by means of loans and/or loan guarantees not otherwise available, or at more favorable terms (i.e., lower interest rates, longer maturities, smaller down payments) than in the private sector; and
5. in insurance, by means of policies and policy guarantees not otherwise available, or available at more favorable terms (i.e., lower premiums, greater coverage) than in the private sector.

To delimit the foregoing further, public income transfer benefits as defined in this study generally do *not* include:

1. government-funded grants or fellowships, not based on financial need, for advanced study and/or research in specified fields, or for participation in international exchange programs, since their primary aim is other than support for the beneficiary's standard of living;
2. government subsidies to business, or to individuals in their roles as producers, investors and factor owners in the marketplace, if the overriding aim is to influence their economic behavior or supplement their presently or potentially inadequate standard of living;
3. government-funded public services, facilities and projects which are accessible to, and for the general benefit of, an entire community or segment thereof and which do not selectively confer discrete and measurable amounts of current income support upon needy individuals; and
4. government-funded protective or custodial services for wards of the state such as homeless children, juvenile offenders, prisoners and mental incompetents.

Programs traditionally considered part of the income security system provide cash or in-kind benefits and fall within the above constraints. With a few exceptions, programs providing tax, credit and insurance benefits, in that order, are less likely to be considered in the income security context.

A somewhat special case included in the state and local inventory is in the Workers' Compensation program. To workers injured on the job, it provides cash benefits in the form of disability compensation, and cash or in-kind benefits, to cover the cost of medical care. While the program is actually state-run in several jurisdictions, in the others it is only state-regulated, but actually run through private insurers. For the sake of consistency, and because program costs are mandated by state law, even if not always paid from state coffers, this study contains Workers' Compensation programs for all states. These programs account for over ten percent of all state and local income transfer outlays.

We noted in our preceding inventory that, despite the evident disagreement among policy analysts regarding which income transfer programs—like Workers' Compensation—to consider in relation to welfare reform, we choose to represent all types of programs. We recognize that the inclusion of some programs in the following pages is sure to engender a measure of debate, but it may also broaden our horizons when we contemplate the directions and dimensions which national welfare reform ought to assume. That, in the final analysis, is what our study is all about.

Project Scope

In the first report on our study, we mentioned the more significant past attempts to identify and describe the nation's public income transfer system. We noted, in passing, that very little work had been done in this regard at the state and local levels where the multiplicity of program approaches defies easy categorization.

We began our study by examining Federal programs before undertaking any analysis of state or local programs. We chose this schedule for several reasons. Obviously, Federal benefits are most immediately relevant to the issues of national welfare reform which were then being deliberated by Congress and the Carter Administration. Federal programs also account for the overwhelming proportion of income transfer expenditures, and the Federal initiatives are much better documented than those of the lower levels of government. Furthermore, the Federal income transfer system largely determines the form and substance of state and local systems since they are typically designed to conform to the funding requirements of, fill in the gaps between, and supplement the effects wrought by, Federal initiatives.

4

Introduction

In order to prescribe manageable limits to the study of state and local programs, we had to reduce the total number of programs to be described. We accomplished this objective in three ways:

1. by excluding descriptions of state and local versions of federally enabled and predominantly federally funded programs, since the overall program aspects have already been described in our Federal report (but state and local contributions to the three largest Federal programs are given for each state);
2. by focusing on state-enabled programs, since local initiatives are generally either nonexistent or of small moment; and
3. by examining only the 25 largest-spending states, since they account for 83 percent of all government expenditures below the Federal level.

While we have not described all state and local programs, we have estimated their total cost on the basis of published data.

Thus, of the $273 billion that state and local governments directly spent for all purposes including income security in fiscal year 1977, almost $65 billion were in Federal intergovernmental grants and aid. While much of these Federal funds went to assist state-run programs, much was also passed on to the localities by the states. Additional billions circumvented state agencies entirely, going straight from the Federal government to local jurisdictions. As a consequence, Federal funds find their way into an incredible variety of state and local programs.

To complicate the pattern of Federal involvement further, in one state a program may be predominantly federally financed, but in another state the same program may have little or no Federal funding. Unfortunately, state and local officials frequently are unable to specify the flow of Federal dollars below the departmental level into various programs under their jurisdiction. This results, in part, from the fact that $77 billion, or 43 percent, of all $180 billion in local general revenue in fiscal year 1977 came from state and Federal aid. Thus, almost half of all funds available to local government do not originate within its jurisdiction. Whenever our analysis of any program's financing revealed that half or more of its funds derived from Federal aid, that program's description was excluded from the inventory.

A somewhat special case, in this regard, is the Supplemental Security Income (SSI) program which provides public assistance to needy aged, blind and disabled persons. The Federal SSI program establishes a national income floor for such persons and requires no state or local matching funds. However, Congress recognized that its national standard might be deemed inadequate by some states; accordingly, they were invited to establish their own, self-financed and regulated programs, in order to raise the level of support within each state. Since state SSI programs are completely optional and fully state-funded, their descriptions are included in the inventory.

We concentrated our analysis on state-enabled programs; one of our feasibility studies had uncovered few significant income transfer programs originating at the county or municipal government level. In most states, in fact, it would be unconstitutional for a local jurisdiction to establish any such program other than pursuant to appropriate state law. Where such legislative authority does exist, it might simply be permissive, allowing localities, if they so choose, to set up and fund a specified program. In other instances, state law is mandatory, even to the point of requiring localities to fund the entire program cost themselves. Generally, however, the state shares the cost of such programs with the local jurisdictions. In any event, identifying every local version of a state-enabled program would be an enormously time-consuming and repetitious task, so we limited ourselves to the more general state-level program descriptions.

Table B lists the 25 states encompassed by our research effort. (They are ranked according to their levels of direct general expenditures by state governments, for all purposes, in fiscal year 1977; and the total of state and local direct expenditures is presented for each state.) The half of the states we examined, together with their local jurisdictions, accounted for five-sixths of all government expenditures below the Federal level in fiscal year 1977. Consequently, while there are surely many income transfer programs also operating in the 25 unexamined states, their outlays are just as surely of minor import, as compared to those covered in the following pages.

We have derived estimates of the total cost of the state and local income transfer systems for programs that implement Federal initiatives as well as for those that address problems and populations disregarded, or at least inadequately addressed, by Federal law.

In essence then, the scope of the second phase of our research has been:

1. to collect illustrative information identifying and describing as many state-enabled and predominantly state-funded income transfer programs as possible, within the 25 states with the greatest direct expenditures, and
2. to compile estimates of 1977 income transfer outlays for these programs and for all similar programs in the 50 states and their local jurisdictions.

Introduction

These estimates of aggregate expenditures were calculated on the basis of data published by the U.S. Census Bureau for its 1977 Government Finances series; by the U.S. Department of Health, Education and Welfare, for its annual Social Welfare Expenditures series; by the U.S. Treasury Department, for its annual Federal Aid to States series; by the Advisory Commission on Intergovernmental Relations, for its studies of property tax circuit-breakers and the intergovernmental grants system; and by the National Technical Information Services office.

TABLE B

Direct General Expenditures, All Purposes
($ in millions)

State	Rank	State Government	State & Local Government
California	1	$ 9,942	$ 32,532
New York	2	8,175	32,178
Pennsylvania	3	6,181	13,747
Illinois	4	5,704	14,237
Texas	5	5,133	12,873
Michigan	6	4,801	12,687
Ohio	7	3,944	11,872
New Jersey	8	3,424	9,723
Massachusetts	9	3,395	7,968
Florida	10	2,885	9,288
Virginia	11	2,456	5,672
Louisiana	12	2,294	4,734
Washington	13	2,268	4,964
North Carolina	14	2,148	5,426
Georgia	15	2,121	5,061
Maryland	16	2,113	6,013
Wisconsin	17	2,089	6,147
Minnesota	18	2.024	5,803
Kentucky	19	1,986	3,480
Alabama	20	1,862	3,696
Indiana	21	1,851	5,080
Tennessee	22	1,833	4,266
Missouri	23	1,741	4,524
Connecticut	24	1,607	3,579
South Carolina	25	1,560	2,814
25-state subtotal		83,538	228,364
50-state total		$103,525	$273,002

Source: Table 4, *Governmental Finances in 1976-77,* GF77 No. 5, U.S. Census Bureau.

Methodological Considerations

We obtained and reviewed all applicable state budgets, annual governor's reports and audits for fiscal years 1977 and 1978. In addition, detailed requests for information were sent to an average of ten department heads in each of the 25 states, in the search for data and programs that might be included in the inventory. All of these sources were utilized to identify state-enabled programs and costs. In order to ascertain the full scale of program characteristics, however, person-to-person discussion with administrative personnel was frequently required.

As a cross-check on our preliminary findings, we examined programs from the perspective of a number of the budgets of major municipalities and counties. By and large, these documents were of minimal value for our purposes. City budgets, for example, typically consist of line-item entries without an accompanying descriptive text.

A further problem at the state and local level stems from the distinctive ways in which each jurisdiction fuses the inherent qualities of its policies with those of a major program, in terms not only of target population and services but also of funding and operation. Given a specific program, in some states, it is actually run by state personnel; in others, it is wholly or partly funded by the state, but run by local officials. In some states, the program purchases a service. In others, it provides the service itself. In some states, the program exists in its own right. In others, it is actually but one function of a larger, more comprehensive program.

All these inconsistencies in approach can make a cross-state comparison virtually meaningless. In examining the inventory, the reader must bear these factors in mind, as well as recognize that the absence of a program description for the state does not necessarily mean that the program is not available there. The program might be predominantly federally funded, or its functions might be subsumed under another program name.

In order to be able to factor out those programs either predominantly of Federal origination or else principally designed to capture Federal matching funds, we attempted with little success to secure audit data, from appropriate Federal officials, relating to required state and local matching contributions. The audit arm of various Federal agencies could not collate most of the needed data on a state-by-state basis. Our concern with this topic stemmed from a desire not to double-count Federal dollars. We wanted to avoid counting the same funds as part of a state or local expenditure in our second phase as were already counted as a Federal expenditure in our first phase.

Introduction

Beyond all these technical and methodological considerations regarding direct expenditures, we were also faced with a major problem regarding indirect, or tax, expenditures. While the concept that differential tax relief for certain groups constitutes an indirect outlay is relatively new among Federal policy analysts, it is generally ignored, if not unheard of, among their state and local counterparts. Therefore, information about tax expenditures (i.e., foregone tax revenue) is typically unavailable below the Federal level of government. For example, among the 25 states surveyed, only the following had any applicable data regarding their personal income tax provisions: Indiana, Minnesota, New Jersey, Ohio and Wisconsin. And, to find cost estimates for property tax measures, we had to turn to the staff of the Advisory Commission on Intergovernmental Relations rather than to the individual states.

While a few states had cost estimates for some specialized exclusions from sales taxation (e.g., food for seeing-eye dogs), we ended up disregarding sales taxes in our study. The major form of "relief" granted under sales tax law comes when dispensations are made excluding such essentials as food, clothing and medical purchases from taxation. Such blanket treatment does not, by our analysis, qualify as an income transfer benefit. Accordingly, sales tax provisions are not described in the inventory.

To recapitulate the funding sources considered in this inventory then, we have fully considered property tax income transfer provisions because solid data were available. Total state and local property tax revenues, in fiscal year 1977, were over $62 billion; and 96 percent went into the treasuries of local jurisdictions. On the other hand, we disregarded general sales taxes, which accounted for over $35 billion in total state and local revenues, 85 percent of which went into state treasuries. Similarly, we did not work with state and local income tax provisions, even though personal income taxation yielded a total of $29 billion in revenues, 90 percent of which went into state coffers. It was necessary to exclude the income tax revenues nonetheless; we could not get consistent or adequate data covering state and local income tax provisions.

Although we were unable to obtain data that would permit us to estimate the cost in foregone revenues of individual income tax provisions, we nevertheless attempted an estimate of the aggregate cost of all such state and local measures. (Three of the states we examined do not have an individual income tax: Florida, Texas and Washington. Two others do not have a broad-based individual income tax, but rather a dividend and interest income tax: Connecticut and Tennessee.) Since most state income transfer provisions in income tax law closely follow those available under Federal tax law, we applied the Federal revenue loss ratio for each provision to the states which have also adopted a version of the Federal provision, and then adjusted the resultant revenue loss downward to reflect the lower tax rates in effect at the state and local levels. For programs with no Federal counterparts, we roughly approximated tax expenditures. In the aggregate. we feel that the overall estimate derived is reasonable, but we do not publish our cost estimates of individual income tax provisions, because they are not sufficiently grounded in firm data.

How the Inventory is Organized

The inventory describes 633 state-enabled programs (This figure is somewhat arbitrary, inasmuch as many programs could have been subdivided further and presented as functional components.) In addition, preceding each state inventory we present a table of estimated state and local contributions, in fiscal year 1977, to the three principal federally enabled income maintenance programs: Aid to Families with Dependent Children, Social Services and Medicaid. These figures are provided solely as reference points to the expenditure estimates for the state and local programs that follow them. Each state's population and total expenditure figures are given to round out the picture.

Within each of the 25 surveyed states, programs are generally arranged in the following order:

I. benefits to replace earnings lost due to the age, disability, death or other absence of the primary earner;
2. benefits to supplement generally the income of the family;
3. benefits to improve the earnings potential of the individual;
4. personal income tax relief, by means of provisions that do not stem from those in Federal tax law.

This presentation of programs has been accomplished with only a moderate amount of "forcing square pegs into round holes." However, the programs could have been arranged just as satisfactorily by target population or type of benefit, by whether or not they are based on financial need, or even alphabetically by the name of the administering agency.

All such sequencing can be equally misleading to the general reader; there is no overriding scheme determining the national income transfer network. For this reason, a rigorous internal organization has been avoided. Programs with similar objectives and target populations tend to be near one another, regardless of their relative acceptability as elements of the income transfer system. We hope the reader will discover some thought-provoking juxtapositions.

At the top of each program description in the inventory is the program name, and underneath it is the state agency (or agencies)

10

responsible for program administration. We have chosen to use the state agency name under which it appears in the proposed 1978 state budget.

The narrative paragraph for each program describes in general terms the program's objective, target population, benefits, administration and financing, numbers of people served, and relation to individual need. In this context, "need" always refers to financial need. Program benefits said to be conditioned on need are provided only to individuals who are able to meet certain income and/or assets criteria for low income. Program benefits said to be conditioned in part on need are provided in relation to such criteria in only some specified instances, or in such a fashion that they also aid, but to a lesser degree, those who do not have low incomes. Program benefits said to be not directly conditioned on need are provided to individuals who are able to satisfy certain demographic requirements frequently related to low income. For program benefits said to be not conditioned on need, none of the above holds true.

At the bottom of each program description, except for those resulting from income tax laws, the estimated fiscal year 1977 expenditure is presented. (Comments, where necessary, are provided underneath that figure.) "Expenditure" in this context means outlay, as used in the Federal Budget, or revenue loss, in the case of tax relief programs. An outlay is the total of checks and cash disbursed during a fiscal year in carrying out a program; as such, it disregards whether the commitments for such disbursements were made in the present year or in the past, by contract or otherwise.

Expenditure figures in the inventory include estimates of each program's direct "overhead" (i.e., its share of administrative staff salaries and expenses,) as well as the costs of operations, maintenance, construction, and similar program support.

Every effort has been made to eliminate double-counting where intra-budget transfers occur. The inventory includes the transferred amount under one or the other of the programs affected by such bookkeeping practices.

Essentially, our estimation procedure for non-tax programs involved four steps:

1. making a first-cut approximation based on the fiscal year 1977 column of the 1978 state budget;
2. comparing such amounts to those in the documents and information received from program administrators;
3. discussing any substantial discrepancies between figures derived above with appropriate state and local officials; and

4. resolving remaining inconsistencies, when possible, with agreement among the various parties.

Any program deriving half or more of its funds from Federal sources has been excluded from the inventory, with the exception of AFDC, Social Services and Medicaid for which we present estimated state and local contributions in the beginning, as reference points for other state and local program expenditures. Programs with lesser proportions of Federal aid remain in the inventory, and the amount of Federal funding where known, is noted in the "Comments" section of the description. Also, we have not included those state and local income tax provisions that accomplish the same purpose as any Federal provisions described in our previous report.

Over all, the programs described in the inventory account for two-thirds of all state and local income transfer outlays, disregarding those expenditures mandated by Federal aid and matching formulas.

SUMMARY

We estimate that income transfer outlays by all levels of government accounted for an aggregate expenditure of $298 billion in fiscal year 1977.

Our analysis of the Federal income transfer system revealed 182 programs providing cash, tax-relief, in-kind, credit, and insurance benefits to individuals. These programs required an estimated $248 billion in direct and indirect Federal outlays. Comparable state and local government outlays amounted to an estimated $50 billion in fiscal year 1977. Thus, of the almost $300 billion spent by public income transfer programs during fiscal year 1977, just one dollar in six originated at the level of state and local government.

TABLE 1

Estimated Federal, State and Local Outlays
for Income Transfer Programs, FY 77
($ in billions)

Source	Outlay
Federal	
Program Outlay	
Direct Expenditure	$181
Intergovernmental aid to states and localities	32
Tax Expenditure	35
Total	$248
State and Local	
Program Outlay	
Share of Federally enabled programs	16
Programs inititated by states and localities	27
Tax Expenditure	7
Total	50
Total of All Programs	**$298**

A third of all state and local income transfer outlays consists of matching contributions to federally enabled programs. In fiscal year 1977, some $16 billion in state and local revenue was used to capture an estimated $32 billion in Federal inter-governmental aid for income transfer programs. In fact, just three programs of the U.S. Department of Health, Education and Welfare (i.e., Aid to Families with Dependent Children, Social Services, and Medicaid) accounted for all but a quarter of total state and local contributions to federally enabled income transfer assistance. While such Federal programs explicitly call for state and local matching funds, other Federal initiatives implicitly necessitate non-Federal contributions by providing insufficient financing to meet eligible program needs.

In summary, Federal programs were responsible for 90 percent of all income transfer outlays in fiscal year 1977:

- direct Federal outlays ($181 billion),
- Federal intergovernmental aid ($32 billion),
- programs requiring state and local matching revenues ($16 billion), and
- Federal tax expenditures ($35 billion).

Due to this virtual domination of the income transfer system by the Federal sector, the major policy options for system reform are inherent in the study of Federal programs rather than state and local operations.

Of the $34 billion expended in fiscal year 1977 by state and local governments on income transfer programs originating below the Federal level, we estimate that approximately $7 billion—or one dollar in five—took the form of tax relief. State and local officials generally do not consider such tax relief measures to constitute outlays. Thus, it seems that only $27 billion, or nine percent of the nation's income transfer outlays, may be attributed to conscious funding decisions by state and local officials. About a third of this amount is appropriated by state and local officials for the retirement and disability benefits of their own employees.

Federal Income Transfer Programs

Before proceeding to a description of state and local programs, a recapitulation of our findings about the Federal income transfer system is in order. At the Federal level, we found that:

- 62 percent of income transfer outlays are for programs providing cash benefits;
- 23 percent, in-kind assistance;
- 14 percent, tax relief; and
- one percent, credit and insurance benefits.

Summary

The predominance of cash aid reflects the presence of a relatively few, very large, social insurance programs. The Social Security system of retirement, survivors and disability payments alone accounts for half of all Federal cash outlays and a third of total Federal income transfer expenditures. Among Federal programs providing in-kind benefits, just two programs, Medicaid and Medicare, account for half the outlays. Among tax, credit and insurance programs, there is no similar domination by a couple of programs.

A fifth of the 182 Federal programs each expended a billion dollars or more in fiscal year 1977. At the other end of the spectrum, almost a third of the Federal programs each cost under $50 million. In 1977, the median Federal outlay for income transfer programs was $149 million.

Less than a fourth of all Federal outlays are provided, even in part, to individuals who must demonstrate inadequate income to qualify for aid. Almost two-thirds of all Federal outlays involve benefits to individuals who merely have to exhibit certain characteristics (e.g. old age, disability, residence in a poverty area) generally associated with lower incomes. And one-eighth of all Federal outlays do not require even this much of a test.

Finally, 70 percent of Federal outlays for income security are designed to replace the lost earnings of retired, disabled or deceased breadwinners; and Social Security accounts for three-fifths of these expenditures.

State and Local Income Transfer Programs

Estimated state and local outlays during fiscal year 1977, for the 633 income transfer programs in the 25-state inventory, total $19 billion. In addition, an estimated $3 billion in state and local income tax benefits are not included in the inventory because their descriptions closely parallel those contained in our preceding report on Federal income tax relief. Thus, the $22 billion in expenditures for income transfer purposes, identified during our study, amount to two-thirds of the $34 billion in total outlays of all state and local governments for non-Federal initiatives in the national income security system.

Although we cannot claim that the programs studied and included in the inventory are representative of all state and local income transfer initiatives, the fact that they account for such a large proportion of aggregate outlays permits us to generalize about our findings.

Among the state and local income transfer programs for which the inventory contains adequate expenditure estimates, the median program outlay, in fiscal year 1977, was $3.9 million. Because of the presence of some relatively very large programs in the inventory, the average outlay is substantially greater than the median; and in fiscal year 1977, the average was $32.4 million. Table 2 presents the distribution of programs for which we have adequate cost data, by their fiscal year 1977 outlay.

TABLE 2

Percentage Distribution of State-Enabled Income Transfer Programs, by Annual Outlay (25 Top States, FY 77)

Outlay[1] ($ in millions)	Distribution of Programs[2]
$ 0.0 - 0.24	10%
0.25 - 0.99	15
1.0 - 2.49	18
2.5 - 9.99	24
10.0 - 24.99	11
25.0 - 99.99	14
100.0 or more	8
	100%

Total Programs—575[2]

Total Outlays—$18,610 million[2]

Average Outlay—$32.4 million

Median Outlay—$3.9 million

[1] State and local funds only, excluding Federal aid and matching contributions.

[2] Excludes income transfer programs stemming from state and local personal income tax systems.

The programs in the 25-state inventory can be categorized by the form of benefit each provides, i.e., cash, in-kind, tax relief, credit or insurance. However, some of the largest programs provide two forms of benefits. Workers' Compensation, for example, provides both cash aid and in-kind medical care; and student financial assistance programs often provide both cash and credit benefits. Since these represent sizeable outlays, we have reallocated the appropriate sums and accordingly present the distribution, by benefit form, in Table 3.

TABLE 3

Percentage Distribution of State-Enabled Income Transfer Programs and Outlays, by Form of Benefit (25 Top States, FY 77)

Form of Benefit	Programs	Outlays[1]
Cash	41%	67%
In-kind	35	15
Tax Relief	20	14
Credit or Insurance	4	4
Total	100%	100%
	(633 programs)	($19.3 billion)

[1] State and local funds only, excluding Federal aid and matching contributions.

Two-thirds of the state-enabled income transfer outlays stem from cash benefits distributed by programs. Tax relief benefits account for one-seventh of outlays, as do in-kind benefits. Credit and insurance benefits account for only four percent of aggregate expenditures. Table 3 presents this distribution, which closely resembles that of Federal outlays.

The predominance of cash outlays results from the benefits of the Public Employee Retirement Systems, Optional SSI, Worker's Compensation, General Assistance, and various student aid grants. Most of the in-kind expenditures derive from health programs, including the medical care portion of Worker's Compensation. The tax relief outlays are mainly a function of property tax benefits for the elderly and disabled, as well as for veterans. In addition, data is provided estimating aggregate income tax relief encompassed in the programs listed in the inventory. Credit and insurance benefits stem from various programs offering student loans and home mortgage assistance.

Similar to what we found in our examination of Federal income transfer programs, state-enabled programs also provide benefits not predominantly as a function of income, but rather as a function of other conditions, such as age or disability.

Table 4 shows that just over one-quarter of the state-enabled income transfer outlays are provided by programs that even partly look into an applicant's financial situation. Two-thirds of the outlays are provided by programs that examine other characteristics. Six percent of the outlays require that neither income nor demographic conditions be satisfied.

TABLE 4

Percentage Distribution of State-Enabled Income Transfer Programs and Outlays, by Benefit Relationship to Financial Need (25 Top States, FY 77)

Relationship of Benefit to Need	Programs	Outlays[1]
Conditioned on need	32%	25%
Conditioned, in part, on need	9	2
Not directly conditioned on need	43	67
Not conditioned on need	16	6
Total	100% (633 programs)	100% ($19.3 billion)

[1] State and local funds only, excluding Federal aid and matching contributions.

As we see in Table 5, almost three-fourths of the state-enabled outlays serve the purpose of replacing income lost through the retirement, disability or death of the breadwinner. One-fourth serves the purpose of supplementing household income generally. Four percent are intended to improve the earning potential of the individual through rehabilitation, training or post-secondary education.

TABLE 5

Percentage Distribution of State-Enabled Income Transfer Programs and Outlays, by Program Rationale (25 Top States, FY 77)

Program Rationale	Programs	Outlays[1]
To replace earnings lost due to age, disability, death, etc.	37%	73%
To supplement generally the income of the family	45	23
To improve the earnings potential of the individual	18	4
Total	100% (575 programs)	100% ($18.6 billion)

[1] State and local funds only, excluding Federal aid and matching contributions.

18

Summary

In most regards, the summary characteristics of the programs included in the 25-state inventory resemble those of the Federal programs described in the previous volume. In the following pages, individual program descriptions give the reader a more detailed impression of what these state-enabled programs are like.

ALABAMA

Population: 3,690,000

Total State and Local Expenditures
for all Purposes:
$3,696,000,000

MAJOR FEDERALLY ENABLED
INCOME TRANSFER PROGRAMS

FY 77 Expenditures (est.)

Program	State	Local
Aid to Families with Dependent Children	$25,010,000	$ 0
Medicaid	54,740,000	0
Social Services	7,150,000	0

OPTIONAL STATE SUPPLEMENTATION FOR SSI

Department of Pensions and Security

The aged, over 65 years old, the blind and the disabled are provided cash supplements to their Federal SSI benefits for basic and special needs. Basic needs are food, shelter, clothing, utilities and daily living necessities. Special needs are those not provided for through monthly or optional SSI payments and include nursing or attendant care services. Benefits are provided to eligible couples living independently, to individuals and couples in personal or foster-care homes, in cerebral palsy treatment centers and in nursing homes or tuberculosis hospitals. Benefits are $35 monthly for couples living independently and vary for other categories. Benefits are in the form of direct cash payments, funded wholly by the state. Payments are administered by the state, but eligibility is determined at the county level. Over 19,500 individuals receive benefits monthly. Benefits are conditioned on need.

FY 77 Expenditure (est.): **$12,540,000**

PEACE OFFICERS' ANNUITY AND BENEFIT FUND

Treasury Department

Full-time peace officers who retire at age 52 with 20 years of service, at age 65 with 15 years of service, or regardless of age with 30 years of service, and their dependents are provided with financial assistance to replace income lost through retirement. Benefits are paid directly to the beneficiary in the form of cash without any restriction on its use. Payments range between $89 and $185 per month. Some 550 individuals benefit from this program. Members contribute $10 a month while the state does not directly contribute. This program is partially financed by court fees. This is a voluntary program whose members may also participate in the Public Employees' Retirement System. Benefits are not directly conditioned on need.

FY 77 Expenditure (est.): **$1,136,500**

Benefits paid total $1,016,000.
Administrative costs total $120,500.

Alabama

TEACHERS' RETIREMENT SYSTEM

Treasury Department

Full-time employees of Alabama public schools, who retire at age 60 with at least ten years of service, or regardless of age with 30 years of service, and their dependents are provided with financial assistance to replace income lost through retirement. Benefits are paid directly to the beneficiary in the form of cash without any restriction on its use. Payments average $376 per month. Some 1,450 individuals benefit from this program. Members contribute five percent of salary while the state contributes about 14 percent. Benefits are not directly conditioned on need.

FY 77 Expenditure (est.): **$63,697,000**

Benefits paid total $62,898,000.
Administrative costs total $799,000.

JUDICIAL RETIREMENT FUND

Treasury Department

State judges who retire at age 65 with at least 12 years of service, or regardless of age with 18 years of service, and their surviving spouses are provided with financial assistance to replace income lost through retirement. Benefits are paid directly to the beneficiary in the form of cash without any restriction on its use. Payments average $1,000 per month. Some 76 individuals benefit from this program. Members contribute six percent of salary while the state contributes 42.5 percent. Benefits are not directly conditioned on need.

FY 77 Expenditure (est.): **$1,007,700**

Benefits paid total $1,000,000.
Administrative costs total $7,700.

PUBLIC EMPLOYEES' RETIREMENT SYSTEM

Treasury Department

Full-time state employees who retire at age 60 (with the exception of state police who can retire at age 52) with at least ten years of service, or regardless of age with 30 years of service, and their dependents are provided with financial assistance to replace income lost through retirement. Benefits are paid directly to the beneficiary in the form of cash without any restriction on its use. Payments average $246 per month. Some 6,800 individuals benefit from this program. Members contribute five percent of salary (except state police who contribute ten percent). The state contributes 9.36 percent for employees and 20.23 percent for state police. Benefits are not directly conditioned on need.

FY 77 Expenditure (est.): **$20,712,000**

Benefits paid total $20,090,000.
Administrative costs total $622,000.
State contributions total about $25,423,000.

LOW-INCOME SENIOR CITIZEN PROPERTY TAX EXEMPTION

Department of Revenue

Indirect financial assistance is provided to low-income homeowners, 65 years and older, whose annual gross household income is less than $5,000. Benefits are in the form of tax relief, funded by allowing the homeowner a total exemption of his local property tax. Some 50,000 persons benefit yearly. Benefits are conditioned on need.

FY 77 Expenditure (est.): **$10,000,000**

Alabama

SENIOR CITIZEN PROPERTY TAX EXEMPTION

Department of Revenue

Indirect financial assistance is provided to homeowners, 65 years and over. Benefits are in the form of tax relief, funded by allowing the senior citizen homeowner to exempt from state property taxes an additional $3,000 of assessed value of his homestead property. Over 100,000 persons benefit yearly. Benefits are not directly conditioned on need.

FY 77 Expenditure (est.): **$1,000,000**

PROPERTY TAX EXEMPTION

Department of Revenue

Indirect financial assistance is provided to all homeowners. Benefits are in the form of tax relief, funded by allowing the homeowner to exempt from state property taxes $2,000 of assessed value of his homestead property. Over a half million persons benefit yearly. Benefits are not conditioned on need.

FY 77 Expenditure (est.): **$3,000,000**

GENERAL ASSISTANCE PROGRAM

Department of Pensions and Security

Short-term or emergency aid to cover the costs of food, shelter, clothing and other items of daily living are made to resident individuals, couples and families with children. Benefits are paid directly to the beneficiary in the form of cash without any restrictions on its use or through vendor payments in the case of medical assistance. Payments are in amounts varying according to each beneficiary's needs as determined under the state law. Benefits are funded by grants to local offices of the state public assistance agency. This program is financed by state funds. A monthly average of 29 recipients are aided. The average benefit payment is $13 monthly. Benefits are conditioned on need.

FY 77 Expenditure (est.): **$4,400**

WORKERS' COMPENSATION PROGRAM

Department of Industrial Relations

Workers injured or disabled on the job, as well as the surviving dependents of workers who die as a result of such injury, are provided financial assistance both as compensation for lost wages and to pay for the cost of any required medical or rehabilitative care. Benefits are in the form of cash payments, funded by means of a state-regulated private insurance program to which each covered employer must contribute a percentage of payroll determined by the employer's experience rating and industrial classification. Beneficiaries receive two-thirds of normal wages, up to a maximum weekly compensation of $120. These benefits may be received for no more than 300 weeks and the total amount of benefits one may receive is unlimited. In addition, a funeral allowance of $1,000 is provided for workers who die on the job. Approximately 15,000 workers and survivors were aided weekly in FY 77. Benefits are not directly conditioned on need.

FY 77 Expenditure (est.): **$64,165,000**

DETECTION AND CONTROL OF PREVENTABLE DISEASES

Department or Health

Victims or potential victims of preventable diseases are provided screening, testing and treatment at clinics and hospitals across the state. Diseases such as tuberculosis, venereal disease, hypertension, cancer, diptheria and other preventable diseases are provided for under this program. Benefits are in kind, funded by payments to treatment centers. Over 250,000 patient-contacts occur yearly under the program. Benefits are conditioned on need.

FY 77 Expenditure (est.): **$4,307,000**

Alabama

HEMOPHILIA PROGRAM

Department of Education

Home treatments are provided to persons with hemophilia in order to limit the deleterious effects of the disease and to lessen their likelihood of hospitalization. Services include blood coagulation, preventive treatment, hospitalization and drugs. Benefits are in kind, funded by payments to service providers. Approximately 100 persons were aided in FY 77. Benefits are not directly conditioned on need.

FY 77 Expenditure (est.): **$300,000**

CRIPPLED CHILDREN'S SERVICES

Department of Education

Indigent children with chronic handicaps are provided diagnostic treatment and follow-up services. Treatment may include medical assistance, prosthesis, appliances, drugs, hospitalization, nursing care and physical therapy. Benefits are in kind, funded by payments to participating institutions. Approximately 14,000 children are aided annually. Benefits are conditioned on need.

FY 77 Expenditure (est.): **$4,479,000**

Federal matching funds are added to the above state expenditure.

MENTAL HEALTH—NON-INSTITUTIONAL

Department of Mental Health

The mentally ill are provided treatment in community-based mental health centers in order to reduce the need for institutional care. Benefits are mainly in kind, funded by grants to area and local non-profit organizations. Services include mental health care, sheltered workshops, daycare and other related mental health care services. Over 50,000 people received services in FY 77. Benefits are not conditioned on need.

FY 77 Expenditure (est.): **$9,596,000**

ALCOHOLISM AND DRUG ABUSE

Department of Mental Health

Alcoholics and persons with serious drug problems are provided diagnostic and primary care at local community-based centers. Benefits are in kind and include detoxification services funded by payments to area hospitals and centers. Approximately 3,500 persons were aided in FY 77. Benefits are not conditioned on need.

FY 77 Expenditure (est.): **$3,044,000**

MENTAL RETARDATION—NON-INSTITUTIONAL

Department of Mental Health

The mentally retarded are provided treatment in community-based mental health centers in order to reduce the need for institutional care. Benefits are mainly in kind, funded by grants to area and local nonprofit organizations. Services include mental health care, sheltered workshops, daycare and other related mental health care services. Approximately 40,000 cases received services in FY 77. Benefits are not directly conditioned on need.

FY 77 Expenditure (est.): **$6,292,000**

VETERANS' AFFAIRS—SPECIAL GRANTS AND SUBSIDIES

Department of Veterans' Affairs

Veterans and the children of deceased or disabled veterans are provided financial assistance to enable them to complete their college education. Benefits are in the form of cash, paid directly to students. Approximately 1,600 persons are aided annually at an average benefit of between $550 and $600 for a maximum of four years. Benefits are not conditioned on need.

FY 77 Expenditure (est.): **$1,250,000**

MEDICAL SCHOLARSHIPS

Department of Education

Students at medical schools within the state are provided loans for tuition based on need and merit. Benefits are in the form of credit, funded by lowered interest rates. Up to 25 percent of the class is expected to receive benefits annually. The maximum loan is $12,000 for four years; and it can be repaid in either cash or service. A small number of non-refundable merit scholarships are available. Benefits are conditioned on need.

FY 77 Expenditure (est.): **$130,000**

PERSONAL INCOME TAX PROVISIONS

Department of Revenue

Low-Income Exemption. Indirect financial assistance is provided to persons whose annual gross income does not exceed $1,500 for single persons and $3,000 for married couples. Benefits are in the form of tax relief, funded by allowing the individual a total exemption of his income from personal income taxation. Benefits are conditioned on need.

Public Employees Retirement Income Exemption. Indirect financial assistance is provided to certain public employees who receive pensions or other retirement income. Benefits are in the form of tax relief, funded by allowing the taxpayer to exempt from income subject to personal income taxation, the payments received from state pension or retirement funds. Benefits are not directly conditioned on need.

Head of Family Exemption. Indirect financial assistance is provided to taxpayers who are single and maintain and support one or more dependents in the home. Benefits are in the form of tax relief, funded by allowing the taxpayer an additional $1,500 exemption from income subject to personal income taxation. Benefits are not conditioned on need.

CALIFORNIA

Population: 21,896,000

Total State and Local Expenditures
for all Purposes:
$32,532,000,000

MAJOR FEDERALLY ENABLED
INCOME TRANSFER PROGRAMS

FY 77 Expenditures (est.)

Program	State	Local
Aid to Families with Dependent Children	$ 576,980,000	$397,020,000
Medicaid	1,188,270,000	373,180,000
Social Services	9,900,000	51,980,000

California

OPTIONAL STATE SUPPLEMENTATION FOR SSI

Department of Benefit Payments

The aged, over 65 years old, the blind and the disabled are provided cash supplements to their SSI benefits for basic and special needs. Basic needs are food, shelter, clothing, utilities and daily living necessities. Special needs are those not provided for through monthly or optional SSI payments and include catastrophic events, housing repairs, moving expenses, food for guide dogs, emergency loans and aid to potentially self-supporting blind. Benefits are provided to eligible persons living independently with or without cooking facilities, those receiving nonmedical board and care, those living in the household of another, and disabled children under age 18 living with their parents, guardian or relative by marriage. Benefits range up to $156 monthly for individuals living independently with cooking facilities and $396 for blind couples. Benefits are proportionately lower for other categories. Benefits are in the form of direct cash payments funded wholly by the state. Payments are administered by the Federal government while eligibility is determined at Social Security district offices. Over 671,000 individuals receive aid monthly. Benefits are conditioned on need.

FY 77 Expenditure (est.): **$896,510,000**

TEACHERS' RETIREMENT SYSTEM

State and Consumer Services

Full-time teachers employed in public schools and individuals associated with teachers (such as counselors) who retire at age 55 with five years of service and their dependents are provided with financial assistance to replace income lost through retirement. Benefits are paid directly to the beneficiary in the form of cash without any restriction on its use. Payments average $458 per month. Some 72,368 individuals benefit from this program. Members contribute eight percent of salary and the state contributes $4,333,000 per year. Local contributions total eight percent of payroll. Benefits are not directly conditioned on need.

FY 77 Expenditure (est.): **$404,630,000**

Benefits paid total $398,042,000.
Administrative costs total $6,588,000.
The state contribution is $130,000,000 for 30 years for
   the unfunded liability of the system (since 1972).

LEGISLATORS' RETIREMENT FUND

State and Consumer Services

Legislators and constitutional officers (except judges) who retire at age 60 with at least four years of service, or at any age with 20 years of service, and their dependents are provided with financial assistance to replace income lost through retirement. Benefits are paid directly to the beneficiary in the form of cash without any restriction on its use. Payments average $682 per month. Some 171 individuals benefit from this program. Members contribute four to eight percent of salary depending upon when they entered the system. The state contributes 18.8 percent. Benefits are not directly conditioned on need.

FY 77 Expenditure (est.): **$1,443,000**

Benefits paid total $1,400,000.
Administrative costs total $43,000.
State contributions total $1,230,000.

PUBLIC EMPLOYEES' RETIREMENT SYSTEM

State and Consumer Services

Full-time state employees who retire at age 50 with at least five years of service and their dependents are provided with financial assistance to replace income lost through retirement. Benefits are paid directly to the beneficiary in the form of cash without any restriction on its use. Payments average $332 per month. Some 124,224 individuals benefit from this program. Members contribute five to eight percent, depending upon class of membership. The state contributes 17 to 30 percent. Benefits are not directly conditioned on need.

FY 77 Expenditure (est.): **$505,629,000**

Benefits paid total $496,080,000.
Administrative costs total $9,549,000.

California

SENIOR CITIZEN PROPERTY TAX ASSISTANCE

State Controller's Office

Indirect financial assistance is provided to low-income homeowners, 62 and older, whose total household income is $12,000 or less. Benefits are in the form of tax relief, funded by rebates of a portion of the property tax bill. The level of benefits ranges, depending on income, from four percent to 96 percent of property taxes paid on the first $8,500 of assessed value. Approximately 320,000 elderly homeowners were aided in FY 77, at an average of $266 each. Benefits are conditioned, in part, on need.

FY 77 Expenditure (est.): **$85,000,000**

SENIOR CITIZEN PROPERTY TAX POSTPONEMENT

State Controller's Office

Indirect financial assistance is provided to elderly homeowners to help pay for the cost of their property taxes. All homeowners 62 or older already receiving standard property tax exemptions and whose homes have liens, mortgages or loans against them amounting to less than 80 percent of their assessed values can qualify for the tax deferral. Benefits are in the form of tax relief, funded by the state's assumption of all or part of the senior citizen's property taxes. Annual interest at seven percent is charged against the share assumed by the state; and the total becomes a lien against the property, which can be paid back in full or in part at any time. About 8,000 homeowners are aided annually. Benefits are not directly conditioned on need.

FY 77 Expenditure (est.): **$5,000,000**

SENIOR CITIZEN RENT ASSISTANCE

State Controller's Office

Indirect financial assistance is provided to low-income renters 62 and over whose total household net income is $5,000 or less. Benefits are in the form of tax relief, funded by rebates based on household income and a statutory property tax equivalent of $220. The level of benefits ranges from four percent to 96 percent of the property tax equivalent, depending on net household income. Approximately 120,000 renters were aided in FY 77, receiving an average of $83 each. Benefits are conditioned on need.

FY 77 Expenditure (est.): **$10,000,000**

WORKERS' COMPENSATION PROGRAM

Department of Industrial Relations

Workers injured or disabled on the job, as well as the surviving dependents of workers who die as a result of such injury, are provided financial assistance both as compensation for lost wages and to pay for the cost of any required medical or rehabilitative care. Benefits are in the form of cash payments, funded by means of state-administered and state-regulated private insurance programs to which each covered employer must contribute a percentage of payroll determined by the employer's experience rating and industrial classification. Beneficiaries receive two-thirds of normal wages, up to a maximum weekly compensation benefit of $154. These benefits may be received for no more than 240 weeks and the total amount of benefits one may receive is unlimited. In addition, a funeral allowance of $1,000 is provided for workers who die on the job. Approximately 163,000 workers and survivors were aided weekly in FY 77. Benefits are not directly conditioned on need.

FY 77 Expenditure (est.): **$927,325,000**

California

GENERAL ASSISTANCE PROGRAM

Health and Welfare Agency

Maintenance payments, short-term or emergency aid to cover the costs of food, shelter, clothing and other items of daily living are made to individuals, couples and families with children. Benefits are paid directly to the beneficiary in the form of cash without any restrictions on its use or through vendor payments (to the suppliers of goods and services including medical). Employable persons must register with the state employment service. Payments are in amounts varying according to each beneficiary's needs as determined under state law. Benefits are funded by grants to county welfare agencies. Each month an average of 50,000 recipients (in some 48,000 cases) are aided. The average monthly benefit per recipient is $103.

FY 77 Expenditure (est.): **$62,000,000**

INDEMNIFICATION OF PRIVATE CITIZENS

General Government

Victims of violent crime and their dependents are provided cash indemnification if they have suffered financial hardship as a result of crime or violence, or if they have sustained injury in performing acts of benefit to the public. Benefits are in the form of cash, paid directly to victims. Benefits consist of cash awards for loss of earnings, medical expenses, rehabilitation services and attorneys' fees. The minimum benefit is $500; the maximum, $23,500. About 2,500 awards are made annually. Benefits are not directly conditioned on need.

FY 77 Expenditure (est.): **$5,305,000**

FARM AND HOME LOANS TO VETERANS

Department of Veterans' Affairs

California veterans are provided the opportunity to own homes and/or farms through long-term, low-interest loans. Benefits are in the form of favorable credit terms. The maximum loan for a farmer is $120,000; for a homeowner $43,000. About 7,000 loans are made annually. Benefits are not conditioned on need.

FY 77 Expenditure (est.): **$443,000,000**

This figure is for property acquisition, loan funding and loan service.

VETERANS' CLAIMS AND RIGHTS

Department of Veterans' Affairs

This program provides information and counseling services to veterans and their dependents concerning the availability of benefits. Benefits are in kind, funded by grants to county offices. Over 7,800 persons were aided in FY 77. Benefits are not conditioned on need.

FY 77 Expenditure (est.): **$1,642,000**

CARE OF SICK AND DISABLED VETERANS

Department of Veterans' Affairs

Sick and/or disabled veterans are provided care at the Veterans' Home in order to promote their overall health. Benefits are in kind, funded by a lump-sum grant to the home. Beneficiaries need never leave the home as long as they are unable to maintain themselves. They must be residents of the state for five years prior to entry. Couples may also qualify. Approximately 1,350 people are aided annually at an average of $32 daily for all types of care, including geriatric, medical, nursing, residential, hospital and social service treatment. Benefits are conditioned on need.

FY 77 Expenditure (est.): **$12,674,000**

Of the above amount, $5,326,000 are Federal funds.

California

INDIAN HEALTH

Department of Health

Indians, in accordance with their cultural needs, are provided health care in addition to those medical services which Medicaid already covers. Benefits are in kind, funded by state grants. The program is open to the 200,000 native American Indians in California. Benefits are not directly conditioned on need.

FY 77 Expenditure (est.): **$2,500,000**

CRIPPLED CHILDREN SERVICES

Department of Health

Children with severe, physically handicapping conditions are provided high quality, comprehensive care, including diagnosis, treatment and therapy. Benefits are in kind, funded by grants to participating care facilities. Approximately 65,000 children were aided in FY 77 at an average cost of $460 per case. Benefits are conditioned, in part, on need.

FY 77 Expenditure (est.): **$26,100,000**

Of the above amount, $3,000,000 are Federal funds.

GENETIC DISEASE PROGRAM

Department of Health

Individuals over age 21 with hemophilia, cystic fibrosis or sickle cell disease are provided preventive care, inpatient and outpatient treatment, surgery, blood derivatives and rehabilitative therapy. Benefits are in kind, funded by grants to treatment facilities. Over 500 persons are aided monthly. Benefits are conditioned, in part, on need.

FY 77 Expenditure (est.): **$536,000**

TAY-SACHS DISEASE PROGRAM

Department of Health

Persons with Tay-Sachs disease are provided medical services through Harbor-UCLA Hospital and through contracts with nine other hospitals and universities. Services include screening, assays, testing, publicity, education and collection of blood. Benefits are in kind, funded by grants to participating institutions. Sixty families are currently on the registry while 10,000 tests were administered in FY 77. Benefits are not conditioned on need.

FY 77 Expenditure (est.): **$349,000**

TUBERCULOSIS CONTROL

Department of Health

Persons with tuberculosis, who are in need, are provided preventive care and prophylactic drugs at outpatient clinics across the state. Benefits are in kind, funded by grants through counties to clinics. The cost of services not covered by medical insurance or other assistance programs are met. Benefits are not conditioned on need.

FY 77 Expenditure (est.): **$350,000**

ALCOHOLISM PROGRAMS—TREATMENT AND REHABILITATION

Department of Alcohol and Drug Abuse

Treatment and rehabilitation services are provided to alcoholics at clinics, hospitals and self-help centers. Benefits are in kind, funded by state grants to various county and local programs. Services include detoxification, medical services, food and shelter at residential facilities. Non-resident services include diagnosis, group and family therapy and day treatment. Approximately 120,000 persons receive services annually. Benefits are not directly conditioned on need.

FY 77 Expenditure (est.): **$20,912,000**

California

EDUCATIONAL ASSISTANCE TO VETERANS' DEPENDENTS

Department of Veterans' Affairs

Dependents of veterans who were killed or totally disabled in service are provided financial assistance for their education. Benefits are in the form of cash, paid directly to beneficiaries. Over 10,300 students received aid in FY 77. The average monthly benefit was $50 for college students and $20 for high school students. Benefits are not conditioned on need.

FY 77 Expenditure (est.): **$2,125,000**

SPECIAL CLIENTELE SERVICES

Department of Education

Blind people are provided talking books and braille books at community colleges to help further their education. Benefits are in kind, funded by grants to community colleges. Benefits are not directly conditioned on need.

FY 77 Expenditure (est.): **$573,000**

EDUCATIONAL OPPORTUNITY GRANTS

Department of Education-Community Colleges

Minority students who would not otherwise qualify for community college entry are provided financial aid and educational support. Benefits are in kind, in the form of guidance counseling, and in cash, paid directly to students to cover the costs of tuition, books and living expenses. Approximately 41,000 received benefits in FY 77. Benefits are conditioned on need.

FY 77 Expenditure (est.): **$5,738,000**

OCCUPATIONAL AND EDUCATIONAL TRAINING GRANTS

Department of Education

Needy and talented students are provided post-secondary, occupational education grants. Benefits are in the form of cash, based on grades, recommendations and demonstrable skill. Almost 1,000 students were aided in FY 77 at an average cost of $1,414 per student. The maximum benefit is $2,000. Benefits are conditioned on need.

FY 77 Expenditure (est.): **$2,404,000**

Of the above amount, $323,000 are Federal funds.

COLLEGE OPPORTUNITY GRANTS

Department of Education

Disadvantaged students who have a potential for college success are provided financial assistance for tuition and living expenses at colleges and universities across the state. Benefits are in the form of cash, funded directly to institutions. Grants are based on need, grades and recommendations. Approximately 12,600 students were aided in FY 77 at an average cost of $1,070 per student. The maximum benefit is $3,600. Benefits are conditioned on need.

FY 77 Expenditure (est.): **$14,281,000**

This figure includes $2,959,000 of Federal funds.

STUDENT FINANCIAL AID—UNIVERSITY OF CALIFORNIA

Department of Education

Graduate and undergraduate college students in need are provided financial aid while attending schools within the state university system. Benefits are in the form of cash, funded to the colleges, for tuition, books and other expenses. The maximum benefit is $1,500. Benefits are conditioned on need.

FY 77 Expenditure (est.): **$471,000**

California

EDUCATIONAL OPPORTUNITY PROGRAM

Department of Education—State Universities and Colleges

Minority students who would not otherwise qualify for four-year college entry are provided financial aid and educational support. Benefits are in kind, in the form of guidance counseling, and in cash, paid directly to students to cover the costs of tuition, books and living expenses. Approximately 12,500 students were aided in FY 77. Benefits are conditioned on need.

FY 77 Expenditure (est.): **$6,069,000**

GRANT PROGRAM—SCHOLARSHIPS

Department of Education

Students in need who are academically qualified are given financial aid for four-year state and private colleges to cover the costs of tuition, books, room and board. Benefits are in the form of cash, paid directly to the colleges and universities. Approximately 39,000 students received aid in FY 77. The minimum benefit is $1,200; the maximum, $2,700. Benefits are conditioned on need.

FY 77 Expenditure (est.): **$47,939,000**

Of the above amount, $3,987,000 are Federal funds.

EDUCATIONAL OPPORTUNITY GRANTS

Department of Education—Hastings College of Law

Minority students who would not otherwise qualify for law school entry are provided financial aid and educational support. Benefits are in kind, in the form of guidance counseling, and in cash, paid directly to students to cover the costs of tuition, books and living expenses. Approximately 280 students received aid at an average benefit of $900. Benefits are conditioned on need.

FY 77 Expenditure (est.): **$202,000**

GRADUATE FELLOWSHIP PROGRAM

Department of Education

Needy graduate and professional students who are in fields where there are manpower shortages are offered financial assistance. Benefits are in the form of cash, for tuition, books and fees. About 275 persons are aided annually at an average cost of $2,012 per student. Benefits are conditioned on need.

FY 77 Expenditure (est.): **$2,107,000**

PERSONAL INCOME TAX PROVISIONS

Franchise Tax Board

Low-Income Exemption. Indirect financial assistance is provided to persons whose annual gross income is $10,000 or under for a single person or $12,000 or under for a married couple. Benefits are in the form of tax relief, funded by allowing the individual total exemption of his income from personal income taxation. Benefits are conditioned, in part, on need.

Exemption Credit for Widow(er) with Dependent Child. Indirect financial assistance is provided to widows and widowers with a dependent child or stepchild. Benefits are in the form of tax relief, funded by allowing the taxpayer a $50 personal exemption credit against income tax liability. Benefits are not directly conditioned on need.

Deduction for Child Adoption Expenses. Indirect financial assistance is provided to taxpayers who adopt a child. Benefits are in the form of tax relief, funded by allowing such taxpayers a deduction from income of those adoption expenses which exceed three percent of the adjusted gross income. This deduction for personal income tax purposes cannot exceed $1,000 per household. The three percent limitation is eliminated if the adopted child is a "hard to place" child. Benefits are not conditioned on need.

Special Low-Income Credit. Indirect financial assistance is provided to low-income taxpayers. Benefits are in the form of tax relief, funded by allowing a credit against personal income tax liability of up to $40 per tax filer. To be eligible, single taxpayers must have an adjusted gross income of $5,080 or less; married taxpayers must have an adjusted gross income of $10,160 or less. Benefits are conditioned on need.

CONNECTICUT

Population: 3,108,000

Total State and Local Expenditures
for all Purposes:
$3,579,000,000

MAJOR FEDERALLY ENABLED
INCOME TRANSFER PROGRAMS
FY 77 Expenditures (est.)

Program	State	Local
Aid to Families with Dependent Children	$ 75,100,000	$ 0
Medicaid	106,310,000	0
Social Services	10,010,000	0

OPTIONAL STATE SUPPLEMENTATION FOR SSI

Department of Social Services

The aged, over 65 years old, the blind, 22 to 65, and the disabled, 22 to 65, are provided cash supplements to their federal SSI benefits for basic and special needs. Basic needs are food, shelter, clothing, utilities and daily living necessities. Special needs are those not provided for through monthly or optional SSI payments and include recurring and nonrecurring expenses for laundry, telephone, moving and home property repairs. Benefits are provided to eligible persons living independently. Benefits are equal to the deficit between monthly SSI benefits, other income and income maintenance needs based on state standards. Benefits are in the form of direct cash payments, funded wholly by the state. Payments are administered by the state; eligibility is determined at local Social Service Department offices. Over 10,500 individuals are aided monthly. Benefits are conditioned on need.

FY 77 Expenditure (est.): **$11,232,000**

TEACHERS' RETIREMENT SYSTEM

Office of the Comptroller

Full-time teachers in public schools who retire at age 60 with at least 20 years of service, or regardless of age with 35 years of service, and their beneficiaries are provided with financial assistance to replace income lost through retirement. Benefits are paid directly to the beneficiary in the form of cash without any restriction on its use. Payments average $570 per month. Some 8,070 individuals benefit from this program. Members contribute two percent of earnings on which Social Security contributions are deducted, plus five percent of salary in excess of that amount which is actuarily determined. Benefits are not directly conditioned on need.

FY 77 Expenditure (est.): **$55,646,000**

Benefits paid total $55,246,000.
Administrative costs total $400,000.
State contributions total $55,042,000.

GENERAL ASSEMBLY PENSION SYSTEM

Office of the Comptroller

Members of the General Assembly who retire at age 65 with at least ten years of service are provided with financial assistance to replace income lost through retirement. Benefits are paid directly to the beneficiary in the form of cash without any restriction on its use. Payments average $60 per month. Some 13 retirees benefit from this program. Members contribute ten percent of salary while the state contributes an amount which is actuarily determined. Benefits are not directly conditioned on need.

FY 77 Expenditure (est.): **$9,720**

This is the total benefits paid.
Administrative costs are not available.
State contributions total about $7,800.

PROBATE JUDGES' AND EMPLOYEES' RETIREMENT SYSTEM

Office of the Comptroller

Probate judges and employees of the probate court who retire at age 65, with 12 years of service for judges and 15 years of service for employees, and their dependents are provided with financial assistance to replace income lost through retirement. Benefits are paid directly to the beneficiary in the form of cash without any restriction on its use. Payments average $232 per month. Some 63 individuals benefit from this program. Members contribute 2.25 percent of earnings covered by Social Security, plus five percent of earnings in excess of that amount. The state contributes an amount which is actuarily determined. Benefits are not directly conditioned on need.

FY 77 Expenditure (est.): **$186,000**

Benefits paid total $176,000.
Administrative costs total $10,000.
State contributions total $311,000.

JUDGES' RETIREMENT SYSTEM

Office of the Comptroller.

State judges who retire at age 65 with at least ten years of service and their dependents are provided with financial assistance to replace income lost through retirement. Benefits are paid directly to the beneficiary in the form of cash without any restriction on its use. Payments range from $1,500 to $2,200 per month. Some 63 individuals benefit from this program. Members contribute about five percent of salary. This is a pay-as-you-go system. The state pays for the pensions out of the general funds as needed. Benefits are not directly conditioned on need.

FY 77 Expenditure (est.): **$1,300,000**

This is the total benefits paid.
Administrative costs are included.

PUBLIC EMPLOYEES' RETIREMENT SYSTEM

Office of the Comptroller

Full-time employees of the state and its political subdivision who retire at age 50 with at least 25 years of service, or at age 60 with ten years of service, (except State police who may retire at age 47 with 20 years of service), and their dependents are provided with financial assistance to replace income lost through retirement. Benefits are paid directly to the beneficiary in the form of cash without any restriction on its use. Payments average $368 per month. Some 13,258 individuals benefit from this program. Members contribute two percent of earnings on which Social Security contributions are deducted plus five percent of earnings in excess of that amount. (State police are not covered by Social Security). The state contributes an amount which is actuarily determined. Benefits are not directly conditioned on need.

FY 77 Expenditure (est.): **$58,484,000**

Benefits paid total $58,484,000.
Administrative costs are paid by the Office of the
    Comptroller.
State contributions total $48,750,000.

Connecticut

LOCAL PROPERTY TAX RELIEF FOR SENIOR CITIZENS

Tax and Revenue Department

Indirect financial assistance is provided senior citizens. Benefits are in the form of tax relief, funded by means of local property assessments being frozen at certain levels. Towns are reimbursed by the state for any revenues lost by this progam. At most, 60,000 elderly homeowners benefit yearly. Benefits are not conditioned on need.

FY 77 Expenditure (est.): **$19,016,000**

SENIOR CITIZEN PROPERTY TAX RELIEF

Tax and Revenue Department

Indirect financial assistance is provided to low-income home-owners and renters, aged 65 and over, whose total household net income is $6,000 or less. Benefits are in the form of tax relief, funded by means of rebates based on the amount that the local property tax bill or rent equivalent (set at 20 percent of rent) exceeds five percent of income. The maximum benefit is $400. Over 101,000 persons were aided in FY 77, at an average of $244 per person. Benefits are conditioned on need.

FY 77 Expenditure (est.): **$24,754,000**

PROPERTY TAX EXEMPTION FOR THE DISABLED

Tax and Revenue Department

Indirect financial assistance is provided to disabled persons receiving Supplemental Security Income. Benefits are in the form of tax relief, funded by allowing eligible homeowners to exempt from local property taxes $1,000 of assessed value of the taxpayer's property. Towns are reimbursed by the state for any loss of revenues incurred by this exemption. About 6,000 persons benefit yearly. Benefits are conditioned on need.

FY 77 Expenditure (est.): **$329,000**

TRIAGE

Department of Aging

Community-based programs are provided for the elderly in order to postpone permanent institutionalization, prevent inappropriate institutionalization and enhance the quality of their lives. Benefits are in kind, funded through grants to local agencies and institutions. Over 1,400 persons are aided annually. Benefits are not directly conditioned on need.

FY 77 Expenditure (est.): **$681,000**

Of the above amount, $267,000 are Federal funds.

ASSISTANCE AND MEDICAL AID PROGRAM FOR THE DISABLED

Department of Social Services

Residents aged 18-65 years who are permanently and totally disabled, who have insufficient means of support and who do not qualify for Supplemental Security Income or Old Age Survivor and Disability Insurance are provided financial assistance and services. Benefits are in the form of cash, and in kind, funded by payments directly to recipients and the purchase of medical care, at an average cost monthly of $180 per case. Over 1,000 persons are aided monthly. Benefits are conditioned on need.

FY 77 Expenditure (est.): **$2,094,000**

ASSISTANCE FOR QUADRAPLEGICS AND TOTALLY INCAPACITATED PERSONS

Department of Social Services

Quadraplegics and totally incapacitated persons who do not qualify for welfare, Medicare, Medicaid or admission to state institutions, or who cannot get other financial assistance, are provided such assistance by the state. Benefits are in the form of cash, paid directly to the institutions or persons. Under 1,000 people received aid in FY 77. Benefits are not directly conditioned on need.

FY 77 Expenditure (est.): **$15,000**

Connecticut

WORKERS' COMPENSATION PROGRAM

Workman's Compensation Commission

Workers injured or disabled on the job, as well as the surviving dependents of workers who die as a result of such injury, are provided financial assistance both as compensation for lost wages and to pay for the cost of any required medical or rehabilitative care. Benefits are in the form of cash payments, funded by means of a state-regulated private insurance program to which each covered employer must contribute a percentage of payroll determined by the employer's experience rating and industrial classification. Beneficiaries receive two-thirds of normal wages, up to a maximum weekly compensation benefit of $147, according to the number of dependents. These benefits may be received for the total period of disability and the total amount of benefits one may receive is unlimited. In addition, a funeral allowance of $1,500 is provided for workers who die on the job. Approximately 11,000 workers and survivors were aided weekly in FY 77. Benefits are not directly conditioned on need.

FY 77 Expenditure (est.): **$74,433,000**

GENERAL ASSISTANCE PROGRAM

Department of Social Services

Maintenance payments—short-term or emergency aid to cover the costs of food, shelter, clothing and other items of daily living—are made to individuals, couples, families with children and fathers unemployed due to a strike. Benefits are paid directly to the beneficiary in the form of cash without any restrictions on its use or through vendor payments (to the suppliers of goods and services including medical care). Shelter and utility payments to vendors are limited to $72. Employable persons must accept work project assignments. Payments are in amounts varying according to each beneficiary's needs as determined under state law. Benefits are funded by grants to local offices of the state public assistance agency. This program is financed by state and local funds. Each month an average of 22,751 recipients (in some 14,517 cases) are aided. The average monthly benefit per recipient is $83 (per case, the average is $130). Benefits are conditioned on need.

FY 77 Expenditure (est.): **$22,599,000**

EMERGENCY FOOD RELIEF

Department of Social Services

Emergency assistance is provided to needy families with dependent children in order to help them secure food when other funds are not available, when an emergency exists and the health and safety of the children is at stake. Benefits are in the form of vouchers for food, funded by payments from the department. The average cost per case is about $20. Over 6,500 cases were aided in FY 77. Benefits are conditioned on need.

FY 77 Expenditure (est.): **$154,000**

EMERGENCY ENERGY ASSISTANCE

Department of Social Services

Emergency assistance is provided to needy families with children in order to prevent shut-off of utilities when non-payment of bills has occurred. Benefits are in the form of cash paid directly to vendors, at an average of $125 per case. Almost 10,000 families are aided annually. Benefits are conditioned on need.

FY 77 Expenditure (est.): **$1,241,000**

SOLDIERS', SAILORS' AND MARINES' FUND

Department of Social Services

Qualified veterans and their dependents are provided temporary financial assistance which includes hospital, medical and miscellaneous aid. Benefits are in the form of cash and in kind, funded by payments from the fund. Over 300 persons receive cash payments weekly at an average cost of $50 per case. The purchase of medical care averages $100 weekly; hospital care, $1000 weekly. Benefits are conditioned on need.

FY 77 Expenditure (est.): **$1,782,000**

SUPPORT OF DEPENDENTS

Department of Health and Hospitals

Dependents of veterans who were killed in service or who are presently being cared for in Veterans' Homes are provided financial assistance to help them meet living expenses. Benefits are in the form of cash, funded by grants paid directly to survivors, not to exceed $35 per week per adult and $15 per week per child. Over 380 persons were aided in FY 77. Benefits are conditioned, in part, on need.

FY 77 Expenditure (est.): **$74,000**

GRANTS FOR ALCOHOLISM AND DRUG-DEPENDENT SERVICES

Department of Mental Health

Health care is provided to drug addicts and alcoholics through non-profit programs run by community agencies and municipalities. Benefits are in kind, funded by grants to the agencies and municipalities. Over 9,500 persons were admitted for treatment in FY 77. Benefits are not conditioned on need.

FY 77 Expenditure (est.): **$2,068,000**

AWARDS TO CHILDREN OF DECEASED OR DISABLED VETERANS

Department of Education

Children of deceased or disabled veterans who were residents at the time of their induction into the armed forces are provided financial assistance for college costs. Benefits are in the form of cash, paid directly to the colleges on behalf of the students. The maximum award is $400. Approximately 150 students were aided in FY 77. Benefits are not directly conditioned on need.

FY 77 Expenditure (est.): **$62,000**

RESTRICTED EDUCATIONAL ACHIEVEMENT

Department of Education

Disadvantaged minority undergraduate students who are qualified residents of the state are provided financial support according to need, individual potential, and academic achievement to enable them to pursue a college education. Benefits are in the form of cash paid directly to the institutions. About 600 persons are aided annually at an average cost of about $400 per semester. Benefits are conditioned on need.

FY 77 Expenditure (est.): **$260,000**

HIGHER EDUCATION GRANTS

Department of Education

Undergraduate students with substantial financial need are provided grants so that they may pursue a full-time college education. Benefits are in the form of cash, paid directly to institutions. Over 1,100 students receive these grants at an average value of $320 per student. Benefits are conditioned on need.

FY 77 Expenditure (est.): **$380,000**

STATE SCHOLARSHIP PROGRAM

Department of Education

Graduate and undergraduate students are provided financial support according to need, individual potential and academic achievement. Benefits are in the form of cash, paid directly to institutions. About 2,900 students received scholarships in FY 77 at an average value of $700. Benefits are conditioned, in part, on need.

FY 77 Expenditure (est.): **$2,063,000**

SCHOLARSHIP AID TUITION REFUNDS

Department of Education

Undergraduate students with substantial financial need are provided financial support through tuition waivers. Benefits are in kind, funded by payments to state and community colleges. Not more than ten percent of the total full-time enrollment may receive waivers in any semester. About 7,000 students are aided annually. Benefits are conditioned on need.

FY 77 Expenditure (est.): **$1,771,000**

COLLEGE CONTINUATION GRANT

Department of Education

Undergraduate students are provided financial support according to need, individual potential and academic achievement to enable them to pursue a college education. Benefits are in the form of cash, paid directly to the institutions. Approximately 800 persons are aided annually at an average cost of about $400 per semester. Benefits are conditioned on need.

FY 77 Expenditure (est.): **$340,000**

FLORIDA

Population: 8,452,000

Total State and Local Expenditures
for all Purposes:
$9,287,000,000

MAJOR FEDERALLY ENABLED
INCOME TRANSFER PROGRAMS
FY 77 Expenditures (est.)

Program	State	Local
Aid to Families with Dependent Children	$ 70,420,000	$ 0
Medicaid	109,760,000	0
Social Services	22,390,000	1,490,000

Florida

OPTIONAL STATE SUPPLEMENTATION FOR SSI

Department of Health and Rehabilitative Services

The aged, 65 years old and over, the blind and the disabled are provided cash supplements to their Federal SSI benefits for basic needs. Basic needs are food, shelter, clothing, utilities and daily living necessities. Benefits are provided to eligible persons living under the Community Care Program (which is room and board facilities providing personal care, and adult foster homes) and under the Community Residential Placement Program for the developmentally disabled (which is foster homes, group homes and residential habilitation centers). Individuals living independently do not receive benefits. Benefits average $41 monthly for individuals living in a group home and vary for other categories. Benefits are in the form of direct cash payments, funded wholly by the state. Payments are administered by the state; eligibility is determined at local Department of Health and Rehabilitation Services offices. Over 2,250 individuals are aided monthly. Benefits are conditioned on need.

FY 77 Expenditure (est.): **$1,104,000**

NATIONAL GUARD RETIREMENT SYSTEM

Division of Retirement

Members of the National Guard who retire regardless of age with 20 years of service, and their dependents are provided with financial assistance to replace income lost through retirement. Benefits are paid directly to the beneficiary in the form of cash without any restriction on its use. Payments average $325 per month. Some 57 individuals benefit from this program. It is noncontributory for members. This is an unfunded, pay-as-you-go system paid for by the state. Benefits are not directly conditioned on need.

FY 77 Expenditure (est.): **$222,500**

Administrative costs are assumed by the Florida Retirement System.

PUBLIC EMPLOYEES' RETIREMENT SYSTEM

State Retirement Commission

Full-time employees of the state and its political subdivisions who retire at age 62 with at least ten years of service, or at any age with 30 years of service, and their dependents are provided with financial assistance to replace income lost through retirement. Benefits are paid directly to the beneficiary in the form of cash without any restriction on its use. Payments average $294 per month. Some 19,170 individuals benefit from this program. This system is non-contributory for members while the state contributes 9.1 percent of total payroll. Benefits are not directly conditioned on need.

FY 77 Expenditure (est.): **$58,780,000**

Benefits paid total $55,000,000.
Administrative costs total $3,780,000.

HOMESTEAD EXEMPTION

Department of Revenue

Indirect financial assistance is provided to all homeowners. Benefits are in the form of tax relief, funded by allowing the individual to exempt from property taxation the first $5,000 of assessed value of his homestead. Some two million homeowners receive benefits under this provision annually. Benefits are not conditioned on need.

FY 77 Expenditure (est.): **$182,000,000**

ADDITIONAL HOMESTEAD EXEMPTION FOR SENIOR CITIZENS

Department of Revenue

Indirect financial assistance is provided to taxpayers, who have been residents of the state for five consecutive years, are 65 years and older and qualify for the standard Homestead Property Tax Exemption. Benefits are in the form of tax relief, funded by allowing the elderly taxpayer to exempt from property taxation an additional $5,000 of assessed value of his homestead property. However, the sum of all exemptions claimed may not exceed $10,000. Close to 400,000 elderly property-owners benefit yearly. Benefits are not directly conditioned on need.

FY 77 Expenditure (est.): **$39,000,000**

WIDOWS' EXEMPTION

Department of Revenue

Indirect financial assistance is provided to widowed taxpayers who reside in Florida and have not remarried. Benefits are in the form of tax relief, funded by allowing the widow to exempt from property taxation an additional $500 of assessed value of her homestead property. However, the sum of all exemptions claimed may not exceed $10,000. Almost 250,000 widows benefit yearly. Benefits are not directly conditioned on need.

FY 77 Expenditure (est.): **$2,000,000**

PROPERTY TAX EXEMPTION FOR THE DISABLED

Department of Revenue

Indirect financial assistance is provided to totally and permanently disabled persons and to veterans with service-related total and permanent disabilities. Benefits are in the form of tax relief, funded by allowing the taxpayer to exempt from property taxation the total value of the resident homestead. To be eligible, taxpayers must have resided in the state for five years and in the case of non-veterans, have an income of $8,200 or less. Approximately 5,000 persons receive benefits. Benefits are conditioned, in part, on need.

FY 77 Expenditure (est.): **$3,000,000**

BLIND AND DISABLED EXEMPTION

Department of Revenue

Indirect financial assistance is provided to permanently disabled and blind taxpayers to help them pay their property taxes. Benefits are in the form of tax relief, funded by allowing the disabled or blind individual to exempt an additional $500 of assessed value of his real holdings from property taxation. However, the sum of all exemptions claimed may not exceed $10,000. Almost 100,000 disabled and blind property owners benefit yearly. Benefits are not directly conditioned on need.

FY 77 Expenditure (est.): **$1,000,000**

ADDITIONAL DISABILITY EXEMPTION

Department of Revenue

Indirect financial assistance is provided to disabled taxpayers, who have been residents of the state for five consecutive years and are qualified for the standard $500 Disability Property Tax Exemption, but are not receiving the $5,000 Senior Additional Property Tax Exemption. Benefits are in the form of tax relief, funded by allowing the individual to exempt from property taxation an additional $4,500 of the value of his homestead property. However, the sum of all exemptions claimed may not exceed $10,000. Over 20,000 disabled property owners benefit yearly. Benefits are not directly conditioned on need.

FY 77 Expenditure (est.): **$2,000,000**

CRIMES COMPENSATION COMMISSION

Department of Health and Rehabilitation Services

Victims of violent crime are provided financial assistance to compensate for their losses. Benefits are in the form of cash and are based on a Commission's determination. Beneficiaries must have sustained loss or injury due to the crime. Benefits are not conditioned on need.

FY 77 Expenditure (est.): **$2,570,000**

GENERAL ASSISTANCE PROGRAM

Department of Health and Rehabilitation Services

Short-term or emergency assistance to cover the costs of food, shelter, clothing and other items of daily living are made to resident individuals, couples and families with children. Benefits are paid directly to the beneficiary in the form of cash, without any restriction on its use, or through vendor payments. These payments are in amounts varying according to each beneficiary's needs, as determined under local law. Benefits are funded by appropriations to the administering local welfare agencies from local revenues. A monthly average of 19,000 recipients (in some 8,000 cases) are aided. The average monthly benefit is $21 per individual. Benefits are conditioned on need.

FY 77 Expenditure (est.): **$4,500,000**

WORKERS' COMPENSATION PROGRAM

Bureau of Workmen's Compensation

Workers injured or disabled on the job, as well as the surviving dependents of workers who die as a result of such injury, are provided financial assistance both as compensation for lost wages and to pay for the cost of any required medical or rehabilitative care. Benefits are in the form of cash payments, funded by means of a state-regulated private insurance program to which each covered employer must contribute a percentage of payroll determined by the employer's experience rating and industrial classification. Beneficiaries receive 60 percent of normal wages, up to a maximum of $119. These benefits may be received for no more than 350 weeks and the total amount of benefits one may receive is unlimited. In addition, a funeral allowance of $1,000 is provided for workers who die on the job. Approximately 70,000 workers and survivors were aided weekly in FY 77. Benefits are not directly conditioned on need.

FY 77 Expenditure (est.): **$307,760,000**

FAMILY PLACEMENT (HOMECARE FOR THE ELDERLY)

Department of Health and Rehabilitation Services

Low-income persons, aged 65 and over, who have been residents of Florida for at least one year, certified by a physician to be in need of services, and who can demonstrate financial need, are provided homecare services in order to prevent institutionalization by making it possible for them to continue living in their homes. Benefits are in the form of cash, funded by direct payments to the elderly, who in turn may pay the individual providing alternative care. Approximately 200 persons are aided annually. Benefits are conditioned on need.

FY 77 Expenditure (est.): **$500,000**

MEDICAL AND SOCIAL SERVICES TO THE BLIND

Department of Education

Medically indigent, blind and visually handicapped persons are provided ambulatory and home health services by county health clinics and hospitals across the state. Benefits are in kind, funded by state payments to county clinics and hospitals. Over 13,600 persons were aided in FY 77. Benefits are conditioned, in part, on need.

FY 77 Expenditure (est.): **$2,843,000**

Of the above amount, $1,200,000 are Federal funds.

AMBULATORY TREATMENT SERVICES

Department of Health and Rehabilitation Services

The residential ambulatory population and the rural poor are provided health care services. Benefits are in kind, funded by the purchase of physical and dental services, as well as primary health care. Benefits are not directly conditioned on need.

FY 77 Expenditure (est.): **$3,982,000**

Florida

CHRONIC DISEASE CONTROL

Department of Health and Rehabilitation Services

This program provides care for those at high risk of contracting non-communicable diseases and provides methods of relieving disability arising from such diseases. Services are for diabetes, kidney disease, and other chronic diseases. Benefits are in kind, funded by a state grant to participating hospitals. Over 250,000 persons received services in FY 77. Services are on both an inpatient and outpatient basis. Benefits are conditioned on need.

FY 77 Expenditure (est.): **$4,000,000**

Of the above amount, almost $2,000,000 are Federal funds.

TUBERCULOSIS ADMINISTRATION AND OUTPATIENT

Department of Health and Rehabilitation Services

Persons with tuberculosis, or who are at risk of contracting tuberculosis, are provided care in community hospitals and outpatient facilities. Benefits are in kind, funded partly by grants to participating facilities. Services include testing, drugs and diagnosis. Over 200 persons received treatment, and 427,000 received screening services in FY 77. Benefits are not directly conditioned on need.

FY 77 Expenditure (est.): **$1,727,000**

COMMUNITY ALCOHOLIC SERVICES

Department of Health and Rehabilitation Services

Alcoholics are provided detoxification, residential and educational services at centers across the state. Benefits are in kind, funded by grants to participating centers. About 58,000 persons received services in FY 77. The average cost per person was $176. Benefits are not directly conditioned on need.

FY 77 Expenditure (est.): **$9,962,000**

DEVELOPMENTAL TRAINING—MENTALLY RETARDED

Department of Health and Rehabilitative Services

Caretaker relatives of mentally retarded children and adults in need of services are provided the opportunity to become employed or enrolled in a training program through the provision of alternate day care, home care and personal care services. The caretaker relatives are thus able to leave the home. Benefits are in kind, funded by payments to approximately 2,000 caretaker individuals in FY 77. Benefits are conditioned, in part, on need.

FY 77 Expenditure (est.): **$9,824,000**

COMMUNITY MENTAL HEALTH SERVICES

Department of Mental Health Services

Persons in need of mental health care and treatment are provided such services at 60 private mental health clinics within the state. Benefits are in kind, funded by grants to the clinics. Approximately 200,000 patient days of treatment were provided in FY 77. Each clinic receives funds quarterly based on services during the previous quarter. Benefits are conditioned, in part, on need.

FY 77 Expenditure (est.): **$2,055,000**

INDIGENT PSYCHIATRIC DRUG PROGRAM

Department of Mental Health Services

Poor people are given drugs for various medical conditions at community centers across the state. Benefits are in kind, funded by the purchase of drugs at low rates, which are then purchased by the specific community center where the drug is dispensed. Approximately 40,000 patients purchased drugs this way in FY 77. Benefits are conditioned on need.

FY 77 Expenditure (est.): **$1,160,000**

STUDENT ASSISTANCE GRANTS

Department of Education

Undergraduate students who have lived in the state for two years and can demonstrate exceptional financial need are provided financial assistance to cover the costs of college expenses. Benefits are in the form of cash, paid directly to institutions. About 8,300 students were aided in FY 77. The minimum benefit is $200 and the maximum is $1,200 per grant. Benefits are conditioned on need.

FY 77 Expenditure (est.): **$7,000,000**

AWARDS TO CHILDREN OF DECEASED OR DISABLED VETERANS

Department of Education

Children whose parents entered military service from Florida, lived in the state for five years, and were killed or disabled in service, are provided financial assistance at state universities and community colleges. Benefits are in the form of cash, paid directly to beneficiaries. Over 70 students between the ages of 16 and 22 were aided in FY 77. Benefits are not conditioned on need.

FY 77 Expenditure (est.): **$50,000**

SEMINOLE-MICCOSUKEE INDIAN SCHOLARSHIPS

Department of Education

Seminole-Miccosukee Indians are provided financial aid in order for them to attend college in the state of Florida. Benefits are in the form of cash, paid directly to institutions. The maximum scholarship is $600 annually for no longer than four academic years. Eight scholarships are granted yearly. Benefits are conditioned on need and merit.

FY 77 Expenditure (est.): **$5,000**

STATE-INSURED STUDENT LOANS

Department of Education

Students who have been residents for one year and can demonstrate need are provided low-interest, long-term loans at colleges across the state. Benefits are in the form of favorable credit terms, funded by the state's insuring against defaults of repayments. Over 16,000 new loans and renewals were granted in FY 77. The maximum loan is $2,500. Benefits are conditioned on need.

FY 77 Expenditure (est.): **$10,000,000**

GEORGIA

Population: 5,048,000

Total State and Local Expenditures
for all Purposes:
$5,061,000,000

MAJOR FEDERALLY ENABLED
INCOME TRANSFER PROGRAMS
FY 77 Expenditures (est.)

Program	State	Local
Aid to Families with Dependent Children	$ 38,970,000	$3,850,000
Medicaid	121,530,000	0
Social Services	14,470,000	0

FIREMEN'S RETIREMENT SYSTEM

Office of Planning and Budget

Regular or volunteer firefighters who retire at age 55 with 25 years of service and their dependents are provided with financial assistance to replace income lost through retirement. Benefits are paid directly to the beneficiary in the form of cash without any restriction on its use. Payments range from $50 to $215 per month. (average $125). Some 741 individuals benefit from this program. Members contribute five percent of salary while the state does not contribute directly. One percent of a sales tax levied on gross premiums of all fire, lightning, extended coverage, inland marine coverage and storm coverage policies of insurance is contributed to the fund. Benefits are not directly conditioned on need.

FY 77 Expenditure (est.): **$1,256,000**

Benefits paid total $1,146,000.
Administrative costs total $110,000.

PEACE OFFICERS' ANNUITY AND BENEFIT FUND

Office of Planning and Budget

Full-time peace officers who retire at age 55 with at least 20 years of service and their dependents are provided with financial assistance to replace income lost through retirement. Benefits are paid directly to the beneficiary in the form of cash without any restriction on its use. Payments average $188 per month. Some 1,730 individuals benefit from this program. Members contribute $7 per month. The state does not directly contribute. Fines and bond forfeitures of criminal cases are contributed to the system. Benefits are not directly conditioned on need.

FY 77 Expenditure (est.): **$2,720,678**

Benefits paid total $2,555,678.
Administrative costs total $165,000.

PUBLIC SCHOOL EMPLOYEES' RETIREMENT SYSTEM

Office of Planning and Budget

All non-teaching public school employees (those not eligible for the teachers' retirement system) who retire at age 60 with 26 years of service, or regardless of age with 31 years of service, and their dependents are provided with financial assistance to replace income lost through retirement. Benefits are paid directly to the beneficiary in the form of cash without any restriction on its use. Payments range from $90 to $160 per month. Some 4,500 individuals benefit from this program. Members contribute $4 per month (maximum of $36 per year). The state contributes 13.1 percent of payroll. Benefits are not directly conditioned on need.

FY 77 Expenditure (est.): **$4,425,000**

Benefits paid total $4,285,000.
Administrative costs total $140,000.
State contributions total $8,270,000.

TEACHERS' RETIREMENT SYSTEM

Office of Planning and Budget

Full-time public school teachers who retire at age 60 with at least 10 years of service and their dependents are provided with financial assistance to replace income lost through retirement. Benefits are paid directly to the beneficiary in the form of cash without any restriction on its use. Payments range from $300 to $500 per month. Some 14,637 individuals benefit from this program. Members contribute six percent of salary while the state contributes 9.35 percent. Benefits are not directly conditioned on need.

FY 77 Expenditure (est.): **$62,093,000**

Benefits paid total $60,835,000.
Administrative costs total $1,258,000.

TRIAL JUDGES' AND SOLICITORS' RETIREMENT FUND

Office of Planning and Budget

Members who retire at age 60 with at least ten years of service and their dependents are provided with financial assistance to replace income lost through retirement. Benefits are paid directly to the beneficiary in the form of cash without any restriction on its use. This fund is newly organized and consequently no benefits have been paid. Members contribute ten percent of their salary, and the state matches this contribution. Benefits are not directly conditioned on need.

FY 77 Expenditure (est.): **$30,000**

The above amount comprises the current administrative expense.

PUBLIC EMPLOYEES' RETIREMENT SYSTEM

Office of Planning and Budget

Employees of the state and its political subdivisions who retire at age 60 with at least five years of service (if a member joined after 1968, with ten years of service) and their dependents are provided with financial assistance to replace income lost through retirement. Benefits are paid directly to the beneficiary in the form of cash without any restriction on its use. Payments average $297 per month. Some 7,234 individuals benefit from this program. Members contribute three percent of the first $350 of monthly salary plus five percent of any additional amount. The state contributes an amount which is actuarially determined. Benefits are not directly conditioned on need.

FY 77 Expenditure (est.): **$25,762,000**

Benefits paid total $24,802,000.
Administrative costs total $960,000.
State contributions total $17,974,000.

Georgia

HOMESTEAD EXEMPTION

Department of Revenue

Indirect financial assistance is provided to all homeowners. Benefits are in the form of tax relief, funded by allowing the homeowner to exempt from local property taxation $2,000 of total assessed value of his homestead property. Approximately 1,000,000 homeowners receive benefits yearly. Benefits are not conditioned on need.

FY 77 Expenditure (est.): **$51,400,000**

SENIOR CITIZEN HOMESTEAD EXEMPTION

Department of Revenue

Indirect financial assistance is provided to homeowners, 65 years and older, whose net household income is $4,000 or less. Benefits are in the form of tax relief, funded by allowing the elderly homeowner to exempt from local property taxation an additional $2,000 of total assessed value of his homestead property. About 100,000 elderly homeowners receive benefits yearly. Benefits are conditioned on need.

FY 77 Expenditure (est.): **$6,100,000**

SENIOR CITIZEN SCHOOL TAX EXEMPTION

Department of Revenue

Indirect financial assistance is provided to low-income homeowners, 62 years and older, whose annual gross household income is less than $6,000. Benefits are in the form of tax relief, funded by allowing the homeowner to exempt from property taxation for school purposes $10,000 of total assessed value of his homestead property. Over 120,000 elderly property-owners benefit yearly. Benefits are conditioned on need.

FY 77 Expenditure (est.): **$2,500,000**

DISABLED VETERANS' HOMESTEAD EXEMPTION

Department of Revenue

Indirect financial assistance is provided to totally disabled veterans such as paraplegics. Benefits are in the form of tax relief, funded by allowing the veteran to exempt from local property taxation an additional $10,500 of total assessed value of his homestead property. Well under 1,000 veterans benefit yearly. Benefits are not directly conditioned on need.

FY 77 Expenditure (est.): **$100,000**

WAR VETERANS' HOME

Veterans' Service

War veterans are provided nursing home care and domiciliary care at state-run veterans' homes across the state. Benefits are in kind, funded by payments to the homes. About 380 persons were aided in FY 77. Benefits are not directly conditioned on need.

FY 77 Expenditure (est.): **$3,149,000**

WAR VETERAN'S NURSING HOME—AUGUSTA

Veterans' Service

Veterans in need of skilled nursing care and related medical services are provided such care at the Veterans' Home in Augusta. The home is run in conjunction with the Medical College of Georgia. Benefits are in kind, funded by payments to the home. About 175 persons are aided there annually. Benefits are not directly conditioned on need.

FY 77 Expenditure (est.): **$1,463,000**

WORKERS' COMPENSATION PROGRAM

State Board of Workman's Compensation

Workers injured or disabled on the job, as well as the surviving dependents of workers who die as a result of such injury, are provided financial assistance both as compensation for lost wages and to pay for the cost of any required medical or rehabilitative care. Benefits are in the form of cash payments, funded by means of a state regulated private insurance program to which each covered employer must contribute a percentage of payroll determined by the employer's experience rating and industrial classification. Beneficiaries receive two-thirds of normal wages, up to a maximum weekly compensation benefit of $95. These benefits may be received for the total period of disability and the total amount of benefits one may receive is unlimited. In addition, a funeral allowance of $750 is provided for workers who die on the job. Approximately 29,000 workers and survivors were aided weekly in FY 77. Benefits are not directly conditioned on need.

FY 77 Expenditure (est.): **$102,510,000**

GENERAL ASSISTANCE PROGRAM

Department of Human Resources

Short-term or emergency aid to cover the costs of food, shelter, clothing and other items of daily living are made to resident individuals, couples and families with children. Benefits are paid directly to the beneficiary in the form of cash without any restrictions on its use or through vendor payments in the case of medical assistance. Payments are in amounts varying according to each beneficiary's needs as determined under state law. Benefits are funded by grants to local offices of the state public assistance agency. This program is financed by state funds. A monthly average of 2,700 recipients (in some 1,600 cases) are aided. The average monthly benefit payment is $33 per individual. Benefits are conditioned on need.

FY 77 Expenditure (est.): **$1,100,000**

SERVICES TO THE AGED—AREA-WIDE AND COMMUNITY GRANTS

Department of Human Resources

Elderly persons are provided general and social services and services to prevent premature or unnecessary institutionalization. Benefits are in kind, funded by payments to community centers. About 19,000 persons received services in FY 77. Benefits are not directly conditioned on need.

FY 77 Expenditure (est.): **$1,457,000**

CANCER CONTROL BENEFITS

Department of Human Resources

Cancer patients who are medically indigent and in need of medical assistance are provided treatment and support services at hospitals across the state. Benefits are in kind, funded by payments to hospitals. About 1,000 persons were aided in FY 77, at an average cost of about $600 per client. Benefits are conditioned on need.

FY 77 Expenditure (est.): **$522,000**

KIDNEY DISEASE BENEFITS

Department of Human Resources

Persons with chronic kidney disease are provided medical services including transplantation, dialysis, hospital care and renal drugs. Benefits are in kind, funded by payments to participating hospitals. About 300 persons are aided annually. Benefits are not conditioned on need.

FY 77 Expenditure (est.): **$300,000**

HEMOPHILIA BENEFITS

Department of Human Resources

Hemophiliacs are provided clotting factor at cheaper rates than they would otherwise encounter if purchased privately. Benefits are in kind, funded by the purchase of appropriate drugs and treatment. Over 300 persons are aided annually at a rate that is determined, in part, by the severity of the case. Benefits are not directly conditioned on need.

FY 77 Expenditure (est.): **$100,000**

BENEFITS FOR MEDICALLY INDIGENT HIGH-RISK PREGNANT WOMEN AND INFANTS

Department of Human Resources

Medically indigent high-risk pregnant women and their infants are provided quality prenatal care, hospital delivery, and newborn care within their health districts at hospitals and clinics. Benefits are in kind, funded by payments to the care facilities. About 2,500 persons are aided annually at an average cost of about $1,100 per patient. Benefits are conditioned on need.

FY 77 Expenditure (est.): **$2,961,000**

REGIONAL GRANTS FOR PRENATAL AND POSTNATAL CARE PROGRAMS

Department of Human Resources

Medically indigent, high-risk mothers and their infants are provided prenatal and follow-up care at five regional treatment centers within the state. Benefits are in kind, funded by grants to the centers. About 2,500 mothers are aided annually. Benefits are conditioned on need.

FY 77 Expenditure (est.): **$5,400,000**

BENEFITS FOR CHILD CARE—MATERNAL CARE SERVICES

Department of Human Resources

Mothers, infants and school-age children are provided comprehensive health services at hospitals and clinics across the state. Benefits are in kind, funded by payments to participating institutions. Over 260 persons and/or families are aided annually, at an average cost of $820 per case. Benefits are conditioned on need.

FY 77 Expenditure (est.): **$218,000**

CRIPPLED CHILDREN BENEFITS

Department of Human Resources

Medically indigent children who are crippled are provided health services at hospitals and clinics within the state. Benefits are in kind, funded by payments to participating programs. About 19,000 children were aided in FY 77. Benefits are conditioned, in part, on need.

FY 77 Expenditure (est.): **$3,035,000**

BENEFITS FOR CHILD CARE—SPECIALIZED FOSTER CARE

Department of Human Resources

Emotionally disturbed children are provided a family living alternative so that they need not be institutionalized. Benefits are in kind, funded by payments to participating households. About 20 children were aided monthly in FY 77, at an average cost of under $3 per client per day. Benefits are not directly conditioned on need.

FY 77 Expenditure (est.): **$22,000**

BENEFITS FOR FAMILY LIVING CARE

Department of Human Resources

Mentally ill persons are provided services in their own communities on an outpatient basis. Services include counseling, placement and medical services at personal care homes. Benefits are in kind, funded by payments to the homes. Almost 1,500 persons were aided in FY 77 at an average cost of $750 per person. Benefits are conditioned, in part, on need.

FY 77 Expenditure (est.): **$1,125,000**

GRANTS FOR CHILD MENTAL HEALTH

Department of Human Resources

Children under 21 years of age are provided services to complement hospital care. Services include inpatient care, oupatient care, consultation and therapeutic treatment. Benefits are in kind, funded by payments to area programs. Approximately 17,000 individuals were aided in FY 77 at an average cost of about $61 per child. Benefits are conditioned, in part, on need.

FY 77 Expenditure (est.): **$1,044,000**

GRANTS FOR ADULT MENTAL HEALTH

Department of Human Resources

The adult mentally ill are provided health services at clinics and hospitals across the state. Approximately 59,000 cases were aided in FY 77 at an average cost of $67 each. Services include counseling and therapeutic services. Benefits are in kind, funded by payments to participating programs. Benefits are not directly conditioned on need.

FY 77 Expenditure (est.): **$3,971,000**

DRUG ABUSE COMMUNITY TREATMENT PROGRAMS

Department of Human Resources

Alcoholics and persons with serious durg problems are provided diagnostic and primary care at local community-based centers. Benefits are in kind and include detoxification services funded by grants to hospitals and centers. Approximately 3,700 persons were aided in FY 77 at an average cost of about $140 per person. Benefits are not conditioned on need.

FY 77 Expenditure (est.): **$515,000**

OUTPATIENT AND AFTERCARE DRUG PURCHASES

Department of Human Resources

Outpatients, ex-drug abusers, and mentally retarded persons in need of drugs are provided these drugs more cheaply than they could otherwise purchase them at community clinics across the state. Benefits are in kind, funded by state grants to local programs. Over 92,000 persons took advantage of this program in FY 77, at an average cost per person of about $8. Benefits are conditioned, in part, on need.

FY 77 Expenditure (est.): **$750,000**

GRANTS FOR ALCOHOLISM—COMMUNITY TREATMENT PROGRAMS

Department of Human Resources

Alcoholics are provided services on a community basis at outpatient clinics and short-term care facilities. Benefits are in kind and include detoxification, medical care and residential services. Funding is directly to area programs. Almost 19,000 persons received benefits annually at an average cost of about $130 per person. Benefits are conditioned, in part, on need.

FY 77 Expenditure (est.): **$2,420,000**

GROUP HOMES FOR THE MENTALLY RETARDED

Department of Human Resources

Mentally retarded persons are provided services so that they can have an option other than institutionalization or remaining in their own homes. Benefits are in kind, funded by payments to group homes. Services include all home services and a 24-hour residential setting. About 240 persons are aided annually at an average cost of about $7,000 per person per year. Benefits are not directly conditioned on need.

FY 77 Expenditure (est.): **$1,707,000**

BENEFITS FOR CHILD CARE—DAYCARE

Department of Human Resources

Preschool children from low-income families are provided protective care and foster care services not related to daycare on the Federal level. Benefits are in kind, funded by payments to the facilities sponsored by this program. Almost 600 children are cared for daily at an average cost of $1,100 per year per child. Benefits are conditioned on need.

FY 77 Expenditure (est.): **$611,000**

TUITION EQUALIZATION GRANTS

State Scholarship Commission

Georgia students who attend private colleges within the state are provided financial assistance to make up the difference in the cost of books, tuition and living expenses between state and private institutions. Benefits are in the form of cash, paid to the institutions. About 16,000 students received benefits in FY 77. Benefits are conditioned on need.

FY 77 Expenditure (est.): **$6,400,000**

REGENTS SCHOLARSHIPS

University System

College students in need are provided scholarships to cover tuition, books and related costs. Benefits are in the form of cash, paid directly to educational institutions. Approximately 500 students were aided at an average of $400 in FY 77. The maximum benefit at University System of Georgia colleges is $500 for junior colleges, $750 for four-year colleges and $1,000 for graduate study. Benefits are conditioned on need.

FY 77 Expenditure (est.): **$200,000**

STATE STUDENT INCENTIVE SCHOLARSHIPS

State Scholarship Commission

Needy college students are provided financial assistance for tuition, books and other related expenses. Benefits are in the form of cash, paid directly to the institutions. Approximately 6,200 students were aided in FY 77. The maximum benefit is $450. Benefits are conditioned on need.

FY 77 Expenditure (est.): **$1,920,000**

DIRECT GUARANTEED LOANS

State Scholarship Commission

Georgia residents who are attending accredited institutions of higher education, preparing for careers in a number of health care or professional fields, and who can demonstrate need, are provided loans to finance their education. Benefits are in the form of favorable credit terms; and loans may be repaid in cash or in service. Approximately 2,000 were aided in FY 77. Benefits are conditioned on need.

FY 77 Expenditure (est.): **$1,935,000**

The above amount represents the value of loans made and administrative costs.

MEDICAL SCHOLARSHIPS

University System

Medical students, in need, who are willing to practice medicine in an approved community after graduation, are provided scholarships not to exceed $12,000 for four years. Benefits are in the form of cash, paid directly to medical institutions. About 140 students were aided in FY 77 at an average cost of $2,500. Aid is for tuition, books, and other college-related expenses. Students may attend any approved medical college in the nation. Benefits are conditioned on need.

FY 77 Expenditure (est.): **$345,000**

PERSONAL INCOME TAX PROVISIONS

Department of Revenue

Low-Income Credit. Indirect financial assistance is provided to low-income taxpayers. Benefits are in the form of tax relief, funded by allowing a credit against personal income tax liability of up to $15 per tax filer. To be eligible, single taxpayers must have an adjusted gross income of $3,014 or less; married taxpayers must have an adjusted gross income of $6,029 or less. Benefits are conditioned on need.

Exemption for Handicapped Dependents. Indirect financial assistance is provided to taxpayers with a physically or mentally handicapped dependent. Benefits are in the form of tax relief, funded by allowing the taxpayer to claim an additional $700 exemption from gross income subject to personal income taxation. Benefits are not directly conditioned on need.

Deduction of Public Employees' Pensions. Indirect financial assistance is provided to certain public employees who receive pensions or other retirement income. Benefits are in the form of tax relief, funded by allowing the taxpayer to deduct pension and retirement income from the gross adjusted income subject to personal income taxation. Benefits are not directly conditioned on need.

ILLINOIS

Population: 11,245,000

Total State and Local Expenditures
for all Purposes:
$14,237,000,000

MAJOR FEDERALLY ENABLED
INCOME TRANSFER PROGRAMS
FY 77 Expenditures (est.)

Program	State	Local
Aid to Families with Dependent Children	$393,340,000	$ 0
Medicaid	484,960,000	0
Social Services	22,840,000	0

OPTIONAL STATE SUPPLEMENTATION FOR SSI

Department of Public Aid

The aged, over 65 years old, the blind, and the disabled are provided cash supplements to their Federal SSI benefits for basic and special needs. Basic needs are food, shelter, clothing, utilities and daily living necessities. Special needs are those not provided for through monthly or optional SSI payments and include moving expenses, repair and maintenance of property and payment of withheld rent. Benefits are provided to eligible persons regardless of living arrangement. Benefits are equal to the deficit between monthly SSI benefits, other income and income maintenance needs based on state standards. Benefits are in the form of direct cash payments, funded wholly by the state. Payments are administered by the state; eligibility is determined at local Department of Public Aid offices. Over 39,500 individuals are aided monthly. Benefits are conditioned on need.

FY 77 Expenditure (est.): **$31,008,000**

TEACHERS' RETIREMENT SYSTEM

Treasury Department

Full-time teachers (excluding those of the Chicago area) who retire at age 55 with at least 20 years of service, at age 60 with ten years of service or at age 62 with five years of service and their dependents are provided with financial assistance to replace income lost through retirement. Benefits are paid directly to the beneficiary in the form of cash without any restriction on its use. Payments average $470 per month. Some 29,000 individuals benefit from this program. Members contribute eight percent of salary while the state contributes an amount to cover costs not met by members' contributions. Benefits are not directly conditioned on need.

FY 77 Expenditure (est.): **$154,154,000**
Benefits paid total $152,691,000.
Administrative costs total $1,463,000.
State contributions total $157,000,000.

TEACHERS' PENSION AND RETIREMENT FUND OF CHICAGO

Teachers' Retirement System

Full-time Chicago public school teachers who retire at age 55 with at least 20 years of service or regardless of age with 25 years of service, and their dependents are provided with financial assistance to replace income lost through retirement. Benefits are paid directly to the beneficiary in the form of cash without any restriction on its use. Payments range from $167 to $1,417 per month. (The average retirement payment is about $617; the average survivor's payment, $183). Some 8,065 individuals benefit from this program. Members contribute 6.5 percent of salary (plus an additional one percent for survivors' coverage). The state contributes 19.9 percent. Benefits are not directly conditioned on need.

FY 77 Expenditure (est.): **$61,228,000**

Benefits paid total $60,665,000.
Administrative costs total $563,000.

STATE UNIVERSITIES' RETIREMENT SYSTEM

Treasury Department

Full-time employees of Illinois state universities who retire at age 62 with at least five years of service or at age 60 with eight years of service and their dependents are provided with financial assistance to replace income lost through retirement. Benefits are paid directly to the beneficiary in the form of cash without any restriction on its use. Payments average $450 per month. Some 7,500 individuals benefit from this program. Members contribute eight percent of salary while the state contributes about 11.93 percent. Benefits are not directly conditioned on need.

FY 77 Expenditure (est.): **$36,899,948**

Benefits paid total $36,000,000.
Administrative costs total $899,948.

GENERAL ASSEMBLY RETIREMENT SYSTEM

Treasury Department

All legislators who retire at age 55 with at least eight years of service, or at age 62 with four years of service and their dependents are provided with financial assistance to replace income lost through retirement. Benefits are paid directly to the beneficiary in the form of cash without any restriction on its use. Benefits average $7,813 annually. Some 142 retirees and 92 survivors receive such monthly benefits. Members contribute ten percent of salary while the state pays the cost of the plan not met by members' contributions. Benefits are not directly conditioned on need.

FY 77 Expenditure (est.): $1,240,205

Benefits paid total $782,300.
Administrative costs total $236,849.
State contributions total $782,300.

JUDGES' RETIREMENT SYSTEM

Treasury Department

Judges who retire at age 60 with at least ten years of service, or at age 62 with six years of service and their dependents are provided with financial assistance to replace income lost through retirement. Benefits are paid directly to the beneficiary in the form of cash without any restriction on its use. Payments average $1,718 per month. Some 186 retirees and 161 survivors benefit from this program. Members contribute 11 percent of salary while the state pays the cost of the plan not met by members' contributions. Benefits are not directly conditioned on need.

FY 77 Expenditure (est.): $4,321,718

Benefits paid to retirees total $3,284,653.
Benefits paid to survivors total $970,165.
Administrative costs total $66,900.
State contributions total $4,047,600.

PUBLIC EMPLOYEES' RETIREMENT SYSTEM

Treasury Department

Full-time state employees who retire at age 60 with at least eight years of service or at age 55 with 30 years of service, or regardless of age with 35 years of service and their dependents are provided with financial assistance to replace income lost through retirement. Benefits are paid directly to the beneficiary in the form of cash without any restriction on its use. Payments average $230 per month. Some 20,906 individuals benefit from this program. Members contribute four percent of salary (eight percent if they do not contribute to Social Security). Police and firefighters contribute 9 to 9.5 percent. The state contributes 7.3 percent. Benefits are not directly conditioned on need.

FY 77 Expenditure (est.): **$65,927,000**

Benefits paid total $64,795,000.
Administrative costs total $1,132,000.

WORKERS' COMPENSATION PROGRAM

Industrial Commission

Workers injured or disabled on the job, as well as the surviving dependents of workers who die as a result of such injury, are provided financial assistance both as compensation for lost wages and to pay for the cost of any required medical or rehabilitative care. Benefits are in the form of cash payments, funded by means of a state-regulated private insurance program to which each covered employer must contribute a percentage of payroll determined by the employer's experience rating and industrial classification. Beneficiaries receive two-thirds of normal wages up to a maximum weekly compensation benefit of $304. These benefits may be received for the total period of disability and the total amount of benefits one may receive is unlimited. In addition, a funeral allowance of $1,750 is provided for workers who die on the job. Approximately 30,000 workers and survivors were aided weekly in FY 77. Benefits are not directly conditioned on need.

FY 77 Expenditure (est.): **$332,728,000**

GENERAL ASSISTANCE PROGRAM

Department of Public Aid

Maintenance payments, short-term or emergency aid to cover the costs of food, shelter, clothing and other items of daily living are made to resident individuals, couples, families with children and fathers unemployed due to a strike. (Short-term assistance is also available to nonresident individuals pending return to their legal place of residence.) Benefits are paid directly to the beneficiary in the form of cash without any restrictions on its use or through vendor payments (to the suppliers of goods and services including medical care). Employable persons must accept work project assignments. Payments are in amounts varying according to each beneficiary's needs as determined under state law. Benefits are funded by grants to the administering local welfare agencies. This program is financed by state and local funds. Each month an average of 7l,650 recipients (in some 71,650 cases) are aided. The average monthly benefit per recipient is $116 (per case, the average is $136). Benefits are conditioned on need.

FY 77 Expenditure (est.): **$117,259,000**

ELDERLY OR DISABLED HOMEOWNERS' AND RENTERS' REBATE

Department of Revenue

Indirect financial assistance is provided to homeowners and renters aged 65 and older, or disabled, whose annual income does not exceed $10,000. Benefits are in the form of a tax relief, funded by rebates based on the amount that local property taxes or their rent equivalents exceed four percent of household income. The maximum benefit is $650. Additional benefits are provided regardless of tax or rent limits in the amount of either $50 or the product of income times a state-mandated percentage, whichever is greater. Approximately 400,000 persons were aided in FY 77, at an average of $250 per person. Benefits are conditioned, in part, on need.

FY 77 Expenditure (est.): **$100,000,000**

SENIOR CITIZEN PROPERTY TAX EXEMPTION

Department of Revenue

Indirect financial assistance is provided to homeowners 65 years and older. Benefits are in the form of tax relief, funded by allowing the homeowner to exempt from local property taxes up to $1,500 of assessed value of his homestead property. Approximately 200,000 homeowners received benefits in FY 77. Benefits are not directly conditioned on need.

FY 77 Expenditure (est.): **$10,000,000**

STUDENT AND ELDERLY REDUCED-FARE PROGRAM

Department of Transportation

Elderly persons and students are provided transportation assistance through provision of half-fares on public transport across the state. Benefits are in kind, funded by grants to public carriers, based on the number of rides. Almost 3,000,000 riders were subsidized in FY 77. Benefits are not directly conditioned on need.

FY 77 Expenditure (est.): **$23,500,000**

MINORITY BUSINESS ENTERPRISE

Department of Business and Economic Development

Minority, small businessmen are provided help in obtaining contracts with private and state agencies. Benefits are in kind, and consist of counseling, help in procurement of contracts and general advice. Over 1,000 persons were aided in FY 77. Benefits are not directly conditioned on need.

FY 77 Expenditure (est.): **$198,000**

CRIME VICTIMS' COMPENSATION

Attorney General's Office

Victims of violent crime are provided financial assistance to compensate for their losses. Benefits are in the form of cash and provide for losses not replaced by insurance or other plans. Claims must be filed within six months of the incident. Losses must be at least $200, and due only to personal injury. The maximum payment is $10,000. About 3,000 claims were filed in FY 77. Benefits are not conditioned on need.

FY 77 Expenditure (est.): **$930,000**

The above figure does not include administration.

AID TO THE MEDICALLY INDIGENT

Department of Public Aid

Those individuals who are not eligible for Medical Assistance or General Assistance, but whose medical bills exceed their ability to pay, are provided financial aid. Benefits are in the form of cash, paid directly to medical vendors, based on medical and financial need. About 16,000 persons were aided at an average cost of $950 per person. Benefits are conditioned on need.

FY 77 Expenditure (est.): **$15,010,000**

HEMOPHILIA PROGRAM

Department of Public Health

Individuals with hemophilia are provided treatment services and support, in the form of drugs and medical and social services. Over 200 persons received treatment services in FY 77. Benefits are in kind, funded by grants to hospitals across the state. Benefits are not directly conditioned on need.

FY 77 Expenditure (est.): **$305,000**

CHRONIC RENAL DISEASE

Department of Public Health

Individuals with chronic renal disease are provided medical services including kidney transplantation, dialysis, hospital care and drugs. Benefits are in kind, funded by payments to hospitals. Approximately 430 persons took advantage of this program in FY 77. Benefits are conditioned, in part, on need.

FY 77 Expenditure (est.): **$1,162,000**

SERVICES TO UNMARRIED MOTHERS

Department of Children and Family Services

Unmarried women in need of financial assistance are provided appropriate parental and child delivery services. Benefits are in kind, funded by grants to clinics and group homes. Services include maternity and foster home care, counseling and medical care. Benefits are conditioned on need.

FY 77 Expenditure (est.): **$728,000**

COMMUNITY SERVICES FOR THE VISUALLY HANDICAPPED

Department of Children and Family Services

Visually handicapped persons, regardless of age or financial condition, are provided services that enable them to adjust to the effects of their handicap. Benefits are in kind, funded by grants to area clinics and programs. Over 1,500 persons are treated annually. Services include training in mobility, personal care, home management and communication skills. Benefits are not conditioned on need, but visual loss must be severe enough to disallow ordinary activities.

FY 77 Expenditure (est.): **$646,000**

VISUALLY HANDICAPPED INSTITUTE

Department of Child and Family Services

Visually handicapped persons are provided special rehabilitation services. Services include training in braille, communication skills, crafts, homemaking and physical mobility. Benefits are in kind, funded by grants to a specialized rehabilitation institute. About 140 persons were aided in FY 77. Benefits are not directly conditioned on need.

FY 77 Expenditure (est.): **$2,109,000**

COMMUNITY-BASED PROGRAM FOR THE MENTALLY ILL

Department of Mental Health and Developmental Disabilities

Mentally ill persons are provided services in their own communities on an outpatient basis. Services include counseling, placement and medical services. Benefits are in kind, funded by state grants to community centers. Over 210,000 persons received services in FY 77. Benefits are conditioned, in part, on need.

FY 77 Expenditure (est.): **$29,877,000**

COMMUNITY-BASED PROGRAM FOR THE ALCOHOLIC

Department of Mental Health and Developmental Disabilities

Alcoholics are provided services on a community basis at outpatient clinics and short-term care facilities. Benefits are in kind and include detoxification, medical care and residential services. Funding is directly to area programs. Over 33,000 persons receive benefits annually. Benefits are conditioned, in part, on need.

FY 77 Expenditure (est.): **$7,700,000**

COMMUNITY-BASED SERVICES FOR THE DEVELOPMENTALLY DISABLED

Department of Mental Health and Developmental Disabilities

The developmentally disabled are provided medical counseling and placement services at the community level on an outpatient basis. Benefits are in kind, funded by grants to community agencies. Over 17,000 persons took advantage of the program in FY 77. Benefits are not directly conditioned on need.

FY 77 Expenditure (est.): **$36,300,000**

Additional Federal funds expended by this program amount to $800,000.

GRANTS-IN-AID

Department of Veterans' Affairs

Veterans and their families are provided assistance in the form of: 1) bonus payments; 2) headstones; 3) adapted housing; 4) educational opportunities for dependents; 5) services from veterans' organizations; and 6) maintenance travel for aided persons. Benefits are mainly in kind, funded by grants directly to persons and to organizations that provide service. The bonus payments are a one-time grant; headstones are subsidized for $30 per claim in addition to Federal monies; adapted housing, to a maximum of $5,000, in supplement to the Federal program; and educational grants, to $150 per year. Over 9,000 persons received one or another of these services in FY 77. Benefits are conditioned, in part, on need.

FY 77 Expenditure (est.): **$788,000**

VETERANS' HOME

Department of Veterans' Affairs

Veterans and their families are provided dormitory and nursing care at the state veterans' home. Benefits are in kind, funded by a state appropriation to the home. Over 700 persons are cared for annually. Benefits are not directly conditioned on need.

FY 77 Expenditure (est.): **$6,157,000**

VETERANS' SCHOLARSHIPS

Department of Veterans' Affairs

Veterans who have been honorably discharged and served at least one year in the armed forces are provided grants for college tuition and fees. Application for such grants must be made within six months of discharge. Benefits are in the form of cash, payable directly to the colleges. Benefits are not conditioned on need.

FY 77 Expenditure (est.): **$11,534,000**

SCHOLARSHIP FOR SURVIVORS/DEPENDENTS OF CORRECTIONAL WORKERS

Illinois State Scholarship Commission

Survivors and dependents of employees of the Department of Corrections who were killed or 90 percent disabled in the line of duty are provided tuition at universities and colleges across the state. Benefits are in the form of cash, payable directly to institutions. The maximum award is $1,350. Benefits are not conditioned on need.

FY 77 Expenditure (est.): **$5,000**

STATE SCHOLARSHIPS

Department of Education

Students with demonstrable need are provided grants for tuition and other expenses at state universities, colleges and community colleges. Benefits are in the form of cash, funded by payments to the institutions. Over 90,000 individuals were aided in FY 77 at an average cost of $760 per student. Benefits are conditioned on need.

FY 77 Expenditure (est.): **$69,100,000**

INDIANA

Population: 5,330,000

Total State and Local Expenditures
for all Purposes:
$5,080,000,000

MAJOR FEDERALLY ENABLED
INCOME TRANSFER PROGRAMS
FY 77 Expenditures (est.)

Program	State	Local
Aid to Families with Dependent Children	$ 31,530,000	$26,430,000
Medicaid	106,830,000	2,350,000
Social Services	1,780,000	2,490,000

OPTIONAL STATE SUPPLEMENTATION FOR SSI

Department of Public Welfare

The aged, over 65 years old, the blind, and the disabled, 18 and older, are provided cash supplements to their Federal SSI benefits for basic needs. Basic needs are food, shelter, clothing, utilities and daily living necessities. Benefits are provided to eligible persons living in licensed residential-care facilities or boarding homes for the aged. Benefits average $100 monthly for individuals living in a care facility or boarding home and may vary depending on the cost of the facility. Benefits are in the form of direct cash payments, funded wholly by the state. Payments are administered by the state; eligibility is determined at local department of Public Welfare offices. Over 250. individuals are aided monthly. Benefits are conditioned on need.

FY 77 Expenditure (est.): **$300,000**

FIREFIGHTERS' PENSION AND DISABILITY FUND

Treasury Department

Firefighters who retire at age 55 and their dependents are provided with financial assistance to replace income lost through retirement. Benefits are paid directly to the beneficiary in the form of cash without any restriction on its use. An average benefit is equal to one-half the salary of a first-class firefighter. This fund is newly organized (as of May 1, 1977) and consequently no benefits have been paid. Entering firefighters join this system. Members of the Pension Relief Fund may elect to join this system in 1980 and automatically receive $10,000. Members contribute six percent of the salary of a first-class firefighter. The state does not contribute directly to the system. Benefits are not directly conditioned on need.

FY 77 Expenditure (est.): **$1,530,000**

$1,500,000 were distributed to local units of the Pension Relief Fund to defray some expenses.
Administrative costs total $30,000.
The state contributes a portion of excise taxes on liquor, cigarettes and gasoline.

POLICE PENSION AND DISABILITY FUND

Treasury Department

Police officers who retire at age 55 and their dependents are provided with financial assistance to replace income lost through retirement. Benefits are paid directly to the beneficiary in the form of cash without any restriction on its use. An average benefit is equal to one-half the salary of a first-class police officer. This fund is newly organized (as of May 1, 1977) and consequently no benefits have been paid. Newly inducted officers join this system. Members of the Pension Relief Fund may elect to join this system in 1980 and automatically receive $10,000. Members contribute six percent of the salary of a first-class police officer. The state does not contribute directly to the system. Benefits are not directly conditioned on need.

FY 77 Expenditure (est.): $1,530,000

$1,500,000 were distributed to local units of the Pension Relief Fund to defray some expenses.
Administrative costs total $30,000.
The state contributes a portion of excise taxes on liquor, cigarettes and gasoline.

CONSERVATION AND EXCISE RETIREMENT SYSTEM

Treasury Department

Excise officers and conservation officers who retire at age 65 with at least ten years of service and their dependents are provided with financial assistance to replace income lost through retirement. Benefits are paid directly to the beneficiary in the form of cash without any restriction on its use. Payments average $225 per month. Some 35 individuals benefit from this program. Members contribute three percent of the first $8,500 earned and the state contributes ten percent. Benefits are not directly conditioned on need.

FY 77 Expenditure (est.): $98,500

Benefits paid total $94,500.
Administrative costs total $4,000.

TEACHERS' RETIREMENT FUND

Treasury Department

Full-time teachers who retire at age 65 with at least ten years of service, or at age 50 with 15 years of service, and their dependents are provided with financial assistance to replace income lost through retirement. Benefits are paid directly to the beneficiary in the form of cash without any restriction on its use. Payments average $335 per month. Some 22,000 individuals benefit from this program. Members contribute three percent of their salary which purchases an annuity. In addition, the state contributes an amount which will pay a retirement benefit equal to 1.1 percent of the average annual salary multiplied by the number of years of service. Benefits are not directly conditioned on need.

FY 77 Expenditure (est.): **$74,395,000**

Benefits paid total $74,000,000.
Administrative costs total $395,000.

PUBLIC EMPLOYEES' RETIREMENT FUND

Treasury Department

Full-time state employees who retire at age 60 with at least ten years of service and their dependents are provided with financial assistance to replace income lost through retirement. Benefits are paid directly to the beneficiary in the form of cash without any restriction on its use. Payments average $176 per month. Some 16,560 individuals benefit from this program. Members contribute three percent of salary while the state contributes about six percent. Benefits are not directly conditioned on need.

FY 77 Expenditure (est.): **$36,215,500**

Benefits paid total $35,578,000.
Administrative costs total $637,500.

SENIOR CITIZEN PROPERTY TAX EXEMPTION

Department of Revenue

Indirect financial assistance is provided to homeowners, 65 years and older, whose annual income is $6,000 or less. Benefits are in the form of tax relief, funded by allowing the homeowner to exempt from local property taxes $1,000 of assessed value of his homestead property. Almost 100,000 persons were aided in FY 77. Benefits are conditioned on need.

FY 77 Expenditure (est.): **$7,000,000**

ELDERLY OR DISABLED HOMEOWNERS' AND RENTERS' REBATE

Department of Revenue

Indirect financial assistance is provided to homeowners and renters aged 65 and older, or disabled, whose annual income does not exceed $5,000. Benefits are in the form of tax relief funded by rebates based on household income. The level of benefits ranges from ten percent to 75 percent of state property taxes or of their rent equivalents (generally calculated at 20 percent of rent). The maximum benefit is $500. Approximately 29,000 persons were aided in FY 77, at an average of $30 per person. Benefits are conditioned on need.

FY 77 Expenditure (est.): **$850,000**

SOLDIERS' AND SAILORS' HOME

Department of Health

Unwanted or orphaned children of veterans receive a high school education and residential care at the Soldiers' and Sailors' Home. Benefits are in kind, funded by a grant to the Home. About 325 children were aided in FY 77. Benefits are not directly conditioned on need.

FY 77 Expenditure (est.): **$3,559,000**

Indiana

WORKERS' COMPENSATION PROGRAM

Industrial Board

Workers injured or disabled on the job, as well as the surviving dependents of workers who die as a result of such injury, are provided financial assistance both as compensation for lost wages and to pay for the cost of any required medical or rehabilitative care. Benefits are in the form of cash payments, funded by means of a state-regulated private insurance program to which each covered employer must contribute a percentage of payroll determined by the employer's experience rating and industrial classification. Beneficiaries receive two-thirds of normal wages, up to a maximum weekly compensation benefit of $120. These benefits may be received for no more than 500 weeks, and the total amount of benefits one may receive is $60,000. In addition, a funeral allowance of $1,500 is provided for workers who die on the job. Approximately 16,000 workers and survivors were aided weekly in FY 77. Benefits are not directly conditioned on need.

FY 77 Expenditure (est.): **$70,628,000**

GENERAL ASSISTANCE PROGRAM

Department of Public Welfare

Short-term or emergency assistance to cover the costs of food, shelter, clothing and other items of daily living are made to resident individuals, couples and families with children. Benefits are paid directly to the beneficiary in the form of cash, without any restriction on its use, or through vendor payments. These payments are in amounts varying according to each beneficiary's needs, as determined under local law. Benefits are funded by appropriations to the administering local welfare agencies from local revenues. A monthly average of 13,000 recipients (in some 10,000 cases) are aided. The average benefit is $67 monthly per individual. Benefits are conditioned on need.

FY 77 Expenditure (est.): **$10,000,000**

HEMOPHILIA PROGRAM

Department of Health

Hemophiliacs are provided care, treatment and blood supplies at area clinics and hospitals. Benefits are in kind, funded by grants to participating programs to pay for the costs of treatment not otherwise met by medical insurance or other assistance programs. About 60 people were aided in FY 77. Benefits are conditioned, in part, on need.

FY 77 Expenditure (est.): **$150,000**

RENAL DISEASE PROGRAM

Department of Health

People with renal disease are provided dialysis, home care, transplantation and drugs. Benefits are in kind, funded by grants to participating institutions. About 110 persons were aided in FY 77. The average cost for hemodialysis per patient is $5,460. Benefits are conditioned, in part, on need.

FY 77 Expenditure (est.): **$153,000**

SICKLE CELL ANEMIA

Department of Health

Persons with, or at risk of having, sickle cell anemia are provided testing services, educational services and treatment at clinics and health department centers across the state. Benefits are in kind, funded by payments to participating institutions. Treatment is provided at the Indiana University Medical Center only; and about 50 persons received treatment in FY 77. Benefits are not conditioned on need.

FY 77 Expenditure (est.): **$121,000**

Indiana

EPILEPSY PROGRAM—CLINIC

Department of Mental Health

Individuals with epilepsy or suspected of having epilepsy are provided treatment and diagnostic care in outpatient clinics across the state. Benefits are in kind, funded by grants to participating clinics and hospitals. About 500 persons were aided in FY 77. Benefits are not conditioned on need.

FY 77 Expenditure (est.): **$443,000**

FAMILY CARE OF PATIENTS

Department of Mental Health

Individuals released from mental hospitals are provided less restrictive environments in community homes. Benefits are in kind, funded by payments directly to participating homes. Approximately 1,100 persons were aided in FY 77. Benefits are not conditioned on need.

FY 77 Expenditure (est.): **$4,750,000**

COMMUNITY MENTAL HEALTH CLINICS

Department of Mental Health

Mentally ill adults and those in need of outpatient mental health services are provided such services at 60 centers across the state. Benefits are in kind, consisting of therapy, counseling and other mental health services and are funded by grants to localities which contract with the centers. About 9,000 persons were aided in FY 77. Benefits are not conditioned on need.

FY 77 Expenditure (est.): **$1,250,000**

COMMUNITY MENTAL HEALTH CENTER

Department of Mental Health

Mentally ill and mentally retarded individuals, as well as alcoholics and drug abusers, are provided inpatient, outpatient and day care services at 26 mental health centers throughout the state. Benefits are in kind, funded by grants to the centers. Over 50,000 persons were aided in FY 77. Benefits are not conditoned on need.

FY 77 Expenditure (est.): **$13,767,000**

The above amount is matched by Federal funds, on a
  varying percentage basis from center to center.

COMMUNITY CENTERS—MENTALLY ILL AND RETARDED

Department of Mental Health

Mentally ill and mentally retarded persons are provided services at 26 centers across the state. Benefits are in kind, funded by grants to localities which contract with these centers. Services are primarily outpatient and include medical care and counseling. Approximately 80,000 persons were aided in FY 77. Benefits are conditioned, in part, on need.

FY 77 Expenditure (est.): **$36,500,000**

Of the above amount, $12,500,000 are Federal funds.

ASSISTANCE TO RETARDED PERSONS IN COMMUNITY HOMES

Department of Mental Health

Mentally retarded persons who have been released from state mental institutions are provided residential care in their communities as an alternative to further institutionalization. Benefits are in kind, and include care and services in boarding homes, adult activity centers and community residential facilities. Approximately 80 persons are aided annually. Benefits are not directly conditioned on need.

FY 77 Expenditure (est.): **$840,000**

Indiana

FREEDOM OF CHOICE GRANTS

Department of Education

Students who qualify for a state scholarship but who do not wish to attend a public college are provided financial assistance to continue their education within the state. The difference between the cost of education at the state college and at the private college of their choice is paid up to an established limit. Benefits are in the form of cash, paid directly to institutions. Over 1,500 students benefited in FY 77. The average benefit was $1,250. Benefits are conditioned on need.

FY 77 Expenditure (est.): **$2,288,000**

SCHOLARSHIP COMMISSION

Department of Education

College students are provided scholarships based on need and class rank at colleges and universities across the state. Benefits are in the form of cash, paid directly to institutions. About 14,000 people received aid in FY 77. The minimum grant is $100; the maximum, $1,400. Benefits are conditioned on need.

FY 77 Expenditure (est.): **$12,171,000**

EDUCATIONAL GRANTS

Department of Education

All students who do not qualify for state scholarships based on merit are eligible to receive awards based on financial need. Benefits are in the form of cash, funded by grants to participating institutions. About 4,500 students are aided annually. The minimum benefit is $100; the maximum, $1,400. Benefits are conditioned on need.

FY 77 Expenditure (est.): **$2,609,000**

MEDICAL DISTRIBUTION LOAN FUND

Department of Health

Students at medical schools are provided loans for tuition based on need and merit. Benefits are in the form of credit funded by lowered interest rates. About 30 students received loans in FY 77. The maximum loan is $3,000; and it need not be repaid if, for every $3,000 borrowed, one year is spent working in a prescribed area within the state. Benefits are conditioned on need.

FY 77 Expenditure (est.): **$185,000**

PERSONAL INCOME TAX PROVISIONS

Department of Revenue

Low-Income Exemption. Indirect financial assistance is provided to persons whose annual gross income is less than $1,000. Benefits are in the form of tax relief, funded by allowing the individual total exemption of income from personal income taxation. Benefits are conditioned on need.

Exemption from Intangibles Tax. Indirect financial assistance is provided to taxpayers owning stocks, bonds, mutual fund shares, etc., whose gross household income is less than $10,000. Benefits are in the form of tax relief, funded by allowing the taxpayer an exemption, for personal income tax purposes, from the tax due on his intangibles. Benefits are conditioned, in part, on need.

KENTUCKY

Population: 3,458,000

Total State and Local Expenditures
for all Purposes:
$3,480,000,000

MAJOR FEDERALLY ENABLED
INCOME TRANSFER PROGRAMS
FY 77 Expenditures (est.)

Program	State	Local
Aid to Families with Dependent Children	$47,020,000	$ 0
Medicaid	56,920,000	0
Social Services	10,440,000	0

OPTIONAL STATE SUPPLEMENTATION FOR SSI

Department of Human Resources

The aged, over 65 years old, the blind, and the disabled are provided cash supplements to their Federal SSI benefits for basic needs. Basic needs are food, shelter, clothing, utilities and daily living necessities. Benefits are provided to eligible persons living in personal-care facilities, in mini-homes for the aged or infirm, or in caretaker homes. Benefits average $101 monthly for individuals living in personal-care facilities, and vary for other categories. Benefits are in the form of direct cash payments, funded wholly by the state. Payments are administered by the state; eligibility is determined at local Department for Human Resources offices. Over 8,500 individuals are aided monthly. Benefits are conditioned on need.

FY 77 Expenditure (est.): **$10,704,000**

TEACHERS' RETIREMENT SYSTEM

Treasury Department

Full-time public school teachers who retire at age 55 with at least five years of service and their dependents are provided with financial assistance to replace income lost through retirement. Benefits are paid directly to the beneficiary in the form of cash without any restriction on its use. Payments range from $55 to $950 monthly (average about $450). Some 13,636 individuals benefit from this program. Members contribute 7.7 percent of salary while the state contributes 10.7 percent. Benefits are not directly conditioned on need.

FY 77 Expenditure (est.): **$63,923,000**

Benefits paid total $63,317,000.
Administrative costs total $606,000.

PUBLIC EMPLOYEES' RETIREMENT SYSTEM

Kentucky Retirement Systems

Public employees of the state and counties, including policemen and firemen, who retire at age 55 with at least five years of service and their dependents are provided with financial assistance to replace income lost through retirement. Benefits are paid directly to the beneficiary in the form of cash without any restriction on its use. Payments range up to $1,270 monthly (average $138). Some 7,800 individuals benefit from this program. Members contribute from four percent to seven percent of wages; and the employing jurisdiction contributes 7.25 percent, or 14 percent for hazardous work. Benefits are not directly conditioned on need.

FY 77 Expenditure (est.): **$12,524,000**

Benefits paid total $12,115,000.
Administrative costs total $409,000.

SENIOR CITIZEN HOMESTEAD EXEMPTION

Department of Revenue

Indirect financial assistance is provided to homeowners, 65 years and older. Benefits are in the form of tax relief, funded by allowing the elderly homeowner to exempt from local and school property taxation $8,900 of the assessed value of his homestead property. Almost 150,000 elderly homeowners benefit yearly. Benefits are not directly conditioned on need.

FY 77 Expenditure (est.): **$12,000,000**

WORKERS' COMPENSATION PROGRAM

Department of Labor

Workers injured or disabled on the job, as well as the surviving dependents of workers who die as a result of such injury, are provided financial assistance both as compensation for lost wages and to pay for the cost of any required medical or rehabilitative care. Benefits are in the form of cash payments, funded by means of a state-regulated private insurance program to which each covered employer must contribute a percentage of payroll determined by the employer's experience rating and industrial classification. Beneficiaries receive two-thirds of normal wages, up to a maximum weekly compensation of $104. These benefits may be received for the total period of disability and the total amount of benefits one may receive is unlimited. In addition, a funeral allowance of $1,500 is provided for workers who die on the job. Approximately 22,000 workers and survivors were aided weekly in FY 77. Benefits are not directly conditioned on need.

FY 77 Expenditure (est.): **$83,434,000**

GENERAL ASSISTANCE PROGRAM

Department of Human Resources

Short-term or emergency assistance to cover the costs of food, shelter, clothing and other items of daily living are made to resident individuals, couples and families with children. Benefits are paid directly to the beneficiary in the form of cash, without restriction on its use, or through vendor payments to the supplier of goods and services (including medical care). Employable persons must register with the state employment service. Payments are in amounts varying according to each beneficiary's needs as determined under state law. Benefits are funded by appropriations to the administering local welfare agencies from local revenues. A monthly average of 5,000 people (in some 2,500 cases) are aided. The average benefit is $25 per individual. Benefits are conditioned on need.

FY 77 Expenditure (est.): **$1,500,000**

ENERGY COST ASSISTANCE PROGRAM

Department of Human Resources

The elderly, blind and disabled are provided supplemental income to assist them in purchasing energy for home consumption purposes. Benefits are in the form of cash, paid directly to recipients. Approximately 64,000 persons are aided annually. Benefits are conditioned on need.

FY 77 Expenditure (est.): **$5,000,000**

CRISIS-ORIENTED PROGRAM FOR EMERGENCIES

Department of Human Resources

Single and married adults whose children, if any, are over 21 years of age are provided financial assistance if they are ineligible for Federally reimbursed public assistance. Benefits are in the form of cash, paid directly to recipients. Over 3,500 persons are aided annually. Benefits are conditioned on need.

FY 77 Expenditure (est.): **$750,000**

CRIME VICTIMS' REPARATIONS

Department of Justice

Victims of violent crime and their families are provided financial assistance to compensate for their losses. Benefits are in the form of cash and provide for losses not replaced by insurance or other plans. Benefit amounts are determined by the Victims' Compensation Board. Under 100 persons receive benefits annually. Benefits are not conditioned on need.

FY 77 Expenditure (est.): **$286,000**

PROJECT INDEPENDENCE FOR THE ELDERLY

Department of Social Services

Elderly individuals and their families are provided services so that the elderly may remain in their own homes or with caretaker relatives. Benefits are in kind, funded by payments for counseling, daycare, consumer protection and homemaker services. There are 24 services offered in all. Approximately 3,000 persons are aided annually. Benefits are not directly conditioned on need.

FY 77 Expenditure (est.): **$1,500,000**

KIDNEY DISEASE SERVICES

Department of Human Resources

Persons with end-stage renal disease are provided supplemental financial support for medical and rehabilitative services, including drugs and dialysis. Benefits are in kind, paid directly to institutions to purchase necessary services.About 1,200 persons were aided in FY 77. Benefits are not directly conditioned on need.

FY 77 Expenditure (est.): **$230,000**

TUBERCULOSIS AND OTHER RESPIRATORY DISEASES

Department of Human Resources

Persons with tuberculosis or at risk of having tuberculosis are provided in- and outpatient treatment and screening at clinics and hospitals throughout the state. Benefits are in kind, funded by payments to participating institutions. Approximately 1,200 persons were aided in FY 77. Benefits are not directly conditioned on need.

FY 77 Expenditure (est.): **$6,240,000**

PREVENTION AND TREATMENT OF ALCOHOL AND DRUG ABUSE

Department of Human Resources.

Alcoholics and drug abusers are provided medical support and rehabilitative services at comprehensive care centers. Benefits are in kind, funded by payments to centers and treatment facilities. Over 3,000 alcoholics and 7,300 drug abusers are provided emergency, in- and outpatient treatment annually. Benefits are conditioned, in part, on need.

FY 77 Expenditure (est.): **$3,006,000**

PREVENTION AND TREATMENT OF MENTAL RETARDATION

Department of Human Resources.

Mentally retarded adults who are treatable at outpatient centers are provided treatment and diagnosis. Services include medical care, rehabilitation services, physical education and vocational education. Benefits are in kind, funded by payments to participating clinics. Over 32,000 treatment services were performed in FY 77. Benefits are not directly conditioned on need.

FY 77 Expenditure (est.): **$2,260,000**

PREVENTION AND TREATMENT OF MENTAL ILLNESS

Department of Human Resources

In order to reduce the incidence of mental illness and to enhance the development of those already suffering from mental illness, patients are provided comprehensive mental health services at outpatient facilities across the state. Benefits are in kind, funded by payments to participating institutions. Over 99,000 patient-days of services were provided in FY 77. Benefits are conditioned, in part, on need.

FY 77 Expenditure (est.): **$2,050,000**

STUDENT ASSISTANCE

Department of Education

Those students in financial need and able to benefit from higher education are provided financial assistance and related services. Benefits are in the form of cash and credit, generally paid directly to colleges and universities. Approximately 2,500 individuals received student loans, 950 received tuition grants, and 4,000 received student incentive awards in FY 77. Benefits are conditioned on need.

FY 77 Expenditure (est.): **$5,088,000**

UNIVERSITY OF LOUISVILLE—SCHOLARSHIPS AND FELLOWSHIPS

Department of Education

Full- and part-time undergraduate and graduate students are provided scholarships, grants and fellowships to cover the cost of education at colleges and universities across the state. Benefits are in the form of cash, paid directly to institutions. Over 3,200 students were assisted in FY 77. The maximum benefit is $800 or the cost of tuition annually. Benefits are conditioned on need.

FY 77 Expenditure (est.): **$952,000**

Of the above amount, $129,000 are Federal funds.

UNIVERSITY OF KENTUCKY—SCHOLARSHIPS AND FELLOWSHIPS

Department of Education

Undergraduate students are provided scholarships, grants and fellowships based on financial need and academic ability. Benefits are in the form of cash, paid directly to the institution. Over 6,700 students received aid in FY 77. Benefits are to cover the costs of tuition, books and fees, and may range from $250 to $800 annually. Benefits are conditioned on need.

FY 77 Expenditure (est.): **$3,646,000**

PERSONAL INCOME TAX PROVISIONS

Department of Revenue

Public Employees' Retirement Income Exemption. Indirect financial assistance is provided to certain public employees who receive pensions or other retirement income. Benefits are in the form of tax relief, funded by allowing the taxpayer to exempt from personal income taxation the income received from teachers', state employees', county employees' or judicial retirement funds. Benefits are not directly conditioned on need.

Low-Income Exemption. Indirect financial assistance is provided to individuals whose annual gross income does not exceed scheduled limits ranging from $1,650, for those who are single and under age 65, to $4,900 for those who are single, age 65 or over, and blind. (Married couples follow a comparable schedule.) Benefits are in the form of tax relief, funded by allowing the individual total exemption of income from personal income taxation. Benefits are conditioned on need.

LOUISIANA

Population: 3,921,000

Total State and Local Expenditures
for all Purposes:
$4,733,000,000

MAJOR FEDERALLY ENABLED
INCOME TRANSFER PROGRAMS
FY 77 Expenditures (est.)

Program	State	Local
Aid to Families with Dependent Children	$35,200,000	$ 0
Medicaid	65,580,000	0
Social Services	7,870,000	830,000

Louisiana

STATE POLICE RETIREMENT SYSTEM

State Police; Payroll Section

Members of the state police who retire at age 55 with at least 20 years of service (or if hired before 1978, regardless of age with 20 years of service) and their dependents are provided with financial assistance to replace income lost through retirement. Benefits are paid directly to the beneficiary in the form of cash without any restriction on its use. Payments range from $300 to $1,000 per month. Some 480 individuals benefit from this program. Members contribute seven percent while the state contributes 24 percent. Benefits are not directly conditioned on need.

FY 77 Expenditure (est.): **$3,353,980**

Benefits paid total $3,353,000.
Administrative costs total $980.
Sources of funds include 50¢ for each driver's license, a
    percentage of the gasoline tax and a surplus of the
    highway department totalling $1,600,000.

SCHOOL EMPLOYEES' RETIREMENT SYSTEM

Treasury Department

Non-teaching employees of Louisiana public schools who retire at age 60 with at least ten years of service, at age 55 with 25 years of service, or regardless of age with 30 years of service, and their dependents are provided with financial assistance to replace income lost through retirement. Benefits are paid directly to the beneficiary in the form of cash without any restriction on its use. Payments average $170 per month. Some 2,500 individuals benefit from this program. Members contribute seven percent of salary. The state makes annual appropriations to the fund. Benefits are not directly conditioned on need.

FY 77 Expenditure (est.): **$5,218,000**

Benefits paid total $5,101,000.
Administrative costs total $117,000.
State contributions total $6,362,000 to help fund reserves.

SCHOOL LUNCH EMPLOYEES' RETIREMENT SYSTEM

Treasury Department

Employees in public school lunch programs and other persons not eligible for benefits other than Social Security who retire at age 65 with at least ten years of service and their dependents are provided with financial assistance to replace income lost through retirement. Benefits are paid directly to the beneficiary in the form of cash without any restriction on its use. Payments average $126 per month. Some 1,394 individuals benefit from this program. Members contribute half of one percent of the first $1,200 earned plus four percent of the balance of their annual earnings. The state contributes 3.5 percent. Benefits are not directly conditioned on need.

FY 77 Expenditure (est.): **$2,204,000**

Benefits paid total $2,115,000.
Administrative costs total $89,000.

TEACHERS' RETIREMENT SYSTEM

Treasury Department

Permanent teachers of public schools, state-supported colleges and trade schools who retire at age 60 with ten years of service, or at any age with 20 years of service, and their dependents are provided with financial assistance to replace income lost through retirement. Benefits are paid directly to the beneficiary in the form of cash without any restriction on its use. Payments average $577 per month. Some 13,842 individuals benefit from this program. Members contribute seven percent of salary while the state contributes eight percent. Benefits are not directly conditioned on need.

FY 77 Expenditure (est.): **$96,444,000**

Benefits paid total $95,764,000.
Administrative costs total $680,000.

MUNICIPAL EMPLOYEES' RETIREMENT SYSTEM

Treasury Department

Employees of member municipalities who retire at age 60 with at least ten years of service, or regardless of age with 30 years of service, and their dependents are provided with financial assistance to replace income lost through retirement. Payments range from $50 to $750 per month, depending upon length of service and class of membership. Some 1,065 individuals benefit from this program. Members contribute $100 plus four percent of their average annual salary. (Members no longer contributing toward Social Security contribute 9.25 percent). The state does not directly contribute. Benefits are not directly conditioned on need.

FY 77 Expenditure (est.): **$6,750,000**

Benefits paid total $6,659,000.
Administrative costs total $91,000.
Some .25 percent of the *ad valorem* tax is contributed to
  the pension accumulation fund.

STATE EMPLOYEES' RETIREMENT SYSTEM
Treasury Department

Full-time state employees (including legislators and judges) who retire at age 55 with 25 years of service, at age 60 with ten years of service, or regardless of age with 30 years of service, and their dependents are provided with financial assistance to replace income lost through retirement. Benefits are paid directly to the beneficiary in the form of cash without any restriction on its use. Payments average $372 per month. Some 11,000 individuals benefit from this program. Regular members contribute seven percent of their compensation (salary plus other benefits). Legislators and judges contribute eight percent. The state contributes eight percent for regular members and eleven percent for legislators and judges. Benefits are not directly conditioned on need.

FY 77 Expenditure (est.): **$45,550,000**

Benefits paid total $45,000,000.
Administrative costs total $550,000.
State contributions total $27,500,000.

HOMESTEAD EXEMPTION

Department of Revenue and Taxation

Indirect financial assistance is provided to all homeowners. Benefits are in the form of tax relief, funded by allowing the homeowner to exempt from property taxes $2,000 of assessed value of his homestead property. Over 600,000 persons benefit yearly. Benefits are not conditioned on need.

FY 77 Expenditure (est.): **$20,000,000**

BUREAU OF AGING SERVICES

Department of Health and Human Services

Elderly persons are provided services through community projects, nutritional programs and services for the homebound. Benefits are in kind, funded by grants to participating organizations. Over 14,000 persons were aided in FY 77. Benefits are not directly conditioned on need.

FY 77 Expenditure (est.): **$1,383,000**

OFFICE OF VETERANS' AFFAIRS

Department of Veterans' Affairs

All veterans and their families are provided financial and other assistance in four state veterans' programs: (1) contact assistance in obtaining and securing benefits; (2) war orphans' educational assistance; (3) Vietnam bonus and (4) the state-operated veterans' home. Benefits are in kind and in the form of cash, depending on the program. Almost 26,000 veterans were contacted in FY 77. Benefits are not directly conditioned on need.

FY 77 Expenditure (est.): **$1,563,000**

Louisiana

GENERAL ASSISTANCE PROGRAM

Department of Health and Human Resources

Maintenance payments, short-term or emergency aid to cover the costs of food, shelter, clothing and other items of daily living are made to resident individuals and couples, if unemployable, and families with children. Benefits are paid directly to the beneficiary in the form of cash without any restrictions on its use or through vendor payments (to the suppliers of goods and services including medical care). Payments are in amounts varying according to each beneficiary's needs as determined under state law. Benefits are funded by grants to local offices of the state public assistance agency. This program is financed by state funds. Each month some 3,000 recipients (in some 2,895 cases) are aided. The average monthly benefit per recipient is $23.65 (per case, the average is $57). Benefits are conditioned on need.

FY 77 Expenditure (est.): **$1,995,000**

WORKERS' COMPENSATION PROGRAM

Department of Labor

Workers injured or disabled on the job, as well as the surviving dependents of workers who die as a result of such injury, are provided financial assistance both as compensation for lost wages and to pay for the cost of any required medical or rehabilitative care. Benefits are in the form of cash payments, funded by means of a state-regulated private insurance program to which each covered employer must contribute a percentage of payroll determined by the employer's experience rating and industrial classification. Beneficiaries receive two-thirds of normal wages, up to a maximum weekly compensation benefit of $95. These benefits may be received for the total period of disability and the total amount of benefits one may receive is unlimited. In addition, a funeral allowance of $1,500 is provided for workers who die on the job. Approximately 31,000 workers and survivors were aided weekly in FY 77. Benefits are not directly conditioned on need.

FY 77 Expenditure (est.): **$150,546,000**

CHARITY HOSPITAL AT NEW ORLEANS

Department of Health and Human Resources

Health care is provided for the medically indigent and for those with obscure and severe medical problems from all parts of the state at Charity Hospital in New Orleans. Benefits are in kind and include diagnosis, medical and mental health care. Over 1,000 patients are aided daily. Benefits are conditioned on need.

FY 77 Expenditure (est.): **$53,831,000**

Of the above amount, $1,056,000 are Federal funds.

E.A. CONWAY MEMORIAL HOSPITAL

Department of Health and Human Resources

Indigent persons in eleven parish areas receive mental health care, as well as medical and surgical treatment. Benefits are in kind, funded by grants to the hospital. About 40,000 inpatient and 164,000 outpatient days of care are provided annually. Benefits are conditioned on need.

FY 77 Expenditure (est.): **$3,870,000**

EARL K. LONG MEMORIAL HOSPITAL

Department of Health and Human Resources

Indigent persons in eight parish areas are provided mental health care, as well as medical and surgical treatment. Benefits are in kind, funded by grants to the hospital. About 60,000 inpatient and 270,000 outpatient days of care are provided annually. Benefits are conditioned on need.

FY 77 Expenditure (est.): **$10,699,000**

Louisiana

HUEY P. LONG MEMORIAL HOSPITAL

Department of Health and Human Resources

Indigent persons in the central portion of the state are provided with medical care, mental health care and outpatient services. Benefits are in kind, funded by grants to the hospital. About 39,000 inpatient and 91,000 outpatient days of care are provided annually. Benefits are conditioned on need.

FY 77 Expenditure (est.): **$4,729,000**

ISAAC DELGADO REHABILITATION CENTER

Department of Education

Severely handicapped persons receive medical, social, physical and mental services at the center. Almost half the services are aimed at those with mental impairments. Benefits are in kind, funded by grants to the center. Over 550 persons were aided in FY 77. Benefits are conditioned on need.

FY 77 Expenditure (est.): **$182,000**

There are Federal matching funds for this program, on an 80/20 basis.

LAFAYETTE CHARITY HOSPITAL

Department of Health and Human Resources

Indigent persons in the south central portion of the state are provided medical care, mental health care and outpatient services. Benefits are in kind, funded by grants to the hospital. About 46,000 inpatient and 153,000 outpatient days of care are provided annually. Benefits are conditioned on need.

FY 77 Expenditure (est.): **$5,883,000**

LAKE CHARLES CHARITY HOSPITAL

Department of Health and Human Resources

Indigent persons who are suffering from alcoholism and drug abuse are provided with general medical care, mental health care and outpatient services. Benefits are in kind, funded by a grant to the hospital. Over 20,000 inpatient and 6,600 outpatient days of care are provided annually. Benefits are conditioned on need.

FY 77 Expenditure (est.): **$4,009,000**

LALLIE KEMP CHARITY HOSPITAL

Department of Health and Human Resources

Indigent persons who are acutely ill and live in rural areas of the state are provided general medical care, mental health care and outpatient services. Benefits are in kind, funded by a grant to the hospital. Over 19,800 inpatient and 134,000 outpatient days of care were provided in FY 77. Benefits are conditioned on need.

FY 77 Expenditure (est.): **$2,729,000**

WASHINGTON-SAINT TAMMANY CHARITY HOSPITAL

Department of Health and Human Resources

The indigent population of the Washington and Saint Tammany parishes are provided general care, mental health care and outpatient services. Benefits are in kind, funded by state grants to the hospital. Over 13,000 days of inpatient care are provided annually with another 40,000 days on an outpatient basis. Benefits are conditioned on need.

FY 77 Expenditure (est.): **$1,725,000**

COMMUNITY MENTAL HEALTH CENTERS

Department of Health and Human Resources

All persons residing in a center's catchment area are eligible for mental health services, including inpatient, outpatient, elderly, children, alcohol and drug abuse services. Benefits are in kind, funded by grants from the state to the centers. About 61,000 persons are aided annually, receiving prevention, detection, treatment and rehabilitation services. Benefits are conditioned, in part, on need.

FY 77 Expenditure (est.): **$8,670,000**

Of the above amount, $1,108,000 are Federal funds.

EXCEPTIONAL CHILDREN'S ACT

Department of Health and Human Resources

Parents of exceptional children are provided financial assistance for the cost of rooms, board, therapy, and in- and outpatient services in private and non-state institutions. Exceptional children are defined as the mentally retarded, emotionally disturbed, learning disabled and other handicapped who for various reasons cannot be placed in state institutions. Benefits are in cash, funded by grants directly to affected families. Over 1,600 children were aided in FY 77. Benefits are conditioned, in part, on need.

FY 77 Expenditure (est.): **$11,763,000**

HIGHER EDUCATION ASSISTANCE COMMISSION

Department of Education

College students who can show substantial need and who maintain high academic standing are provided loans or grants so that they may pursue a college education. Benefits are in the form of cash and credit, funded by payments directly to students. Over 7,500 persons were aided in FY 77 in amounts ranging from $200 to $500 for scholarships and varying amounts for grants and loans. Benefits are conditioned on need and academic standing.

FY 77 Expenditure (est.): **$595,000**

T.H. HARRIS SCHOLARSHIP PROGRAM

Superintendent of Education

Undergraduate students, enrolled on a full-time basis at public or private institutions, are provided scholarships based on merit, not to exceed $300 yearly. Benefits are in the form of cash, funded by payments to institutions. Over 1,300 students received scholarships in FY 77. Benefits are not conditioned on need.

FY 77 Expenditure (est.): **$341,000**

PERSONAL INCOME TAX PROVISIONS

Department of Revenue and Taxation

Low-Income Exemption. Indirect financial assistance is provided to persons whose annual gross income is less than $6,000. Benefits are in the form of tax relief, funded by allowing the individual a total exemption of his income from personal income taxation. Benefits are conditioned on need.

Credit for Disabled Taxpayers. Indirect financial assistance is provided to the taxpayer who is deaf or mentally incapacitated, who has lost the use of a limb, or who has a spouse or dependent with any of these disabilities. Benefits are in the form of tax relief, funded by allowing a credit of $20 against the taxpayer's income tax liability for each disabled person in the household. Benefits are not directly conditioned on need.

Public Employees' Retirement Income Credit. Indirect financial assistance is provided to certain public employees who receive pensions or other retirement income. Benefits are in the form of tax relief, funded by allowing the taxpayer a credit against his personal income tax liability equal to 1.5 percent of such retirement income. Benefits are not directly conditioned on need.

MARYLAND

Population: 4,139,000

Total State and Local Expenditures
for all Purposes:
$6,013,000,000

MAJOR FEDERALLY ENABLED
INCOME TRANSFER PROGRAMS

FY 77 Expenditures (est.)

Program	State	Local
Aid to Families with Dependent Children	$ 84,600,000	$2,040,000
Medicaid	176,830,000	4,460,000
Social Services	12,370,000	380,000

OPTIONAL STATE SUPPLEMENTATION FOR SSI

Department of Human Resources

The aged, over 65 years old, the blind and the disabled are provided cash supplements to their Federal SSI benefits for basic and special needs. Basic needs are food, shelter, clothing, utilities and daily living necessities. Special needs are those not provided for through monthly or optional SSI payments and include disaster assistance, emergency assistance, fuel assistance, home allowances and eviction-foreclosure allowances. Benefits are provided to eligible persons living in a domiciliary-care facility. Benefits average $32 monthly for those individuals who receive Federally administered benefits and $89 monthly for those who receive state-administered benefits. Benefits are in the form of direct cash payments funded wholly by the state. Payments are administered by both the state and Federal government; eligibility is determined at local Social Security Agency offices. Over 1,000 individuals receive Federally administered benefits and 300 receive state-administered benefits monthly. Benefits are conditioned on need.

FY 77 Expenditure (est.): **$795,000**

STATE POLICE RETIREMENT SYSTEM

Personnel Department

All full-time state police who retire at age 50, or regardless of age with 25 years of service, and their dependents are provided with financial assistance to replace income lost through retirement. Benefits are paid directly to the beneficiary in the form of cash without any restriction on its use. Payments, depending upon length of service, average $809 per month. Some 174 individuals benefit from this program. Members contribute eight percent of salary. The state contributes 15.77 percent. Benefits are not directly conditioned on need.

FY 77 Expenditure (est.): **$2,070,000**

Benefits paid total $1,689,000.
Administrative costs total $381,000.

TEACHERS' RETIREMENT SYSTEM

Personnel Department

All public school teachers and various other school employees who retire at age 60, or regardless of age with 30 years of service, and their dependents are provided with financial assistance to replace income lost through retirement. Benefits are paid directly to the beneficiary in the form of cash without any restriction on its use. Payments average $595 per month. Some 10,293 individuals benefit from this program. Members contribute five percent of salary. The state contributes 5.73 percent. Benefits are not directly conditioned on need.

FY 77 Expenditure (est.): **$75,348,000**

Benefits paid total $74,967,000.
Administrative costs total $381,000.
State contributions total $94,106,000 to help fund reserves.

JUDGES' PENSION PLAN

Personnel Department

All judges who retire at age 60 with at least 16 years of service, or who are ordered to retire by the Court of Appeals, and their dependents are provided with financial assistance to replace income lost through retirement. Benefits are paid directly to the beneficiary in the form of cash without any restriction on its use. Payments average $1,019 per month. Some 88 individuals benefit from this program. Members contribute six percent of salary. The state pays the cost of the plan not met by members' contributions. This is an unfunded, pay-as-you-go system. Benefits are not directly conditioned on need.

FY 77 Expenditure (est.): **$1,076,000**

Benefits paid total $1,076,000.
Administrative costs are paid through the state retirement
    system.
State contributions total $1,036,000.

PUBLIC EMPLOYEES' RETIREMENT SYSTEM

Personnel Department

All full-time state employees and eligible municipal employees who retire at age 60 with at least five years of service, or regardless of age with 30 years of service, and their dependents are provided with financial assistance to replace income lost through retirement. Benefits are paid directly to the beneficiary in the form of cash without any restriction on its use. Payments, depending upon length of service, average $254 per month. Some 9,936 individuals benefit from this program. Members contribute 4.3 percent of salary. The state contributes 5.26 percent (local contribution is 4.29 percent). Benefits are not directly conditioned on need.

FY 77 Expenditure (est.): **$31,695,000**

Benefits paid total $31,314,000.
Administrative costs total $381,000.

HOMEOWNER TAX CREDIT

Department of Assessments and Taxation

Indirect financial assistance is provided to homeowners meeting certain income criteria. Benefits are in the form of tax relief, funded by allowing a credit based on the excess of property taxes over a percentage of income. A graduated schedule of percentages is used, ranging from 1.5 to nine percent of household income for persons 60 years and older, with a maximum benefit set at $900. Homeowners under 60 years of age receive 50 percent of above benefits, with a maximum of $450. Approximately 84,000 homeowners were aided in FY 77, at an average benefit of $248 per person. Benefits are conditioned, in part, on need.

FY 77 Expenditure (est.): **$20,808,000**

WORKERS' COMPENSATION PROGRAM

Workman's Compensation Commission

Workers injured or disabled on the job, as well as the surviving dependents of workers who die as a result of such injury, are provided financial assistance both as compensation for lost wages and to pay for the cost of any required medical or rehabilitative care. Benefits are in the form of cash payments, funded by means of state-administered and state-regulated private insurance programs to which each covered employer must contribute a percentage of payroll determined by the employer's experience rating and industrial classification. Beneficiaries receive two-thirds of normal wages, up to a maximum weekly compensation benefit of $188. These benefits may be received for the total period of disability and the total amount of benefits one may receive is unlimited. In addition, a funeral allowance of $1,200 is provided for workers who die on the job. Approximately 14,000 workers and survivors were aided weekly in FY 77. Benefits are not directly conditioned on need.

FY 77 Expenditure (est.): **$95,220,000**

GENERAL ASSISTANCE PROGRAM

Department of Human Resources

Maintenance payments, short-term or emergency aid to cover the costs of food, shelter, clothing and other items of daily living are made to individuals and couples, usually if unemployable, and families with children. Benefits are paid directly to the beneficiary in the form of cash without any restrictions on its use. Employable persons must accept work project assignments. Payments are in amounts varying according to each beneficiary's needs as determined under state law. Benefits are funded by grants to local offices of the state public assistance agency. This program is financed by state funds. Localities may elect to participate in a special program for employables where state and local funds cover the assistance payments and state funds cover the administrative expenses. Medical care is provided under the state's medical assistance program and is not paid from general assistance funds. Each month some 20,140 recipients (in some 18,913 cases) are aided. The average monthly benefit per recipient is $108 (per case, the average is $115). Benefits are conditioned on need.

FY 77 Expenditure (est.): **$26,104,000**

CRIMINAL INJURIES COMPENSATION BOARD

Department of Public Safety and Convention

Victims of violent crime are provided financial assistance to compensate for their losses. Benefits are in the form of cash and provide for losses not replaced by insurance and other plans. Victims must have suffered serious financial hardship, lost at least two weeks' work, or incurred over $100 in medical costs. About 500 persons received benefits in FY 77. The maximum benefit is $45,000 per claimant. Benefits are not conditioned on need.

FY 77 Expenditure (est.): **$1,361,000**

TREATMENT SERVICES—AGED AND CHRONICALLY ILL

Department of Health and Mental Hygiene

Individuals who are chronically ill, disabled, or suffering from tuberculosis or kidney disease are provided diagnosis, treatment rehabilitation, hemodialysis and related services, drugs and transplantation, as appropriate. Benefits are in kind, funded by payments to participating institutions. About 450 persons received kidney disease treatment in FY 77, at an average cost of $1,300 per patient. Payments varied for other catergories. Benefits are not directly conditioned on need.

FY 77 Expenditure (est.): **$776,000**

RENAL DIALYSIS

Department of Health and Mental Hygiene

To ensure that persons with serious kidney disease receive life-sustaining treatment at the lowest possible cost, this program pays participating renal disease facilities the cost of dialysis and end-stage treatment not paid for by other sources (i.e., Medicare, Medicaid and private insurance). Benefits are in kind, funded by payments to participating institutions. About 30 people receive benefits yearly at an average cost of $10,000 per patient. Benefits are not conditioned on need.

FY 77 Expenditure (est.): **$344,000**

TUBERCULOSIS TREATMENT—INPATIENT

Department of Health and Mental Hygiene

Persons suffering from tuberculosis are provided medical treatment and care. Most patients are elderly persons with chronic problems associated with aging. Many of them are also alcoholics. Benefits are in kind, funded by payments to the Mount Wilson Center. Over 200 persons received benefits in FY 77. Benefits are not conditioned on need.

FY 77 Expenditure (est.): **$744,000**

CRIPPLED CHILDREN'S SERVICE—PREVENTIVE MEDICINE ADMINISTRATION

Department of Health and Mental Hygiene

Needy children with handicapping conditions are provided services in order to prevent permanent disability and to assure that every child will ultimately reach his fullest potential. Services include inpatient and outpatient treatment, purchase of appliances and prostheses, and diagnostic care. Benefits are in kind, funded by payments to hospitals and clinics. About 500 inpatients (at $2,608 per person), 1,000 outpatients (at about $200), and 2,000 specialty patients (at about $50) are treated annually. Benefits are conditioned on need.

FY 77 Expenditure (est.): **$3,245,000**

Of the above amount, $626,000 are Federal funds.

COMMUNITY SERVICES TO ALCOHOLICS

Department of Health and Mental Hygiene

Alcoholics in need of community health services are provided detoxification treatment and general health care at community clinics throughout the state. Benefits are in kind, funded by state grants to the centers. Approximately 15,000 persons were aided in FY 77. Services include in- and outpatient care. Benefits are not directly conditioned on need.

FY 77 Expenditure (est.): **$1,694,000**

EDUCATION OF WAR ORPHANS AND CHILDREN OF DISABLED VETERANS

Department of Public Education

Orphans and children of disabled veterans are provided financial assistance for post-secondary education. Benefits are in the form of cash, paid directly to students. The average benefit is $500 and is paid to over 250 students between the ages of 16 and 23, or up to 27 years old if they have served in the armed forces. Benefits are not conditioned on need.

FY 77 Expenditure (est.): **$119,000**

GENERAL STATE SCHOLARSHIPS

Department of Public Education

Students who can demonstrate financial need and show satisfactory scholastic achievement are provided financial assistance for study at public and private colleges throughout the state. Benefits are in the form of cash, paid directly to institutions. Over 3,200 students were aided in FY 77. Awards range from $200 to $1,500. Half of the funds are for need-based grants and half are for merit-based awards. Benefits are conditioned, in part, on need.

FY 77 Expenditure (est.): **$1,728,000**

Of the above amount, $801,000 are Federal funds.

HIGHER EDUCATION LOAN CORPORATION

Department of Public Education

College students who can demonstrate need are provided low-interest, college-deferred loans at an average of $1,430 per year. Benefits are in the form of favorable credit terms and loan guarantees, to cover the cost of tuition, books and living expenses. About 6,700 students were aided in FY 77. Benefits are conditioned on need.

FY 77 Expenditure (est.): **$469,000**

DELEGATE SCHOLARSHIPS

Department of Public Education

Undergraduate students, enrolled on a full-time basis at public or private institutions, are provided full scholarships for four years. The scholarships are assigned at the discretion of each member of the Maryland House of Delegates who may assign up to two during his term of office. Benefits are in the form of cash, up to a pre-determined level, covering tuition and mandatory fees at any private or public college or university in the state. Approximately 400 students were aided by this program in FY 77. Benefits are not conditioned on need.

FY 77 Expenditure (est.): **$283,000**

LEGISLATIVE SCHOLARSHIPS

Department of Public Education

Undergraduate students, enrolled on a full-time basis at public or private institutions, are provided scholarships which are allocated to each state senator for selection. Benefits are in the form of cash, paid directly to institutions. Each senator compiles a roster of applicants and then submits them to the State Scholarship Commission where they are reviewed for eligibility. Students must demonstrate need and satisfactory achievement. Students must also be Maryland residents and live in the sponsoring senator's district. Over 6,500 students were aided in FY 77. The minimum scholarship is $200; the maximum is $1,500. Scholarships are renewable for up to four years. Benefits are conditioned on need.

FY 77 Expenditure (est.): **$2,668,000**

PERSONAL INCOME TAX PROVISIONS

Department of Treasury

Low-Income Exemption. Indirect financial assistance is provided to persons whose annual gross income is less than $2,950 for a single person or $4,700 for a married couple. Benefits are in the form of tax relief, funded by allowing the individual a total exemption of his income from personal income taxation. Benefits are conditioned on need.

Exemption for Disabled Policemen and Firemen. Indirect financial assistance is provided to firemen and policemen receiving pensions for employment-connected injuries or disabilities. Benefits are in the form of tax relief, funded by allowing the taxpayer to exclude from personal income taxation up to $3,200 of pension income. Benefits are not directly conditioned on need.

MASSACHUSETTS

Population: 5,782,000

Total State and Local Expenditures
for all Purposes:
$7,968,000,000

MAJOR FEDERALLY ENABLED
INCOME TRANSFER PROGRAMS

FY 77 Expenditures (est.)

Program	State	Local
Aid to Families with Dependent Children	$243,780,000	$ 0
Medicaid	402,860,000	0
Social Services	17,190,000	0

OPTIONAL STATE SUPPLEMENTATION FOR SSI
Department of Public Welfare

The aged, over 65 years old, the blind and the disabled are provided cash supplements to their SSI benefits for basic and special needs. Basic needs are food, shelter, clothing, utilities and daily living necessities. Special needs are those not provided for through monthly or optional SSI payments and include disaster benefits, burial expenses, rest home subsidies, moving expenses and home-maker and housekeeper services. Benefits are provided to eligible persons living independently, sharing living expenses, living in the household of another or living in domiciliary-care homes. Benefits range up to $144 monthly for blind individuals and $377 for blind couples living independently, and are proportionately lower for other categories. Benefits are in the form of direct cash payments funded wholly by the state. Payments are administered by the Federal government; eligibility is determined at local Social Security district offices. Over 123,500 individuals are aided monthly. Benefits are conditioned on need.

FY 77 Expenditure (est.): **$155,610,000**

PUBLIC EMPLOYEES' RETIREMENT SYSTEM

Treasury Department

Full-time employees (except elected or appointed officials) who retire at age 55 with 20 years of service and their dependents are provided with financial assistance to replace income lost through retirement. Benefits are paid directly to the beneficiary in the form of cash without any restriction on its use. Payments average $375 per month. Some 23,000 individuals benefit from this program. Most members contribute five percent of salary (the rate for new members is seven percent). The state pays the cost of the plan not met by members' contributions (about 16.3 percent). This is an unfunded pay-as-you-go system. Benefits are not directly conditioned on need.

FY 77 Expenditure (est.): **$100,567,000**

Benefits paid total approximately $100,000,000.
Administrative costs total $567,000 which does not include the cost incurred through the use of the state treasurer's computer system.
State contributions are approximately 85-87 percent of the total benefits.

Massachusetts

EXEMPTION FOR SENIOR CITIZENS

Department of Revenue

Indirect financial assistance is provided to homeowners, 70 years and older, who have resided in the state for ten years, whose gross annual income is less than $6,000 ($7,000 if married) and whose total worth does not exceed $40,000 ($45,000 if married). Benefits are in the form of tax relief, funded by allowing the elderly home-owner an abatement from local property taxes of $4,000 of assessed value or $350, whichever is greater. Approximately 68,000 persons were aided in FY 77. Benefits are conditioned, in part, on need.

FY 77 Expenditure (est.): **$39,400,000**

SENIOR CITIZEN PROPERTY TAX DEFERRAL

Department of Revenue

Indirect financial assistance is provided to homeowners, 65 years and older, who have resided in the state for at least ten years and whose gross incomes do not exceed $20,000. Benefits are in the form of tax relief, funded by the state's assumption of a home-owner's local property taxes, in amounts up to 50 percent of the homeowner's equity in the property. Annual interest at eight per-cent is charged against the share assumed by the state and the total becomes a lien against the property. Some 350 persons were aided in FY 77. Benefits are not directly conditioned on need.

FY 77 Expenditure (est.): **$443,668**

EXEMPTION FOR ELDERLY, INFIRM AND POOR

Department of Revenue

Indirect financial assistance is provided to persons who are elderly, infirm and poor, meeting certain income criteria. Benefits are in the form of tax relief, funded by allowing an abatement from local pro-perty taxes in such amounts and for such periods as may be neces-sary. Approximately 5,000 persons were aided in FY 77. Benefits are conditioned on need.

FY 77 Expenditure (est.): **$2,000,000**

EXEMPTION FOR SURVIVING SPOUSES AND CHILDREN, AND PERSONS 70 YEARS OR OLDER

Department of Revenue

Indirect financial assistance is provided to surviving spouses, minors of deceased parents, and persons 70 years or older, who have been domiciled in the property for at least ten years and whose property value does not exceed $20,000. Benefits are in the form of tax relief, funded by allowing an abatement from local property taxes of $2,000 of assessed value or $175, whichever is greater. Approximately 20,000 persons were aided in FY 77. Benefits are not directly conditioned on need.

FY 77 Expenditure (est.): **$9,900,000**

EXEMPTION FOR WIDOWS AND/OR CHILDREN OF FIREMEN AND POLICEMEN

Department of Revenue

Indirect financial assistance is provided to widows and/or children of firemen or policemen killed in the line of duty. Benefits are in the form of tax relief, funded by allowing the survivor an abatement from local property taxes of $8,000 of assessed value or $700, whichever is greater. Over 150 persons were aided in FY 77. Benefits are not directly conditioned on need.

FY 77 Expenditure (est.): **$140,000**

EXEMPTION FOR BLIND PERSONS

Department of Revenue

Indirect financial assistance is provided to totally blind persons. Benefits are in the form of tax relief, funded by allowing the blind person an abatement of $5,000 of assessed value or $437.50, whichever is greater. Over 3,100 persons were aided in FY 77. Benefits are not directly conditioned on need.

FY 77 Expenditure (est.): **$2,750,000**

TAX RELIEF FOR VETERANS

Department of Revenue

Indirect financial assistance is provided to disabled veterans; veterans from the Spanish-American War, Philippine Insurrection or Chinese Relief Expedition, if honorably discharged; veterans awarded the Purple Heart; wives and widows of qualified veterans who have resided in the state for five years; and mothers and fathers of soldiers and sailors who died in war service. Benefits are in the form of tax relief, funded by allowing an abatement from local property taxes of $2,000 of assessed value or $175, whichever is greater. Approximately 70,000 persons were aided in FY 77. Benefits are not directly conditioned on need.

FY 77 Expenditure (est.): **$18,700,000**

EXEMPTION FOR DISABLED VETERANS

Department of Revenue

Indirect financial assistance is provided to veterans who lost or suffered permanent loss of use of a foot, hand or eye, or who were awarded the Congressional Medal of Honor, Distinguished Service Cross, Navy Cross or Air Force Cross. Benefits are in the form of tax relief, funded by allowing an abatement from local property taxes of $4,000 of assessed value or $350, whichever is greater. Approximately 1,200 persons were aided in FY 77. Benefits are not directly conditioned on need.

FY 77 Expenditure (est.): **$580,000**

EXEMPTION FOR DISABLED VETERANS

Department of Revenue

Indirect financial assistance is provided to veterans who lost or suffered permanent loss of use of both feet or hands, or one foot and one hand, or the sight of both eyes. Benefits are in the form of tax relief, funded by allowing an abatement from local property taxes of $8,000 of assessed value or $700, whichever is greater. Over 150 persons were aided in FY 77. Benefits are not directly conditioned on need.

FY 77 Expenditure (est.): **$130,000**

EXEMPTION FOR 100 PERCENT-DISABLED VETERANS

Department of Revenue

Indirect financial assistance is provided to veterans with a 100 percent, war-service-connected disability, who are incapable of working. Benefits are in the form of tax relief, funded by allowing an abatement from local property taxes of $6,000 of assessed value or $525, whichever is greater. Approximately 1,800 persons were aided in FY 77. Benefits are not directly conditioned on need.

FY 77 Expenditure (est.): **$1,180,000**

EXEMPTION FOR PARAPLEGIC VETERANS

Department of Revenue

Indirect financial assistance is provided to paraplegic veterans. Benefits are in the form of tax relief, funded by allowing the veteran a total exemption from local property taxes. Over 300 persons were aided in FY 77. Benefits are not directly conditioned on need.

FY 77 Expenditure (est.): **$510,000**

EXEMPTION FOR VETERANS IN SPECIAL HOUSING

Department of Revenue

Indirect financial assistance is provided to disabled veterans entitled to specially adapted housing. Benefits are in the form of tax relief, funded by allowing an abatement from local property taxes of $10,000 of assessed value or $875, whichever is greater. Less than 100 persons were aided in FY 77. Benefits are not directly conditioned on need.

FY 77 Expenditure (est.): **$80,000**

GENERAL ASSISTANCE PROGRAM

Executive Office of Human Services

Short-term or emergency assistance to cover the costs of food, shelter, clothing and other items of daily living are made to resident individuals and couples, if unemployable, and families with children. Benefits are paid directly to the beneficiary in the form of cash without any restrictions on its use or through vendor payments in the case of medical assistance. Payments are in amounts varying according to each beneficiary's needs as determined under state law. Benefits are funded by grants to local offices of the state public assistance agency. This program is financed by state funds. Veterans' benefits are also available to a veteran or his dependents administered by a veterans' benefits office in each city or town. (State reimburses cities and towns 50 percent of the benefits payments.) Each month an average of 23,744 recipients (in some 21,578 cases) are aided. The average benefit payment per recipient is $133 (per case the average is $146). Benefits are conditioned on need.

FY 77 Expenditure (est.): **$37,826,000**

WORKERS' COMPENSATION PROGRAM

Industrial Accident Board

Workers injured or disabled on the job, as well as the surviving dependents of workers who die as a result of such injury, are provided financial assistance both as compensation for lost wages and to pay for the cost of any required medical or rehabilitative care. Benefits are in the form of cash payments, funded by means of a state-regulated private insurance program to which each covered employer must contribute a percentage of payroll determined by the employer's experience rating and industrial classification. Beneficiaries receive two-thirds of normal wages, up to a maximum benefit of $150 plus a $6 allowance for each dependent. These benefits may be received for the total period of disability and the total amount of benefits one may receive is $37,500. In addition, a funeral allowance of $1,000 is provided for workers who die on the job. Approximately 30,000 workers and survivors were aided weekly in FY 77. Benefits are not directly conditioned on need.

FY 77 Expenditure (est.): **$168,653,000**

VICTIMS OF VIOLENT CRIME

Treasury Department

Victims of violent crime are provided assistance to compensate for their losses. Benefits are in the form of cash and provide for losses not replaced by insurance or other plans. Victims must have incurred an out-of-pocket loss of at least $70. The maximum payment is $10,000. Benefits are not conditioned on need.

FY 77 Expenditure (est.): **$1,250,000**

HOME CARE SERVICES FOR THE AGED

Department of Elder Affairs

Low-income persons aged 60 and over, at risk of institutionalization, are provided home care services in order to prevent institutionalization by making it possible for them to continue living in their homes. Benefits are in kind, funded by state payments to home care corporations. The income ceilings for eligibility are $4,800 for an individual and $7,200 for a couple. About 27,000 elderly persons were aided in FY 77. Benefits are conditioned on need.

FY 77 Expenditure (est.): **$8,271,000**

HOME TEACHING FOR THE BLIND

Department of Human Resources

Adult blind persons are provided services in order to teach handicrafts, home management, and reading and writing in braille. Benefits are in kind, funded by payments to various service programs. Approximately 900 persons were aided in FY 77. Benefits are not directly conditioned on need.

FY 77 Expenditure (est.): **$199,000**

Massachusetts

CHRONIC DISEASE CONTROL

Department of Public Health

Victims of chronic disease, like venereal disease, epilepsy, alcoholism and heart disease are provided screening, testing and maintenance services at clinics and hospitals within the state. Benefits are in kind, funded by payments to participating institutions. Benefits are conditioned, in part, on need.

FY 77 Expenditure (est.): **$14,015,000**

Of the above amount, $2,419,000 are Federal funds.

ENDSTAGE CHRONIC RENAL DIALYSIS

Department of Public Health

Individuals with chronic renal disease are provided medical services including kidney transplantation, dialysis, hospital care and drugs. Benefits are in kind, funded by payments to treatment centers in hospitals and clinics. Approximately 700 persons take advantage of this program yearly. Benefits are conditioned, in part, on need.

FY 77 Expenditure (est.): **$1,457,000**

COMMUNITY SERVICES FOR CHILDREN—EARLY INTERVENTION

Department of Mental Health

Children under three years of age who are mentally retarded or developmentally disabled are provided treatment, vocational training and nursing care in their homes. Benefits are in kind, funded by payments to 41 area programs which serve families with these children. Over 12,000 individuals are aided annually. Benefits are not directly conditioned on need.

FY 77 Expenditure (est.): **$1,187,000**

MEDICAL EXAMINATIONS FOR THE MENTALLY RETARDED

Department of Mental Health

Mentally retarded individuals are provided medical examinations, in order to monitor and maintain their physical health, at clinics and hospitals throughout the state. Benefits are in kind, funded by payments to participating programs. Over 5,000 inpatients are aided annually. Benefits are not directly conditioned on need.

FY 77 Expenditure (est.): **$405,000**

COMMUNITY PROGRAMS FOR THE MENTALLY RETARDED

Department of Mental Health

Mentally retarded persons are provided various services through programs designed to enable them to exist outside of institutional settings. Benefits are in kind, funded by payments to participating programs. Programs include residences for those who attend day programs, staffed and cooperative apartment residences, home-care, respite care, day activities and sheltered workshops. Over 6,000 individuals are aided at some 500 sites annually. Benefits are not directly conditioned on need.

FY 77 Expenditure (est.): **$4,145,000**

ASSISTANCE TO CHILDREN OF WAR VETERANS

Department of Higher Education

Children aged 16-24 of veterans killed in service, who have lived in the state for not less than five years, are provided financial assistance at state higher educational institutions. Benefits are in the form of cash, paid directly to the students. About 150 students were aided in FY 77. The maximum benefit is $750 per year. Benefits are not directly conditioned on need.

FY 77 Expenditure (est.): **$112,000**

STATE HIGHER EDUCATION GRANTS

Department of Higher Education

Students in need, who have lived in the state for at least one year, are provided financial assistance to cover the costs of a higher education. Benefits are in the form of cash, paid directly to the institutions. About 23,000 students are assisted annually, with awards ranging from $300 to $900 depending, in part, on whether the college is private or public. Benefits are conditioned on need.

FY 77 Expenditure (est.): **$14,250,000**

PERSONAL INCOME TAX PROVISIONS

Department of Corporations and Taxation

Low-Income Exemption. Indirect financial assistance is provided to persons whose annual gross income is $3,000 or less for a single person or $5,000 or less for a married couple. Benefits are in the form of tax relief, funded by allowing the individual a total exemption of his income from personal income taxation. Persons with slightly higher incomes, whose computed income tax liability would reduce their total income to below the $3,000 or $5,000 limit, as appropriate, are also exempted from payment of taxation. Benefits are conditioned on need.

Low-Income Credit. Indirect financial assistance is provided to taxpayers whose total household income is $5,000 or less. Benefits are in the form of tax relief funded by allowing the taxpayer a $4 credit for himself, $4 for his dependent spouse and $8 for every other dependent, to be deducted from his personal income tax liability. Benefits are conditioned on need.

Adoption Fee Exemption. Indirect financial assistance is provided to taxpayers who paid fees to a licensed adoption agency to adopt a minor child. Benefits are in the form of tax relief, funded by allowing the taxpayer to exempt from personal income taxation the portion of the fees in excess of three percent of the adjusted gross income. Benefits are not conditioned on need.

Public Employees' Retirement Income Exemption. Indirect financial assistance is provided to certain public employees who receive pensions or other retirement income. Benefits are in the form of tax relief, funded by allowing the taxpayer to deduct from his gross adjusted income subject to taxation, pensions or retirement fund income from the state or other states with reciprocal provisions. Benefits are not directly conditioned on need.

MICHIGAN

Population: 9,129,000

Total State and Local Expenditures
for all Purposes:
$12,687,000,000

MAJOR FEDERALLY ENABLED
INCOME TRANSFER PROGRAMS
FY 77 Expenditures (est.)

Program	State	Local
Aid to Families with Dependent Children	$406,880,000	$ 0
Medicaid	446,750,000	0
Social Services	27,180,000	0

OPTIONAL STATE SUPPLEMENTATION FOR SSI

Department of Social Services

The aged, over 65 years old, the blind and the disabled are provided cash supplements to their SSI benefits for basic and special needs. Basic needs are food, shelter, clothing, utilities and daily living necessities. Special needs are those not provided for through monthly or optional SSI payments and include emergency home repairs and repairs or replacement of essential home appliances. Benefits are provided to eligible persons living independently, living in the household of another, in domiciliary or personal care facilities and in homes for the aged. Benefits are $25 for individuals and $38 for couples living independently and vary for other categories. Benefits are in the form of direct cash payments, funded wholly by the state. Payments are administered by the Federal government; eligibility is determined at local Social Security district offices. Over 106,500 individuals are aided monthly. Benefits are conditioned on need.

FY 77 Expenditure (est.): **$56,232,000**

STATE POLICE RETIREMENT SYSTEM

Bureau of Retirement Systems

Members of the state police who retire regardless of age with 25 years of service and their dependents are provided with financial assistance to replace income lost through retirement. Benefits are paid directly to the beneficiary in the form of cash without any restriction on its use. Payments range from $200 to $1200 per month (average $623). Some 616 individuals benefit from this program. This system is noncontributory for members while the state contributes 23.43 percent of total payroll (100 percent of total cost). Benefits are not directly conditioned on need.

FY 77 Expenditure (est.): **$4,271,000**

Benefits paid total $4,271,000.
Administrative costs are absorbed by the Treasury Department.

JUDGES' RETIREMENT FUND

Bureau of Retirement Systems

Judges of the various courts of the state who retire at age 60 with at least 12 years of service, at age 55 with 18 years of service, or regardless of age with 25 years of service, and their dependents are provided with financial assistance to replace income lost through retirement. Benefits are paid directly to the beneficiary in the form of cash averaging $781 per month depending upon length of service. Some 50 judges and 43 beneficiaries receive such monthly payments. Members contribute 3.5 percent of salary while the state makes no direct contribution. This system is also financed by various court fees.

FY 77 Expenditure (est.): **$893,000**

Benefits paid total $871,000.
Administrative costs total $22,000.

PUBLIC SCHOOL EMPLOYEES' RETIREMENT FUND

Bureau of Retirement Systems

Public school employees (including teachers) who retire at age 60 with at least ten years of service, or at age 55 with 30 years of service, and their dependents are provided with financial assistance to replace income lost through retirement. Benefits are paid directly to the beneficiary in the form of cash without any restriction on its use. Payments average $284 per month depending upon length of service. Some 36,000 individuals benefit from this program. This system is noncontributory (since June 1977). The state contributes an amount which is actuarily determined. Benefits are not directly conditioned on need.

FY 77 Expenditure (est.): **$123,715,000**

Benefits paid total $122,802,000.
Administrative costs total $913,000.

STATE EMPLOYEES' RETIREMENT FUND

Bureau of Retirement Systems

State employees who retire at age 60 with at least ten years of service, or at age 55 with 30 years of service, and their dependents are provided with financial assistance to replace income lost through retirement. Benefits are paid directly to the beneficiary in the form of cash without any restriction on its use. Payments average $250 per month. Some 11,566 individuals benefit from this program. This system is noncontributory for members. The state contributes about ten percent of total payroll. Benefits are not directly conditioned on need.

FY 77 Expenditure (est.): **$29,641,000**

Benefits paid total $29,257,000.
Administrative costs total $383,800.

TAX RELIEF FOR HOMEOWNERS AND RENTERS

Department of Treasury

Indirect financial assistance is provided to homeowners and renters. Benefits are in the form of tax relief, funded by means of a credit against state income taxes equal to 60 percent of the individual's property tax bill or rent equivalent (set at 17 percent of rent) in excess of 3.5 percent of taxpayer's income. (The elderly receive a proportionately larger credit.) The maximum benefit is $1,200. Should the homeowner or renter not file a state income tax, a rebate is issued. Approximately 1,235,000 persons were aided in FY 77, at an average of $223 each. Benefits are not conditioned on need.

FY 77 Expenditure (est.): **$275,580,000**

TAX RELIEF FOR SENIOR CITIZENS

Department of Treasury

Indirect financial assistance is provided to homeowners and renters, 65 years and older. Benefits are in the form of tax relief, funded by means of an income tax credit based on the amount by which property taxes (or 17 percent of rent) exceed the percentage of income determined by a progressive scale set up by the state. Should the homeowner or renter not file a state income tax, a rebate is issued. Approximately 359,000 persons were aided in FY 77, at an average of $335 each. Benefits are not directly conditioned on need.

FY 77 Expenditure (est.): **$120,250,000**

TAX RELIEF FOR DISABLED PERSONS AND/OR PARAPLEGICS

Department of Treasury

Indirect financial assistance is provided to totally and permanently disabled persons, paraplegics and quadraplegics. Benefits are in the form of tax relief, funded by means of additional state income tax credits equal to 60 percent of the property tax bill (or 17 percent of rent) in excess of an established percentage of income. The maximum credit is $1,200. Should the homeowner or renter not file a state income tax, a rebate is issued. Approximately 32,000 persons were aided in FY 77, at an average of $183 each. Benefits are not directly conditioned on need.

FY 77 Expenditure (est.): **$5,810,000**

148

Michigan

TAX RELIEF FOR BLIND PERSONS

Department of Treasury

Indirect financial assistance is provided to blind persons. Benefits are in the form of tax relief, funded by means of a credit against state income taxes based on a state-equalized value allowance of $3,500 ($7,000 for a married couple if both persons are blind). If the state-equalized value of the property is less than the allowance, all property taxes are refunded up to a maximum of $1,200. If the property value is more than the allowance, a credit is calculated. Should the homeowner or renter not file a state income tax, a rebate is issued. Approximately 3,200 persons were aided in FY 77, at an average of $210 each. Benefits are not directly conditoned on need.

FY 77 Expenditure (est.): **$670,000**

TAX RELIEF FOR SERVICEMEN, VETERANS AND THEIR WIDOWS

Department of Treasury

Indirect financial assistance is provided to servicemen, veterans and their widows, having a maximum household income of $7,500, and to all disabled veterans and their widows, regardless of income. Benefits are in the form of tax relief, funded by means of a credit against state income taxes based on that percentage of the property taxes that the state-equalized value allowance bears to the state-equalized value of the property. The maximum credit is $1,200. Should the homeowner or renter not file a state income tax, a rebate is issued. Approximately 57,000 persons were aided in FY 77, at an average of $193 each. Benefits are conditioned, in part, on need.

FY 77 Expenditure (est.): **$10,980,000**

WORKERS' COMPENSATION PROGRAM

Department of Labor

Workers injured or disabled on the job, as well as the surviving dependents of workers who die as a result of such injury, are provided financial assistance both as compensation for lost wages and to pay for the cost of any required medical or rehabilitative care. Benefits are in the form of cash payments, funded by means of state-administered and state-regulated private insurance programs to which each covered employer must contribute a percentage of payroll determined by the employer's experience rating and industrial classification. Beneficiaries receive two-thirds of normal wages, up to a maximum benefit of $127 to $156 according to the number of dependents. These benefits may be received for the total period of disability and the total amount of benefits one may receive is unlimited. In addition, a funeral allowance of $1,500 is provided for workers who die on the job. Approximately 81,000 workers and survivors were aided weekly in FY 77. Benefits are not directly conditioned on need.

FY 77 Expenditure (est.): **$418,008,000**

GENERAL ASSISTANCE PROGRAM

Department of Social Services

Maintenance payments, short-term or emergency aid to cover the costs of food, shelter, clothing and other items of daily living are made to individuals, couples and families with children. Emergency aid is also available to nonresident individuals pending return to their legal place of residence. Benefits are paid directly to the beneficiary in the form of cash without any restrictions on its use or through vendor payments (to the suppliers of goods and services including medical assistance). Employable persons must accept work project assignments. Payments are in amounts varying according to each beneficiary's needs as determined under state law. Benefits are funded by grants to local offices of the state public assistance agency. This program is financed by state and local funds. Each month an average of 59,343 recipients (in some 47,820 cases) are aided. The average monthly benefit per recipient is $147 (per case, the average is $182). Benefits are conditioned on need.

FY 77 Expenditure (est.): **$104,694,000**

Michigan

GRANTS FOR VETERANS' ORGANIZATIONS AND DEPENDENT ASSISTANCE

Department of Grants and Debt Services

Veterans are assisted in obtaining services and education at state schools and emergency assistance for their dependents in time of need. Benefits are in kind for the educational function and in the form of cash for emergency assistance. Benefits are funded through earnings on trust funds. Over 1,100 veterans and children of veterans were aided in FY 77. Benefits are conditioned on need.

FY 77 Expenditure (est.): **$4,129,000**

VIETNAM VETERANS' BONUS ADMINISTRATION

Department of Military Affairs

Michigan residents who served in the armed forces during 1961-1973 are provided financial assistance. Benefits are in the form of cash, paid directly to the veterans. The minimum annual award is $15, the maximum $600, based on length of service and other related military factors. Some 400,000 veterans were eligible to receive bonuses in FY 77. Benefits are not conditioned on need.

FY 77 Expenditure (est.): **$396,000**

VETERANS' FACILITY

Department of Public Health

Veterans are provided nursing and domiciliary care due to their disability or inability to earn a livelihood. Benefits are in kind, funded by payments to the facilities. About 700 persons are aided annually. Benefits are conditioned on need.

FY 77 Expenditure (est.): **$4,264,000**

Of the above amount, $1,327,000 are Federal funds.

CRIPPLED CHILDREN SERVICES

Department of Public Health

Crippled children are provided medical services, clinical services, nursing care, social services and appliances. Benefits are in kind, funded by payments directly to service providers. Over 16,000 children received some treatment annually. Benefits are not conditioned on need.

FY 77 Expenditure (est.): **$13,841,000**

Of the above amount, $5,147,000 are in Federal funds.

COMMUNITY PLACEMENT FOR MENTALLY ILL AND MENTALLY RETARDED

Department of Mental Health

Mentally ill and mentally retarded persons who have been released from state mental institutions are provided residential care in their communities. Benefits are in kind and include boarding homes, adult activity centers and community residential facilities. Benefits are conditioned, in part, on need.

FY 77 Expenditure (est.): **$10,667,000**

SUBSTANCE ABUSE SERVICES

Department of Public Health

Drug abusers and potential drug abusers are provided services like prevention, outpatient care, methadone maintenance and other medical procedures. Benefits are in kind, funded by payments to co-ordinating agencies which then contract for services locally. Some 57,000 persons are treated annually. Benefits are conditioned, in part, on need.

FY 77 Expenditure (est.): **$11,353,000**

STATE CLINICS—MENTALLY RETARDED

Department of Mental Health

Mentally retarded persons who can be cared for on an outpatient basis are provided medical and clinical services. Benefits are in kind, funded by state grants to local programs. Over 1,100 persons were aided at an average cost of $40 per visit. Benefits are conditioned, in part, on need.

FY 77 Expenditure (est.): **$4,207,000**

GRANTS AND FINANCIAL AID

Department of Education

Students in need are provided grants, scholarships and loans in order to enable them to attend college. Benefits are in the form of cash and credit, paid directly to beneficiaries. Benefits include tuition grants, scholarships based on merit, academic achievement awards and loans. About 5,200 persons received scholarships, 7,000 received grants, and 2,000 received loans in FY 77. The average award for scholarships and grants is $1,200. For the achievement award, the average is $500. Benefits are conditioned on need.

FY 77 Expenditure (est.): **$26,800,000**

PERSONAL INCOME TAX PROVISIONS

Department of Treasury

Low-Income Exemption. Indirect financial assistance is provided to persons whose annual gross income does not exceed scheduled limits ranging from $1,500 for those who are single and under age 65 to $6,000 for those who are married and both over age 65. Benefits are in the form of tax relief, funded by allowing the individual a total exemption of his income from personal income taxation. Benefits are conditioned on need.

Disabled Taxpayer Exemption. Indirect financial assistance is provided to taxpayers who are paraplegic, quadraplegic or hemiplegic, or whose spouse is similarly disabled. Benefits are in the form of tax relief, funded by allowing the individual an additional $1,500 exemption of his income from personal income taxation for each disabled person in the household. Benefits are not directly conditioned on need.

MINNESOTA

Population: 3,975,000

Total State and Local Expenditures
for all Purposes:
$5,803,000,000

MAJOR FEDERALLY ENABLED
INCOME TRANSFER PROGRAMS
FY 77 Expenditures (est.)

Program	State	Local
Aid to Families with Dependent Children	$ 36,080,000	$44,470,000
Medicaid	148,820,000	22,300,000
Social Services	1,190,000	10,760,000

OPTIONAL STATE SUPPLEMENTATION FOR SSI

Department of Public Welfare

The aged, over 65 years old, the blind and the disabled are provided cash supplements to their SSI benefits for basic and special needs. Basic needs are food, shelter, clothing, utilities and daily living necessities. Special needs are those not provided for through monthly or optional SSI payments and include recurring needs like transportation, newspapers and telephones, and nonrecurring needs like major housing repairs, moving expenses, furniture replacement, and fuel and utility adjustments. Benefits are provided to eligible persons according to geographic area. Benefits are $33 for individuals and $44 monthly for couples living independently. Benefits vary within allowable standards according to shelter needs and size of assistance households. Benefits are in the form of direct cash payments, funded 50 percent by the state and 50 percent by localities. Payments are administered by the counties except for salaries which are shared 50 percent by the state. Eligibility is determined at County Welfare and Human Services Boards. Over 5,500 individuals are aided monthly. Benefits are conditioned on need.

FY 77 Expenditure (est.): **$3,192,000**

HIGHWAY PATROLMEN'S RETIREMENT FUND

Commissioner of Finance

State troopers, conservation officers and crime bureau personnel who retire at age 55 with at least ten years of service and their dependents are provided with financial assistance to replace income lost through retirement. Benefits are paid directly to the beneficiary in the form of cash ranging from $209 to $511 (average $455) per month. Some 289 individuals benefit from this program. Members contribute eight percent of salary while the state contributes 22 percent. Benefits are not directly conditioned on need.

FY 77 Expenditure (est.): **$1,082,000**

Benefits paid total $1,047,000.
Administrative costs total $35,000.

TEACHERS' RETIREMENT FUND

Commissioner of Finance

Full-time public school teachers (except in the areas of Duluth, Minneapolis and St. Paul) who retire at age 55 with at least ten years of service, or regardless of age with 30 years of service, and their dependents are provided with financial assistance to replace income lost through retirement. Benefits are paid directly to the beneficiary in the form of cash, averaging $300 per month. Some 9,300 individuals benefit from this program. Members contribute four or eight percent of salary while the state contributes seven or eleven percent (depending on whether or not the teacher is covered by Social Security). Benefits are not directly conditioned on need.

FY 77 Expenditure (est.): **$25,800,000**

Benefits paid total $25,000,000.
Administrative costs total $800,000.

STATE LEGISLATURE RETIREMENT SYSTEM

Treasury Department

Members of the state legislature who retire at age 60 with at least eight years of service, and their dependents are provided with financial assistance to replace income lost through retirement. Benefits are paid directly to the beneficiary in the form of cash without any restriction on its use. Payments average $1,089 per month. Some 195 individuals benefit from this program. Members contribute eight percent of salary while the state contributes any amount not met by members' contributions, to fund any past service liability. Benefits are not directly conditioned on need.

FY 77 Expenditure (est.): **$2,556,000**

Benefits paid total $2,548,000.
Administrative costs total $8,000.

JUDGES' RETIREMENT FUND

Treasury Department

All judges (except seven justices of the Supreme Court) who retire at age 62 with at least ten years of service and their beneficiaries are provided with financial assistance to replace income lost through retirement. Benefits are in the form of cash without any restriction on its use. Payments average $800 per month. Some 43 individuals benefit from this program. Members contribute between 4.2 and 4.8 percent of salary. The state contributes between 8.1 and 8.6 percent. Benefits are not directly conditioned on need.

FY 77 Expenditure (est.): **$369,800**

Benefits paid total $356,800.
Administrative costs total $13,000.
State contributions total $1,198,000 paid from the state
    general fund and the Judges' Retirement Fund, some of
    which is to fund reserves.

PUBLIC EMPLOYEES' RETIREMENT ASSOCIATION

Treasury Department

Local government employees (who are not members of any other retirement system) who retire at age 65 with at least ten years of service, or at age 62 with 30 years of service, and their dependents are provided with financial assistance to replace income lost through retirement. Benefits are paid directly to the beneficiary in the form of cash without any restriction on its use. Payments average $390 per month. Some 7,100 individuals benefit from this program. Members contribute four percent of salary while the state contributes six percent. Benefits are not directly conditioned on need.

FY 77 Expenditure (est.): **$29,900,000**

Benefits paid total $28,824,000.
Administrative costs total $1,076,000.

STATE EMPLOYEES' RETIREMENT SYSTEM

Treasury Department

Full-time state employees who retire at age 65 with at least ten years of service, or at age 62 with 30 years of service (police and firefighters may retire at age 55 with ten years of service), and their dependents are provided with financial assistance to replace income lost through retirement. Benefits are paid directly to the beneficiary in the form of cash without any restriction on its use. Payments average $156 per month. Some 8,084 individuals benefit from this program. Members contribute four to eight percent of salary (police and firefighters contribute eight percent while the state contributes 5.5 to 10.5 percent (12 percent for police and firefighters). Benefits are not directly conditioned on need.

FY 77 Expenditure (est.): **$15,892,000**

Benefits paid total $15,171,000.
Administrative costs total $721,000.

CREDIT FOR HOMEOWNERS AND RENTERS

Department of Revenue

Indirect financial assistance is provided to homeowners and renters on their property taxes. Benefits are in the form of tax relief, funded by means of rebates or—only for senior citizens, renters and disabled persons—income tax credits. The rebate or credit is based on the amount by which local property taxes or rent equivalents (set at 22 percent of rent) exceed a percentage (from one to four percent) of the taxpayer's income. The maximum benefit is $475. Approximately 860,000 persons were aided in FY 77, at an average of $156 each. Benefits are conditioned, in part, on need.

FY 77 Expenditure (est.): **$134,200,000**

GENERAL ASSISTANCE PROGRAM

Department of Public Welfare

Maintenance payments, short-term or emergency aid to cover the costs of food, shelter, clothing and other items of daily living are made to individuals, couples, families with children and fathers unemployed due to a strike. Emergency aid is also available to non-resident individuals pending return to their legal place of residence. Benefits are paid directly to the beneficiary in the form of cash without any restrictions on its use or through vendor payments (to the suppliers of goods and services). Employable persons must accept work project assignments. Payments are in amounts varying according to each beneficiary's needs as determined under state law. Benefits are funded by grants to local offices of the state public assistance agency. This program is financed by state and local funds. Medical care is provided under the state's medical assistance program. Each month an average of 16,687 recipients (in some 13,505 cases) are aided. The average monthly benefit per recipient is $113 (per case, the average is $140). Benefits are conditioned on need.

FY 77 Expenditure (est.): **$22,625,000**

WORKERS' COMPENSATION PROGRAM

Department of Labor and Industry

Workers injured or disabled on the job, as well as the surviving dependents of workers who die as a result of such injury, are provided financial assistance both as compensation for lost wages and to pay for the cost of any required medical or rehabilitative care. Benefits are in the form of cash payments, funded by means of a state-regulated private insurance program to which each covered employer must contribute a percentage of payroll determined by the employer's experience rating and industrial classification. Beneficiaries receive two-thirds of normal wages, up to a maximum weekly compensation benefit of $197. These benefits may be received for the total period of disability and the total amount of benefits one may receive is unlimited. In addition, a funeral allowance of $1,000 is provided for workers who die on the job. Approximately 16,000 workers and survivors were aided weekly in FY 77. Benefits are not directly conditioned on need.

FY 77 Expenditure (est.): **$118,249,000**

VETERANS' BENEFITS

Department of Veterans' Affairs

Disabled and needy veterans and their dependents are provided short-term financial assistance for hospitalization, medical and dental treatment. Also, children of veterans who died of service-connected disabilities are provided financial assistance for higher education. Benefits are in the form of cash, paid to veterans or their families. About 11,000 veterans and their dependents are aided annually, 116 of them being war orphans who receive $250 each for education. Benefits are conditioned on need.

FY 77 Expenditure (est.): **$1,068,000**

VETERANS' SERVICES

Department of Veterans' Affairs

Veterans who are incompetent and are in need of general support are provided fiscal supervision and general support if their income ranges from $173 to $1,000 per month. Benefits are in kind, funded by the purchase of the services of guardians. Approximately 500 individuals are aided annually. Benefits are conditioned on need.

FY 77 Expenditure (est.): **$200,000**

LONG-TERM SHELTERED EMPLOYMENT AND WORK ACTIVITY

Department of Vocational Rehabilitation

Disabled, handicapped or mentally retarded individuals are provided opportunities to work and to support themselves through jobs in sheltered workshops where they are employed in conjunction with local business. Benefits are in the form of both cash compensation for work performed and in kind, including self-care skills, socialization and educational skills. In FY 76 the workshops produced $10.5 million in goods and paid $4.5 million in wages. One hundred of the persons working in the facilities entered private employment in FY 77. Benefits are not directly conditioned on need.

FY 77 Expenditure (est.): **$4,234,000**

Of the above amount, $1,350,000 are Federal funds.

Minnesota

DISEASE CONTROL

Department of Health

Individuals who have contracted, or who are at risk of contracting, tuberculosis, cancer, hypertension and similar diseases, are provided diagnostic services, follow-up preventive care, inpatient and outpatient treatment. Benefits are in kind, funded by grants to treatment facilities. Over 80,000 patient care procedures were provided in FY 77. Benefits are not conditioned on need.

FY 77 Expenditure (est.): **$1,543,000**

Of the above amount, $500,000 are Federal funds.

SERVICES TO CHILDREN WITH HANDICAPS

Department of Health

Children with severe, physically handicapping conditions are provided high quality, comprehensive care, including diagnosis, treatment and therapy. Benefits are in kind, funded by grants to participating care facilities. Approximately 14,000 children were aided in FY 77, at an average cost of almost $400 per case. Benefits are conditioned, in part, on need.

FY 77 Expenditure (est.): **$5,476,000**

Of the above amount, $1,500,000 are Federal funds.

STATE STUDENT LOAN PROGRAM

Department of Higher Education

Postsecondary students are provided long-term, low-interest loans to defray the cost of their education. Benefits are in the form of favorable credit terms. Loans can be up to $2,500 per year and $7,500 cumulatively for undergraduate students and up to $5,000 per year and $15,000 cumulatively for graduate students. Approximately 15,000 students received loans in FY 77. Benefits are conditioned on need.

FY 77 Expenditure (est.): **$26,500,000**

The above amount represents the value of loans disbursed.

STATE SCHOLARSHIPS AND GRANTS-IN-AID

Department of Higher Education

Academically talented students in need are provided financial assistance toward the cost of tuition, books and living expenses in order for them to attend college within the state. Benefits are in the form of cash, funded by payments to higher education institutions. Over 25,000 students received either a scholarship or a grant-in-aid in FY 77. The maximum payment is $1,100. Benefits are conditioned on need.

FY 77 Expenditure (est.): **$17,000,000**

NURSING SCHOLARSHIP PROGRAM

Department of Higher Education

Nursing students with limited financial resources are provided scholarships in varying amount if they are not receiving aid from other sources. Benefits are in the form of cash, paid directly to the students. Approximately 200 students were aided in FY 77. The maximum benefit is $1,100 or 75 percent of need. Benefits are conditioned on need.

FY 77 Expenditure (est.): **$125,000**

MEDICAL STUDENT LOANS

Department of Higher Education

Medical students at the University of Minnesota, Minneapolis, Duluth or the Mayo Medical school, or any interested osteopathy student, are provided long-term low-interest loans to finance their education. Benefits are in the form of favorable credit terms, and loans may be repaid in full through service in a designated rural area for three years. Approximately 65 students receive loans annually at a maximum of $6,000 per year. Benefits are conditioned on need.

FY 77 Expenditure (est.): **$481,000**

PERSONAL INCOME TAX PROVISIONS

Department of Revenue

Low-Income Exemption. Indirect financial assistance is provided to persons whose annual gross income does not exceed scheduled limits ranging from $1,000 for those who are single and under age 65, to $2,400 for those who are single, blind and age 65 or over, and to $3,600 for married couples in which both members are age 65 or over and blind. Benefits are in the form of tax relief, funded by allowing the individual a total exemption of his income from personal income taxation. Benefits are conditioned on need.

Low-Income Credit. Indirect financial assistance is provided to taxpayers whose income does not exceed scheduled limits ranging from $4,400 for single persons to $7,800 for those with five or more dependents. Fifteen percent of personal income is subtracted from the computed tax liability. Benefits are in the form of tax relief, funded by allowing the taxpayer a credit against his personal income tax liability based on the above formula. Benefits are conditioned on need.

Public Employee Retirement Pay Deduction. Indirect financial assistance is provided to certain public employees who receive pensions or other retirement income. Benefits are in the form of tax relief, funded by allowing the taxpayer to deduct pension and retirement income from his gross adjusted income subject to personal income taxation. Benefits are not directly conditioned on need.

Deduction of Adoption Expenses. Indirect financial assistance is provided to taxpayers who adopted a child. Benefits are in the form of tax relief, funded by allowing the taxpayer a deduction from gross annual income of up to $1,250 for expenses relating to the adoption. Benefits are not conditioned on need.

Deaf Credit. Indirect financial assistance is provided to taxpayers who are deaf or who have a deaf spouse or dependent. Benefits are in the form of tax relief, funded by allowing the taxpayer a $25 credit against his personal income tax liability for each deaf member of the household. Benefits are not directly conditioned on need.

MISSOURI

Population: 4,801,000

Total State and Local Expenditures
for all Purposes:
$4,524,000,000

MAJOR FEDERALLY ENABLED
INCOME TRANSFER PROGRAMS
FY 77 Expenditures (est.)

Program	State	Local
Aid to Families with Dependent Children	$70,920,000	$ 0
Medicaid	85,000,000	0
Social Services	8,260,000	0

OPTIONAL STATE SUPPLEMENTATION FOR SSI

Department of Social Services

The aged, over 65 years old, blind and disabled are provided cash supplements to their SSI benefits for special needs only. Special needs are nursing home care and a monthly blind pension. Benefits are provided to eligible persons living in licensed domiciliary or licensed practical or professional nursing homes. Benefits average $33 monthly for individuals living in a licensed practical or professional nursing home and are proportionately lower for other categories. The blind pension is $135 monthly for individuals and $270 for couples. Benefits are in the form of direct cash payments funded wholly by the state. Payments are administered by the state; eligibility is determined at local Department of Social Services offices. Over 40,500 individuals are aided monthly. Benefits are conditioned on need.

FY 77 Expenditure (est.): **$16,296,000**

STATE EMPLOYEES' RETIREMENT FUND

Treasury Department

Employees of the state (except those of the Highway Patrol and certain colleges) who retire at age 55 with at least 15 years of service, or at age 65 with less than 15 years of service, and their dependents are provided with financial assistance to replace income lost through retirement. Benefits are paid directly to the beneficiary in the form of cash. Payments average $120 per month. Some 6,204 individuals benefit from this program. This program is noncontributory (except for covered members of the General Assembly who contribute five percent). The state contributes seven percent of each member's salary. Benefits are not directly conditioned on need.

FY 77 Expenditure (est.): **$10,062,123**
Benefits paid total $9,620,066.
Administrative costs total $422,057.
State contributions total $21,217,755 to fund reserves.

SENIOR HOMEOWNERS AND RENTERS

Department of Revenue

Indirect financial assistance is provided to elderly low-income homeowners and renters. Benefits are in the form of tax relief, funded by providing eligible persons with income tax credits or rebates equal to the amount by which local property taxes or rent equivalents (set at 20 percent of rent) exceed a graduated percentage of annual income. Approximately 56,000 persons were aided in FY 77, receiving an average of $124 each. Benefits are conditioned, in part, on need.

FY 77 Expenditure (est.): **$7,010,000**

GENERAL ASSISTANCE PROGRAM

Department of Social Services

Maintenance payments, short-term or emergency aid to cover the costs of food, shelter, clothing and other items of daily living are made to individuals and couples, if unemployable, and families with children. Benefits are paid directly to the beneficiary in the form of cash without any restrictions on its use. Payments are in amounts varying according to each beneficiary's needs as determined under state law. Benefits are funded by grants to local offices of the state public assistance agency. This program is financed by state funds. Medical assistance is provided under the state's medical assistance program. Each month an average of 6,570 recipients (in some 6,063 cases) are aided. The average monthly benefit per recipient is $63 (per case, the average is $68). Benefits are conditioned on need.

FY 77 Expenditure (est.): **$4,952,000**

WORKERS' COMPENSATION PROGRAM

Department of Labor and Industrial Relations

Workers injured or disabled on the job, as well as the surviving dependents of workers who die as a result of such injury, are provided financial assistance both as compensation for lost wages and to pay for the cost of any required medical or rehabilitative care. Benefits are in the form of cash payments, funded by means of a state-regulated private insurance program to which each covered employer must contribute a percentage of payroll determined by the employer's experience rating and industrial classification. Beneficiaries receive two-thirds of normal wages, up to a maximum weekly compensation benefit of $95. These benefits may be received for no more than 400 weeks and the total amount of benefits one may receive is unlimited. In addition, a funeral allowance of $2,000 is provided for workers who die on the job. Approximately 23,000 workers and survivors were aided weekly in FY 77. Benefits are not directly conditioned on need.

FY 77 Expenditure (est.): **$79,346,000**

NURSING CARE

Department of Family Services

Nursing home care is provided to elderly, blind and disabled individuals who do not qualify for Medicaid. Benefits are in kind, funded by state payments to approved nursing homes. Approximately 9,000 persons were aided in FY 77, at an average cost of $200 per month. Benefits are conditioned on need.

FY 77 Expenditure (est.): **$18,982,000**

INDEMNITY PAYMENTS—LIVESTOCK

Department of Agriculture

Farmers are reimbursed for a portion of their losses when livestock is condemned by the state. Benefits are in the form of direct cash payments to farmers. Benefits are not conditioned on need.

FY 77 Expenditure (est.): **$201,000**

VETERANS' AFFAIRS

Division of Veterans' Affairs

Veterans are assisted so that they may file claims for Federal veterans' benefits. Included in this program is a soldiers' home for indigent veterans and their dependents. Benefits are in kind, through the payment of the salaries and expenses required in providing nursing care and benefit services. Almost 300 veterans and their families were provided nursing home care in FY 77. Benefits are conditioned, in part, on need.

FY 77 Expenditure (est.): **$1,156,000**

KIDNEY PROGRAM

Department of Higher Education

To ensure that persons with serious kidney disease receive life-sustaining treatment at the lowest possible cost, this program pays 12 participating renal disease facilities the costs of dialysis or kidney transplantation not paid for by other sources (i.e., Medicare, Medicaid and private insurance). Benefits are in kind, in the form of medical procedures such as home dialysis and transplantation. Approximately 700 persons received benefits under this program in FY 77. Benefits are not directly conditioned on need.

FY 77 Expenditure (est.): **$1,415,000**
Of the above amount, $74,000 are Federal funds.

Missouri

CYSTIC FIBROSIS PROGRAM

Department of Health

In order to ensure that medically needy persons with cystic fibrosis receive proper treatment, five treatment centers provide in kind benefits which include diagnosis, drugs, follow-up and outpatient care. Inhalation equipment is also loaned to patients requiring it. Approximately 250 persons were aided in FY 77. Benefits are directly conditioned on need.

FY 77 Expenditure (est.): **$111,000**

HEMOPHILIA PROGRAM

Department of Health

Home treatments are provided to persons with hemophilia. Services include blood coagulation and preventive treatment in order to limit the deleterious effects of the disease and to lessen the likelihood of hospitalization. Benefits are in kind, funded by the state payments to service providers. Approximately 70 persons were aided in FY 77. Benefits are not directly conditioned on need.

FY 77 Expenditure (est.): **$137,000**

CANCER TREATMENT AND RESEARCH

Department of Health

Cancer diagnostic and treatment services are provided to residents and their families. Screening is provided for the total population. Treatment includes surgery, radiation and chemotherapy. Benefits are in kind, funded through the Cancer Hospital Fund. Benefits are not conditioned on need.

FY 77 Expenditure (est.): **$3,372,000**

RESPIRATORY DISEASE—INPATIENT RESPIRATORY CARE

Department of Health

Persons are provided diagnosis, treatment and screening for tuberculosis and other respiratory diseases. Benefits are in kind, funded by grants to the state Chest Hospital and the University of Missouri. About 1,800 persons received services in FY 77. Benefits are not directly conditioned on need.

FY 77 Expenditure (est.): **$5,323,000**

SICKLE CELL ANEMIA

Department of Health

Individuals with sickle cell anemia are provided inpatient and outpatient treatment. Screening is provided to all persons and especially to members of ethnic groups in which the incidence of sickle cell anemia is high. Benefits are in kind, funded through state grants to various institutions. Approximately 2,500 persons were treated in FY 77. Benefits are not conditioned on need.

FY 77 Expenditure (est.): **$182,000**

TUBERCULOSIS CHARITY PATIENTS

Department of Health

Persons with tuberculosis are provided treatment to supplement the cost of services at public hospitals in Kansas City, St. Louis City and St. Louis County. Benefits are in kind, consisting of hospitalization, outpatient treatment, drugs and follow-up care. The average cost of such services per day is $25 for hospitalized patients and $8 per day for outpatients. Over 53,000 outpatient weeks were paid for in FY 77. Benefits are conditioned on need.

FY 77 Expenditure (est.): **$612,000**

COMPREHENSIVE PSYCHIATRIC SERVICE—OUTPATIENT

Department of Mental Health

Assistance is provided for mentally ill persons who are capable of achieving a level of independence but who also need psychiatric and follow-up care in order to function within the community. Benefits are in kind, consisting mostly of diagnostic, psychiatric and treatment services. About 45,000 persons received treatment monthly in FY 77. Benefits are not conditioned on need.

FY 77 Expenditure (est.): **$5,469,000**

Of the above amount, $964,000 are Federal funds.

PATIENT PLACEMENT

Department of Mental Health

Mentally ill, developmentally disabled, and alcoholic and/or drug dependent persons are placed in appropriate living facilities within their communities. Benefits are in kind, funded by the purchase of care for patients transferred from large institutions to specialized nursing facilities. Over 10,000 individuals are transferred to these community facilities yearly. Benefits are not conditioned on need.

FY 77 Expenditure (est.): **$8,591,000**

Of the above amount, $1,991,000 are Federal funds

ALCOHOL AND DRUG ABUSE—OUTPATIENT GRANTS

Department of Mental Health

Alcoholics and problem drinkers are provided outpatient services including counseling and detoxification. Benefits are in kind, funded through grants to participating institutions. Services were provided to approximately 4,000 persons in FY 77. Benefits are conditioned, in part, on need.

FY 77 Expenditure (est.): **$4,320,000**

Of the above amount, $929,000 are Federal funds.

FAMILY MEDICAL SERVICES—MENTAL RETARDATION

Department of Mental Health

Pregnant women, infants and women at risk are provided obstetric and pediatric care aimed at reducing the incidence of mental retardation. Benefits are in kind, and include hyalin membrane disease care purchased at an average cost of $2,700 for obstetrical and $9,500 for pediatric services (the most expensive part of the program). Over 350 persons are aided annually. Benefits are not directly conditioned on need.

FY 77 Expenditure (est.): **$1,564,000**

MENTAL RETARDATION AND DEVELOPMENTAL DISABILITIES—OUTPATIENT

Department of Mental Health

The mentally retarded and developmentally disabled (i.e., those suffering substantial handicaps resulting from mental retardation, cerebral palsy, epilepsy or other neurological conditions developed in childhood) are helped to function normally within the community despite their developmental problems. Benefits are in kind, consisting of outpatient, psychiatric and follow-up care. Over 6,000 persons received services in FY 77. Benefits are not directly conditioned on need.

FY 77 Expenditure (est.): **$2,388,000**

Of the above amount, $932,000 are Federal funds.

BLIND PENSION

Department of Family Services

Monthly payments are made to blind residents who are ineligible for other public assistance. Benefits are in the form of cash at an average payment of $152 per month for each recipient. Approximately 216 blind people were aided in FY 77. Benefits are conditioned, in part, on need.

FY 77 Expenditure (est.): **$394,000**

SERVICES FOR THE BLIND AND PHYSICALLY HANDICAPPED

Department of Higher Education

Library services are provided to the blind and physically handicapped so that they may utilize the resources available in state and local libraries. Benefits are in kind, funded by direct state grants. An average of $25 is spent on each blind or handicapped person who uses the program services. Approximately 8,000 persons took advantage of the program in FY 77. Benefits are not directly conditioned on need.

FY 77 Expenditure (est.): **$193,000**

SHELTERED WORKSHOPS FOR THE HANDICAPPED

Department of Elementary and Secondary Education

Handicapped individuals are provided opportunities to work and to support themselves through jobs in sheltered workshops where they are employed in conjunction with local business. Benefits are in the form of cash compensation for work performed and in kind, including organization and supervision. Over 3,700 persons took advantage of the workshop program in FY 77. Benefits are not directly conditioned on need.

FY 77 Expenditure (est.): **$2,995,000**

STUDENT GRANT PROGRAM

Department of Higher Education

Undergraduate residents, enrolled on a full-time basis at approved public or private institutions within the state, are provided financial aid as needed, not to exceed one-half the tuition and required fees, up to a maximum of $900. Benefits are in the form of cash, funded by direct state payments to the student. Over 10,000 students received aid in FY 77. Benefits are conditioned on need, and satisfactory continuance of education.

FY 77 Expenditure (est.): **$3,364,000**

SCHOLARSHIPS AND FELLOWSHIPS UNIVERSITY OF MISSOURI

Department of Higher Education

Undergraduate residents are provided financial support for attendance at the University of Missouri, in order to equalize opportunity and access to the university. Benefits are in the form of cash assistance including grants, trainee stipends, prizes, awards and tuition or fee remissions. Over 4,000 needy students are assisted annually. Benefits are conditioned on need and on satisfactory continuance of education

FY 77 Expenditure (est.): **$1,921,000**

PERSONAL INCOME TAX PROVISIONS

Department of Revenue

Public Employees' Retirement Pay Deduction. Indirect financial assistance is provided to certain public employees who receive pensions or other retirement income. Benefits are in the form of tax relief, funded by allowing the taxpayer to deduct such pension and retirement income from his gross adjusted income subject to personal income taxation. Benefits are not directly conditioned on need.

NEW JERSEY

Population: 7,329,000

Total State and Local Expenditures
for all Purposes:
$9,723,000,000

MAJOR FEDERALLY ENABLED
INCOME TRANSFER PROGRAMS
FY 77 Expenditures (est.)

Program	State	Local
Aid to Families with Dependent Children	$165,710,000	$73,540,000
Medicaid	251,210,000	90,000
Social Services	15,010,000	6,860,000

OPTIONAL STATE SUPPLEMENTATION FOR SSI

Division of Public Welfare

The aged, over 65 years old, the blind and the disabled are provided cash supplements to their SSI benefits for basic and special needs. Basic needs are food, shelter, clothing, utilities and daily living necessities. Special needs are those not provided for through monthly or optional SSI payments and include emergency assistance for catastrophic events and burial payments. Benefits are provided to eligible persons living independently, in licensed boarding homes, in incorporated homes for the aged, in residential facilities for the mentally retarded, living with an ineligible spouse or living in the household of another. Benefits are $22 monthly for individuals and $10 monthly for couples living independently and vary for other categories. Benefits are in the form of direct cash payments funded 75 percent by the state and 25 percent by counties. Payments are administered by the Federal government; eligibility is determined at local Social Security district offices. Over 50,000 individuals are aided monthly. Benefits are conditioned on need.

FY 77 Expenditure (est.): **$21,288,000**

CONSOLIDATED POLICE AND FIREMEN'S PENSION FUND

Treasury Department

Police officers and firefighters appointed prior to July 1944 who retire at age 55 and their dependents are provided with financial assistance to replace income lost through retirement. Benefits are paid directly to the beneficiary in the form of cash without any restriction on its use. Payments average $373 per month. Some 7,409 individuals benefit from this program. Members contribute six to 12 percent of salary, depending upon their age at the time of enrollment. The employing unit of government contributes 17 percent. Benefits are not directly conditioned on need.

FY 77 Expenditure (est.): **$33,694,000**

Benefits paid total $33,166,000.
Administrative costs total $528,000, which is funded by
    state, county and municipal contributions of .2 percent of
    the total eligible payroll.

176

New Jersey

STATE POLICE RETIREMENT SYSTEM

Treasury Department

All uniformed officers and troopers of the state police who retire at age 55 with 25 years of service and their dependents are provided with financial assistance to replace income lost through retirement. Benefits are paid directly to the beneficiary in the form of cash without any restriction on its use. Payments average $600 per month. Some 514 individuals benefit from this program. Members contribute about six percent of salary while the state contributes about 17 percent. Benefits are not directly conditioned on need.

FY 77 Expenditure (est.): **$3,803,000**

Benefits paid total $3,686,000.
Administrative costs total $117,000, which Is funded by a
    state contribution of .2 percent of the total eligible
    payroll.

TEACHERS' RETIREMENT SYSTEM

Treasury Department

Teachers and certain other public school employees who retire at age 60 and their dependents are provided with financial assistance to replace income lost through retirement. Benefits are paid directly to the beneficiary in the form of cash without any restriction on its use. Payments average $460 per month. Some 22,000 individuals benefit from this program. Members contribute four to ten percent of salary, depending upon their age at the time of enrollment. The employing unit of government contributes about 9.5 percent. Benefits are not directly conditioned on need.

FY 77 Expenditure (est.): **$122,963,000**

Benefits paid total $121,040,000.
Administrative costs total $1,923,000, which is funded by
    state, county and municipal contributions of .2 percent of
    the total eligible payroll.

JUDGES' RETIREMENT SYSTEM

Treasury Department

Judges who retire at age 65 with 15 years of service and their dependents are provided with financial assistance to replace income lost through retirement. Benefits are paid directly to the beneficiary in the form of cash without any restriction on its use. Payments average $1,650 per month. Some 146 individuals benefit from this program. The system is noncontributory for members. The state contributes about 15 percent of payroll. Benefits are not directly conditioned on need.

FY 77 Expenditure (est.): **$2,934,000**

Benefits paid total $2,888,000.
Administrative costs total $46,000.

PUBLIC EMPLOYEES' RETIREMENT SYSTEM

Treasury Department

Full-time state, county and municipal employees who retire at age 60 and their dependents are provided with financial assistance to replace income lost through retirement. Benefits are paid directly to the beneficiary in the form of cash without any restriction on its use. Payments average $232 per month. Some 26,300 individuals benefit from this program. Members contribute four to ten percent of salary, depending upon their age at the time of enrollment. The state contributes up to 9.5 percent of total payroll. Benefits are not directly conditioned on need.

FY 77 Expenditure (est.): **$74,664,000**

Benefits paid total $73,497,000.
Administrative costs total $1,167,000, which is funded by
    state, county and municipal contributions of .2 percent of
    the total eligible payroll.

CENTRAL PENSION FUND

Treasury Department

This program administers a series of noncontributory pension acts for disabled war veterans and governors' widows. Benefits are paid directly to the beneficiary in the form of cash without any restriction on its use. Payments average $90 per month. Some 447 individuals benefit from this program. The state pays the total cost of the system. Benefits are not directly conditioned on need.

FY 77 Expenditure (est.): **$467,000**
Benefits paid total $467,000.

HOMESTEAD REBATE

Division of Taxation

Indirect financial assistance is provided to homeowners or condominium owners. Benefits are in the form of tax relief, funded by means of rebates based on scheduled local property tax exemptions. About 200,000 residents, 65 years and older, or permanently or totally disabled, are entitled to an additional $50 rebate. The total exemption shall not exceed 50 percent of the property tax bill. Approximately 1,400,000 persons, in all, were aided in FY 77, at an average of $187 each ($227 for those 65 and over). Benefits are not conditioned on need.

FY 77 Expenditure (est.): **$274,000,000**

TENANT REBATES

Division of Taxation

Indirect financial assistance is provided to tenants. Benefits are in the form of tax relief, funded by requiring a landlord to pass on to the tenants 65 percent of any reduction in the landlord's local property tax bill brought about by the Homestead Rebate program. There are no state-allocated funds. Approximately 545,000 tenants were aided in FY 77. Benefits are not conditioned on need.

FY 77 Expenditure (est.): **$36,000,000**

PROPERTY TAX DEDUCTIONS FOR SENIOR CITIZENS AND VETERANS

Division of Taxation

Indirect financial assistance is provided to persons 65 years and older, or to certain of their surviving spouses, and to qualified veterans and servicemen, or to their surviving spouses. To be eligible, the elderly and their surviving spouses must have annual incomes of $5,000 or less. Benefits are in the form of tax relief, funded by means of property tax deductions of up to $160 yearly for senior citizens and up to $50 yearly for veterans. About 500,000 persons receive benefits yearly. Benefits are conditioned, in part, on need.

FY 77 Expenditure (est.): **$58,000,000**

PROPERTY TAX DEDUCTION FOR PERMANENTLY AND TOTALLY DISABLED

Division of Taxation

Indirect financial assistance is provided to permanently and totally disabled persons. Benefits are in the form of tax relief, funded by means of a deduction from local property taxes of up to $160 yearly. Approximately 35,000 persons were aided in FY 77. Benefits are not directly conditioned on need.

FY 77 Expenditure (est.): **$5,960,000**

VIOLENT CRIMES COMPENSATION BOARD

Department of Law and Public Safety

Victims of violent crime and their dependents are provided assistance to compensate for their losses. Benefits are in the form of cash and provide for losses not replaced by insurance or other plans. The Board determines the amount of each award, ranging from $100 to $10,000 per case. Approximately 300 persons are aided annually. Benefits are not conditioned on need.

FY 77 Expenditure (est.): **$1,020,728**

New Jersey

REDUCED FARE ON RAILROADS AND BUSES FOR THE ELDERLY AND HANDICAPPED

Department of Transportation

Elderly and/or handicapped persons are provided transportation assistance to utilize buses and railroads. A half-fare program is in effect during off-peak hours. Special equipment is also provided to non-profit organizations to assist those persons who cannot use scheduled services. Benefits are in kind, funded by state grants to both public and private carriers. Over 390,000 riders took advantage of the half-fare program at an average cost of $8.97. Benefits are not directly conditioned on need.

FY 77 Expenditure (est.): **$3,400,000**

WORKERS' COMPENSATION PROGRAM

Department of Labor and Industry

Workers injured or disabled on the job, as well as the surviving dependents or workers who die as a result of such injury, are provided financial assistance both as compensation for lost wages and to pay for the cost of any required medical or rehabilitative care. Benefits are in the form of cash payments, funded by means of a state-regulated private insurance program to which each covered employer must contribute a percentage of payroll determined by the employer's experience rating and industrial classification. Beneficiaries receive two-thirds of normal wages, up to a maximum weekly compensation benefit of $138. These benefits may be received for no more than 300 weeks and the total amount of benefits one may receive is unlimited. In addition, a funeral allowance of $750 is provided for workers who die on the job. Approximately 47,000 workers and survivors were aided weekly in FY 77. Benefits are not directly conditioned on need.

FY 77 Expenditure (est.): **$236,349,000**

GENERAL ASSISTANCE PROGRAM

Department of Human Services

Maintenance payments, short-term or emergency aid to cover the costs of food, shelter, clothing and other items of daily living are made to individuals, couples, families with children and fathers unemployed due to a strike. Benefits are paid directly to the beneficiary in the form of cash without any restrictions on its use or through vendor payments (to the suppliers of goods and services including medical). Employable persons must register with the state employment service. Payments are in amounts varying according to each beneficiary's needs as determined under state law. Benefits are funded by grants to local welfare agencies. The state provides 75-80 percent of the assistance costs but not all localities receive state aid or are under state supervision. Each month an average of 50,313 recipients (in some 30,357 cases) are aided. The average monthly benefit per recipient is $98 (per case, the average is $162).

FY 77 Expenditure (est.): **$59,042,000**

ASSISTANCE FOR DEPENDENT CHILDREN— INSUFFICIENT EMPLOYMENT OF THE PARENTS

Department of Human Services

Assistance to cover the minimum costs of food, shelter, clothing and other items of daily living is provided on behalf of needy dependent children in intact families. Such children must be deprived of support due to insufficient employment of their parents, when either one or both are working full-time but due to inadequate wages cannot support the family. Benefits are in the form of cash, paid directly to the children's parents. Benefits are funded 75 percent by the state and 25 percent by the counties. Over 3,000 cases receive aid monthly. Benefits are conditioned on need.

FY 77 Expenditure (est.): **$9,386,000**

TUBERCULOSIS SERVICES

Department of Health

Persons with tuberculosis are provided preventive care and prophylactic drugs at clinics and hospitals across the state. Benefits
are in kind, funded by payments to participating programs. The cost
of services not covered by medical insurance or other assistance
programs are met. Benefits are not conditioned on need.

FY 77 Expenditure (est.): **$1,800,000**

Of the above amount, $400,000 are Federal funds.

CHRONIC RENAL DISEASE

Department of Health

To ensure that persons with serious kidney disease receive life-
sustaining treatment at the lowest possible cost, this program pays
participating renal disease facilities the cost of dialysis and related
medical procedures not paid for by other sources (i.e. Medicare,
Medicaid and private insurance). Benefits are in kind, in the form of
medical procedures such as home dialysis and kidney transplantation. Approximately 450 persons received benefits under this program in FY 77. Benefits are not conditioned on need.

FY 77 Expenditure (est.): **$872,000**

HEMOPHILIA PROGRAM

Department of Health

Individuals with hemophilia are provided treatment services and
support in the form of drugs, medical and social services. Services
are aimed at needy persons. Benefits are in kind, funded by payments to hospitals and treatment centers. Over 200 persons are aided annually. Benefits are not directly conditioned on need.

FY 77 Expenditure (est.): **$571,000**

GRANTS TO BLIND VETERANS

Department of Human Services

Honorably discharged blind veterans are provided grants in order to help them meet the costs of living within their handicap. Benefits are in the form of cash, paid directly to the veterans. About 70 persons are aided annually at a yearly rate of $750 each. Benefits are not directly conditioned on need.

FY 77 Expenditure (est.): **$56,000**

VETERANS' ORPHANS FUND— EDUCATIONAL GRANTS

Department of Human Services

Children, aged 16-21, of disabled or deceased veterans are provided financial aid to assist them in completing their higher education while attending college within New Jersey. Benefits are in the form of cash, paid directly to the students. About 150 persons were aided annually at a maximum rate of $500. Benefits are not conditioned on need.

FY 77 Expenditure (est.): **$72,000**

TUITION AID GRANTS

Department of Higher Education

Graduates of New Jersey Community Colleges who are educationally and/or financially disadvantaged are provided financial support for attendance at postsecondary four-year educational institutions. Benefits are in the form of cash, funded by payments to institutions. Over 5,000 students are aided annually. Grants range from $100 to full tuition or $1,000, whichever is less. Award amounts decrease as one's ability to pay increases. Determination of ability to pay is made by the College Scholarship Service. Grants may be held in conjunction with Federal aid or Garden State Scholarships. Benefits are conditioned on need.

FY 77 Expenditure (est.): **$4,087,000**

New Jersey

OPPORTUNITY PROGRAM GRANTS

Department of Higher Education

Graduate and undergraduate students who are educationally and/or financially disadvantaged are provided financial support for attendance at postsecondary educational institutions. Benefits are in the form of cash, funded by payments to institutions. Over 12,500 students are aided annually at a maximum of $1,000 per year for undergraduates and $1,500 per year for graduates. To be eligible, family income may not exceed $10,000. Benefits are conditioned on need.

FY 77 Expenditure (est.): **$12,630,000**

PERSONAL INCOME TAX PROVISIONS

Treasury Department

Low-Income Exemption. Indirect financial assistance is provided to persons whose annual gross household income is $3,000 or less. Benefits are in the form of tax relief, funded by allowing the individual a total exemption of his income from personal income taxation. Benefits are conditioned on need.

Retirement Income Exclusion. Indirect financial assistance is provided to taxpayers age 62 and older and to those disabled and receiving Social Security. Benefits are in the form of tax relief, funded by allowing the taxpayer to exclude from his annual gross income up to $7,500 for single persons and up to $5,000 for each member of a married couple. The excludable amount may be comprised of taxable pension and annuity benefits, as well as wages, salaries and net business income, if such earnings do not exceed $3,000. Benefits are not directly conditioned on need.

NEW YORK

Population 17,924,000

Total State and Local Expenditures
for all Purposes:
$9,723,000,000

MAJOR FEDERALLY ENABLED
INCOME TRANSFER PROGRAMS
FY 77 Expenditures (est.)

Program	State	Local
Aid to Families with Dependent Children	$481,500,000	$482,790,000
Medicaid	1,223,070,000	592,470,000
Social Services	22,340,000	32,520,000

New York

OPTIONAL STATE SUPPLEMENTATION FOR SSI

Department of Social Services

The aged, over 65 years old, the blind and the disabled are provided cash supplements to their SSI benefits for basic and special needs. Basic needs are food, shelter, clothing, utilities and daily living necessities. Special needs are those not provided for through monthly or optional SSI payments and include moving-related expenses, replacement of basic needs items, repair or replacement of major appliances and "other" expenses. Benefits are provided to eligible persons, according to the geographic areas in which they live, who are living alone, with others, in the household of another, in foster homes, or in residential facilities for the mentally disabled or retarded. Benefits are $61 monthly for individuals and $76 monthly for couples living independently and vary for other categories. Benefits are in the form of direct cash payments, funded by the state and localities. Payments are administered by the Federal government; eligibility is determined at local Social Security district offices. Over 359,000 individuals are aided monthly. Benefits are conditioned on need.

FY 77 Expenditure (est.): **$224,016,000**

POLICEMEN'S AND FIREMEN'S RETIREMENT SYSTEM

Comptroller's Office

All paid policemen and firemen employed by the state and its political subdivisions, except New York City, who retire at age 55 with 20 to 25 years of service, depending on the plan, and their dependents, are provided with financial assistance to replace income lost through retirement. Benefits are paid directly to the beneficiary in the form of cash without any restriction on its use. Payments average $562 per month. Some 8,100 individuals benefit from this program. The system is noncontributory for 99 percent of the members. The employing jurisdiction contributes from 15 to 47 percent. Benefits are not directly conditioned on need.

FY 77 Expenditure (est.): **$55,641,000**

Benefits paid total $54,500,000.
Administrative costs total $1,141,000.
State contributions total $25,200,000.

TEACHERS' RETIREMENT FUND

Comptroller's Office

All teachers in the state and local school systems, except those in New York City, who retire at age 55 to 62 years, with from 20 to 30 years of service, depending on the plan, and their dependents are provided with financial assistance to replace income lost through retirement. Benefits are paid directly to the beneficiary in the form of cash without any restriction on its use. Payments average $460 per month. Some 40,000 individuals benefit from this program. The system is noncontributory for members. The state contributes approximately 19.4 percent of wages. Benefits are not directly conditioned on need.

FY 77 Expenditure (est.): **$227,110,000**

Benefits paid total $221,109,000.
Administrative costs total $6,001,000.
State contributions total $499,000,000 to help fund reserves.

PUBLIC EMPLOYEES' RETIREMENT SYSTEM

Comptroller's Office

Employees of the state, public authorities and hospitals, and municipalities electing to participate, who retire at age 62, or at any age with 35 years of service, and their dependents are provided with financial assistance to replace income lost through retirement. Benefits are paid directly to the beneficiary in the form of cash without any restriction on its use. Payments average $280 per month. Some 121,000 individuals benefit from this program. The system is noncontributory for 87 percent of the members. The state contributes 25 percent of total covered payroll. Benefits are not directly conditioned on need.

FY 77 Expenditure (est.): **$415,000,000**

Benefits paid total $406,800,000.
Administrative costs total $8,200,000.
State contributions total $426,900,000 to help fund reserves.

New York

PROPERTY TAX EXEMPTION FOR AGED

State Board of Equalization and Assessment

Indirect financial assistance is provided to homeowners and renters, 65 years and older, with annual incomes not exceeding $3,000 to $7,200, depending on the locality. Benefits are in the form of tax relief, funded by means of a 50 percent exemption on local property taxes for homeowners and a rent freeze at one-third of household income for renters. This program is adopted for use and administered by individual localities. Income ceilings are determined by the localities but cannot exceed $7,200. Over 250,000 elderly persons benefit yearly. Benefits are conditioned on need.

FY 77 Expenditure (est.): **$60,000,000**

PROPERTY TAX EXEMPTION FOR VETERANS

State Board of Equalization and Assessment

Indirect financial assistance is provided to veterans, to certain disabled veterans or to their surviving spouses. Benefits are in the form of tax relief, funded by means of exemptions to local property taxes, excluding school taxes, in amounts up to a maximum of $5,000 of assessed value ($10,000 for disabled veterans requiring specially adapted housing). This program is administered primarily by local tax assessors who determine eligibility and process applications. Some 300,000 persons are aided annually. Benefits are not directly conditioned on need.

FY 77 Expenditure (est.): **$30,000,000**

VETERANS' BLIND ANNUITY ASSISTANCE

Department of Veterans' Affairs

Blind veterans and their widows are provided financial assistance in order to help them maintain their living standard. Benefits are in the form of cash, funded by payments directly to veterans or their widows. Approximately 2,000 persons are aided annually, at an average cost of $500 per person. Benefits are not conditioned on need.

FY 77 Expenditure (est.): **$1,105,000**

VETERAN COUNSELING

Department of Veterans' Affairs

Veterans and their families are provided assistance in obtaining and establishing entitlement to benefits through counseling services at 82 counseling centers within the state. Benefits are in kind and include services relating to taxes, insurance, compensation, loans, medical and dental benefits, employment services, education and rehabilitation services. Approximately 9,210,000 services were recorded at division counseling centers in 1977. Benefits are not conditioned on need.

FY 77 Expenditure (est.): **$2,195,000**

CRIME VICTIMS' COMPENSATION

Executive Department

Victims of violent crime who suffer physical injury, disability or death and their dependents are provided assistance to compensate for loss of earnings or support. Benefits are in the form of cash and provide for losses not replaced by insurance or other plans. The maximum total award is $20,000. Benefits range from $135 to $250 weekly for as long as the payments are awarded. About 5,000 persons filed for compensation in FY 77. Benefits are not conditioned on need.

FY 77 Expenditure (est.): **$3,043,000**

EMPLOYMENT FOR THE DISADVANTAGED

Department of Civil Service

Disadvantaged persons, particularly within minority groups, are provided entry-level positions in the public sector. Benefits are in kind, funded by payments to the Career Opportunities Division, which identifies and develops jobs for minority group members, recruits and refers minority group members for placement in these jobs and trains minority group members for jobs in the public sector. Over 2,000 minority group members were provided clerical and secretarial jobs. Benefits are conditioned on need.

FY 77 Expenditure (est.): **$1,029,000**

Of the above amount, $304,000 are Federal funds.

New York

WORKERS' COMPENSATION PROGRAM

Workmen's Compensation Board

Workers injured or disabled on the job, as well as the surviving dependents of workers who die as a result of such injury, are provided financial assistance both as compensation for lost wages and to pay for the cost of any required medical or rehabilitative care. Benefits are in the form of cash payments, funded by means of state-administered and state-regulated private insurance programs to which each covered employer must contribute a percentage of payroll determined by the employer's experience rating and industrial classification. Beneficiaries receive two-thirds of normal wages, up to a maximum weekly compensation benefit of $125. These benefits may be received for the total period of disability and the total amount of benefits one may receive is unlimited. In addition, a funeral allowance of $750 is provided for workers who die on the job. Approximately 107,000 workers and survivors were aided weekly in FY 77. Benefits are not directly conditioned on need.

FY 77 Expenditure (est.): **$512,897,000**

HOME RELIEF PROGRAM

Department of Social Services

Maintenance payments, short-term or emergency aid to cover the costs of food, shelter, clothing and other items of daily living are made to individuals, couples and families with children. Benefits are paid directly to the beneficiary in the form of cash without any restrictions on its use. Employable persons must accept work project assignments. Payments are in amounts varying according to each beneficiary's needs as determined under state law. Benefits are funded by grants to local offices of the state public assistance agency. This program is financed by state and local funds. Medical assistance is not paid from general assistance funds. Each month an average of 195,618 recipients (in some 148,361 cases) are aided. The average monthly benefit per recipient is $148 (per case, the average is $195.) Benefits are conditioned on need.

FY 77 Expenditure (est.): **$346,964,000**

ALL OTHER INCOME MAINTENANCE

Department of Social Services

Those persons in need of financial assistance and ineligible for all other types of state and Federally funded income maintenance programs are provided short-term aid until their cases are properly disposed. Benefits are in the form of cash, funded by payments directly to both beneficiaries and the providers of such services as lodging care in public homes and burial of the dead. The return of persons to other states or counties is also financed. Benefits are conditioned on need.

FY 77 Expenditure (est.): **$31,000,000**

MEDICAL ASSISTANCE HOME RELIEF AND HOME RELIEF CASH ASSISTANCE

Department of Social Services

Persons 21 to 65 years of age who do not qualify for Federal assistance are provided medical assistance services in order to maintain themselves. Benefits are in kind, funded by purchase of services. Over 180,000 individuals are aided by these programs monthly. The state and localities fund this program on a 50-50 basis. Benefits are conditioned on need.

FY 77 Expenditure (est.): **$126,300,000**

MEDICAL ASSISTANCE CATASTROPHIC ILLNESS PROGRAM

Department of Social Services

Persons 21 to 65 years of age who cannot qualify for public assistance but have outstanding inpatient medical bills are provided financial assistance to help pay these outstanding bills due to catastrophic illness. Catastrophic illness is when care costs exceed 25 percent of an individual's income. Benefits are in the form of cash, paid directly to providers. Over 7,000 patients were aided in FY 77. Benefits are conditioned on need.

FY 77 Expenditure (est.): **$66,700,000**

New York

STATE ALCOHOLISM SERVICES

Department of Alcohol and Substance Abuse

Alcoholics are provided services on a community basis at outpatient and short-term care facilities. Services include detoxification, medical care and residential services. Benefits are in kind, funded by grants to area programs. Over 20,000 persons receive benefits annually. Benefits are conditioned, in part, on need.

FY 77 Expenditure (est.): **$9,000,000**

YOUTHFUL DRUG ABUSER (YDA) PROGRAM

Department of Alcohol and Substance Abuse

Youthful drug and other substance abusers are provided drug-free treatment and prevention services throughout the state. The program includes residential and ambulatory drug-free treatment, prevention programs and volunteer Narcotics Guidance Councils. Benefits are in kind, funded by payments to area programs. Over 40,000 persons received benefits in FY 77. Benefits are not directly conditioned on need.

FY 77 Expenditure (est.): **$53,786,000**
Of the above amount, $14,786,000 are Federal funds.

STATE SUBSTANCE ABUSE SERVICES

Department of Alcohol and Substance Abuse

Persons with serious drug problems, who would otherwise receive prison sentences, are provided diagnostic and primary care at local state drug rehabilitation centers. Benefits are in kind, funded by payments to centers. Approximately 34,000 persons were aided in FY 77. Benefits are not conditioned on need.

FY 77 Expenditure (est.): **$20,000,000**

PREVENTION AND TREATMENT OF MENTAL ILLNESS—OUTPATIENT SERVICES

Department of Mental Hygiene

Mentally ill persons are provided services in their own communities on an outpatient basis in order to prevent institutionalization. Services include counseling, placement and medical services. Benefits are in kind, funded by payments to community centers. About 35,000 persons are aided annually. Benefits are not conditioned on need.

FY 77 Expenditure (est.): **$65,000,000**

PREVENTION AND TREATMENT—MENTAL ILLNESS IN YOUTH

Department of Mental Hygiene

Children and youth who are mentally ill are provided community-based services including diagnosis, treatment, education assistance, therapy, group homes, vocational training and counseling. Benefits are in kind, funded by payments through area agencies to local programs. Over 40,000 persons were aided in FY 77. Benefits are conditioned on need.

FY 77 Expenditure (est.): **$39,286,000**

PHYSICALLY HANDICAPPED CHILDREN

Department of Health

Physically handicapped children who are not eligible for Medicaid are provided rehabilitation services at hospitals and clinics across the state. The purpose of this program is to reimburse 50 percent of the costs to New York City and 57 counties for services to these children. Benefits are in kind, funded 50 percent by localities and 50 percent by the state. Over 30,000 children are aided annually. Benefits are conditioned on need.

FY 77 Expenditure (est.): **$5,100,000**

Of the above amount, $250,000 are Federal funds.

New York

KIDNEY DISEASE INSTITUTE

Department of Health

To ensure that persons with serious kidney disease receive life-sustaining treatment at the lowest possible cost, this program provides victims of kidney disease home dialysis treatment. Benefits are in kind, in the form of payments for the cost of home dialysis and administration of the program. Approximately 250 persons were aided in FY 77. Benefits are not directly conditioned on need.

FY 77 Expenditure (est.): **$2,800,000**

SHELTERED EMPLOYMENT PROGRAM

Department of Education

Mentally retarded and severely handicapped individuals who are considered uneducable and who cannot obtain employment in business or industry are provided jobs and care within sheltered facilities. Benefits are in the form of cash compensation for work performed, and in kind, consisting mainly of supervision in 100 sheltered workshops. Funding is on a per-client basis directly to private, non-profit workshop facilities. Approximately 4,600 individuals were aided in FY 77 at an average cost of $1,000 per person. Benefits are not directly conditioned on need.

FY 77 Expenditure (est.): **$4,300,000**

PREKINDERGARTEN PROGRAM

Department of Education

Children of low-income families are provided educational and social services to discover if education at an early age will overcome educational disadvantages associated with low income. Benefits are in kind, in the form of services provided by staff, and are not connected with either the traditional Daycare or Headstart programs. Over 6,500 children were aided in FY 77. Benefits are conditioned on need.

FY 77 Expenditure (est.): **$8,960,000**

COLLEGE AID FOR NATIVE AMERICANS

Department of Education

Native Americans who live on state reservations are provided financial aid for attendance at postsecondary educational institutions within the state. Benefits are in the form of cash, paid directly to the institutions. Over 300 Native Americans are aided annually at an average cost of $1,100 per year. Benefits are not directly conditioned on need.

FY 77 Expenditure (est.): **$330,000**

SEEK PROGRAM

City University of New York (CUNY)

Residents who are educationally and/or economically disadvantaged are provided financial support for pursuing a postsecondary educational program at the City University of New York. Benefits in cash are in the form of payments to institutions for tuition, books and other college-related costs. Benefits are also in kind, through the funding of administrative and teaching positions. Approximately 10,000 students are aided annually. Benefits are conditioned on need.

FY 77 Expenditure (est.): **$20,200,000**

EDUCATIONAL OPPORTUNITY PROGRAM

State University of New York (SUNY)

Residents who are educationally and/or economically disadvantaged are provided financial support for pursuing a postsecondary educational program at the State University of New York. Benefits are in the form of cash, funded by payments to institutions. Benefits are for tuition, books and other college-related costs. Approximately 8,000 students are aided annually at an average payment of $540 per semester. Benefits are conditioned on need.

FY 77 Expenditure (est.): **$8,000,000**

TUITION ASSISTANCE PROGRAM (TAP)

Higher Education Services Corporation

Undergraduate and graduate residents who can demonstrate financial need are provide financial assistance for attendance at colleges, universities and technical schools within the state. Benefits are in the form of cash, paid directly to institutions. Over 360,000 individuals received aid in FY 77. Undergraduate awards range from $100 to $1,500 yearly, while for graduates the range is $100 to $600 per year. Benefits are conditioned on need.

FY 77 Expenditure (est.): **$184,000,000**

STATE UNIVERSITY SCHOLARSHIPS

State University of New York (SUNY)

Lower-income residents who wish to pursue a higher education are provided supplemental financial aid to make up the difference between their TAP award and SUNY tuition. Benefits are in the form of cash, paid directly to institutions. Over 89,000 students received aid in FY 77. Benefits are conditioned on need.

FY 77 Expenditure (est.): **$1,852,000**

HIGHER EDUCATION OPPORTUNITY PROGRAM

Department of Education

Financially and educationally disadvantaged residents are provided financial aid for attendance at state colleges and universities within New York. Benefits are in the form of cash, paid directly to institutions. Over 5,000 students receive aid annually for tuition, counseling, guidance, remedial courses and tutoring. Benefits may also supplement Basic Education Opportunity Grants and other Federal award programs. The average benefit is approximately $1,400 per year. Benefits are conditioned on need.

FY 77 Expenditure (est.): **$7,591,000**

SCHOLARSHIPS

Department of Education

Undergraduate residents are provided financial assistance according to demonstrable need and achievement, in order to equalize opportunity and access to the State University. Benefits are in the form of cash, paid directly to institutions. Benefits include the Regent's State Scholarship, fellowships, scholarships to children of veterans and nursing scholarships. Approximately 87,000 students are aided annually. Benefits are conditioned, in part, on need.

FY 77 Expenditure (est.): **$24,000,000**

ENROLLMENT EXPANSION AID

Department of Education

State residents attending medical schools outside the United States are provided financial assistance in order to enable them to pursue a medical education within New York State. Benefits are in the form of cash, paid directly to institutions. About 150 persons are aided annually at an average cost of $6,000. Benefits are not conditioned on need.

FY 77 Expenditure (est.): **$900,000**

PERSONAL INCOME TAX PROVISIONS

Department of Taxation and Finance

Deduction of Public Employees' Pensions. Indirect financial assistance is provided to certain public employees who receive pensions or other retirement income. Benefits are in the form of tax relief, funded by allowing the taxpayer to deduct such pension and retirement income from his gross adjusted income subject to personal income taxation. Benefits are not directly conditioned on need.

Low-Income Exemption. Indirect financial assistance is provided to persons whose annual gross income is $2,500 or less for single persons, or $5,000 less for married persons. Benefits are in the form of tax relief, funded by allowing the individual a total exemption of his income from personal income taxation. Benefits are conditioned on need.

NORTH CAROLINA

Population 5,525,000

Total State and Local Expenditures
for all Purposes:
$5,426,000,000

MAJOR FEDERALLY ENABLED
INCOME TRANSFER PROGRAMS
FY 77 Expenditures (est.)

Program	State	Local
Aid to Families with Dependent Children	$23,000,000	$25,020,000
Medicaid	79,770,000	15,290,000
Social Services	9,840,000	6,470,000

OPTIONAL STATE SUPPLEMENTATION FOR SSI

Department of Human Resources

The aged, over 65 years old, the blind and the disabled are provided cash supplements to their SSI benefits for basic and special needs. Basic needs are food, shelter, clothing, utilities and daily living necessities. Special needs are those not provided for through monthly or optional SSI payments and include medical expenses for the blind not covered by Medicaid or other programs. Benefits are provided to eligible persons living independently in domiciliary-care facilities, in multiple households or living with a sighted spouse. Benefits average $157 monthly for all categories. Benefits are in the form of direct cash payments funded 50 percent by the state and 50 percent by counties. Payments are administered by the county government; eligibility is determined at local offices of the Division of Social Services and the Division of Services for the Blind. Over 9,500 individuals are aided monthly. Benefits are conditioned on need.

FY 77 Expenditure (est.): **$18,528,000**

FIREFIGHTERS' DEFERRED COMPENSATION FUND

State Auditor's Office

All firepersons, whether paid or volunteer, belonging to eligible fire departments of the state or its political subdivisions, who retire at age 55 with at least 20 years of service are provided with financial assistance to replace income lost through retirement. Benefits are paid directly to the beneficiary in the form of cash without any restriction on its use. Payments range from $36 to $50 per month, depending upon the age of the recipient. Some 1,500 retirees benefit from this program. Members contribute $5 per month for 20 years. The state contribution equals one percent of fire insurance premiums collected. Benefits are not directly conditioned on need.

FY 77 Expenditure (est.): **$875,000**

Benefits paid total $854,000.
Administrative costs total $21,000.
State contributions total $886,000 to help fund reserves.

North Carolina

UNIFORM JUDICIAL RETIREMENT SYSTEM

Treasury Department

Judges of the General Court of Justice as of 1974 or later, who retire at age 65, or at age 50 with 24 years of service, and their dependents are provided with financial assistance to replace income lost through retirement. Benefits are paid directly to the beneficiary in the form of cash without any restriction on its use. Payments average $975 per month. Some 75 individuals benefit from this program. Members contribute six percent of salary while the state contributes 30 percent. Benefits are not directly conditioned on need.

FY 77 Expenditure (est.): **$820,600**

Benefits paid total $817,000.
Administrative costs total $3,600.
State contributions total $966,000 to help fund reserves.

LOCAL GOVERNMENTAL EMPLOYEES' RETIREMENT SYSTEM

Treasury Department

Employees of local governments who retire at age 65, or regardless of age with 30 years of service, and their dependents are provided with financial assistance to replace income lost through retirement. Benefits are paid directly to the beneficiary in the form of cash without any restriction on its use. Payments average $168 per month. Some 5,969 individuals benefit from this program. Members contribute six percent of salary while the state contributes seven percent. Benefits are not directly conditioned on need.

FY 77 Expenditure (est.): **$12,494,000**

Benefits paid total $12,416,000.
Administrative costs total $348,000.

TEACHERS' AND STATE EMPLOYEES' RETIREMENT SYSTEM

Treasury Department

Full-time state and public school employees who retire at age 65 with at least five years of service, or regardless of age with 30 years of service, and their dependents are provided with financial assistance to replace income lost through retirement. Benefits are paid directly to the beneficiary in the form of cash without any restriction on its use. Payments average $315 per month. Some 30,250 individuals benefit from this program. Members contribute six percent of salary while the state contributes 9.12 percent. Benefits are not directly conditioned on need.

FY 77 Expenditure (est.): **$117,613,000**

Benefits paid total $116,144,000.
Administrative costs total $1,469,000.

PROPERTY TAX RELIEF FOR SENIOR CITIZENS OR TOTALLY DISABLED PERSONS

Department of Revenue

Indirect financial assistance is provided to persons totally and permanently disabled and to those aged 65 or older, with incomes under $9,000 yearly. Benefits are in the form of tax relief, funded by allowing an exemption from property taxes on the first $7,500 of assessed value of the taxpayer's property. About 25,000 persons received benefits in FY 77. Benefits are conditioned, in part, on need.

FY 77 Expenditure (est.): **$1,000,000**

WORKERS' COMPENSATION PROGRAM

Department of Commerce

Workers injured or disabled on the job, as well as the surviving dependents of workers who die as a result of such injury, are provided financial assistance both as compensation for lost wages and to pay for the cost of any required medical or rehabilitative care. Benefits are in the form of cash payments, funded by means of a state-regulated private insurance program to which each covered employer must contribute a percentage of payroll determined by the employer's experience rating and industrial classification. Beneficiaries receive two-thirds of normal wages, up to a maximum weekly compensation benefit of $168. These benefits may be received for the total period of disability and the total amount of benefits one may receive is unlimited. In addition, a funeral allowance of $500 is provided for workers who die on the job. Approximately 11,000 workers and survivors were aided weekly in FY 77. Benefits are not directly conditioned on need.

FY 77 Expenditure (est.): **$68,142,000**

GENERAL ASSISTANCE PROGRAM

Department of Human Resources

Short-term or emergency assistance to cover the costs of food, shelter, clothing and other items of daily living are made to resident individuals, couples and families with children. Benefits are paid directly to the beneficiary in the form of cash, without any restriction on its use, or through vendor payments. These payments are in amounts varying according to each beneficiary's needs, as determined under state law. Benefits are funded by appropriations to the administering local welfare agencies from local revenues. A monthly average of 5,330 recipients (in some 2,436 cases) are aided. The average benefit is $19 per individual. Benefits are conditioned on need.

FY 77 Expenditure (est.): **$1,239,000**

SERVICES TO THE BLIND AND HANDICAPPED

Department of Library Resources—Cultural Resources

Physically and visually handicapped persons are provided library services so that they may take advantage of libraries across the state. Services include books in braille, recordings and large-type books. Benefits are in kind, funded by grants to libraries. Over 12,900 individuals were aided in FY 77. Benefits are not directly conditioned on need.

FY 77 Expenditure (est.): **$270,000**

JOB ORIENTATION AND MOTIVATION

Department of Education

Chronically unemployed and underemployed people are provided educational assistance designed to motivate them towards permanent jobs and thus reduce their dependence on public assistance. Benefits are in kind, funded by grants to educational units. Over 2,200 individuals were aided in FY 77. Services include literacy skills, financial management, and family and consumer counseling. Benefits are conditioned, in part, on need.

FY 77 Expenditure (est.): **$2,168,000**

NORTH CAROLINA REHABILITATION CORPORATION

Department of Agriculture

People planning to purchase farms and students from rural families who cannot afford college are provided financial assistance in order to stimulate rural enterprise and reduce the number of needy and jobless people in the state. Benefits are in the form of favorable credit terms, funded by state loans to individuals up to amounts of $40,000 per loan. About 30 persons were aided in FY 77. Benefits are not directly conditioned on need.

FY 77 Expenditure (est.): **$600,000**

Administrative costs are $10,660

SERVICES FOR VETERANS AND THEIR DEPENDENTS

Department of Veterans and Veterans' Affairs

Veterans and their dependents are aided in securing the privileges, rights and benefits due them under Federal, state and local laws. Benefits are in kind, funded by payment of salaries to personnel. Services include scholarship coordination, administration and field service for examining claims. Over 30,000 persons were assisted in FY 77. Benefits are not conditioned on need.

FY 77 Expenditure (est.): **$1,200,000**

RURAL HEALTH CLINICS

Department of Human Resources

Primary health care services are rendered to people in small towns and rural areas in order to replace services that doctors who no longer practice in these areas might provide. Benefits are in kind, including nursing and family medicine. About 70,000 persons from rural areas benefited in FY 77. Benefits are not directly conditioned on need.

FY 77 Expenditure (est.): **$1,341,000**

CANCER CONTROL

Department of Human Resources

Medically indigent adults are provided early care in order to reduce cancer deaths and disabilities. Benefits are in kind, funded by grants to participating institutions. Over 1,800 adults were aided in FY 77 at an average cost of $990. Benefits are conditioned on need.

FY 77 Expenditure (est.): **$1,706,000**

CHEST HOSPITALS—TREATMENT SERVICES

Department of Human Resources

Persons with tuberculosis, emphysema, chronic bronchitis, asthma and lung cancer are provided diagnosis and treatment at three chest hospitals across the state. Services also include rehabilitation and dental care. Benefits are in kind, funded by grants to the three hospitals. About 3,500 were aided FY 77. Benefits are conditioned, in part, on need.

FY 77 Expenditure (est.): **$3,921,000**

Of the above amount, $1,796,000 are Federal funds.

KIDNEY DISEASE CONTROL

Department of Human Resources

Persons with serious kidney disease receive life-sustaining treatment at the lowest possible cost. Services include financial assistance for treatment, medicine, dialysis and transplants. Benefits are in kind, funded by grants to participating institutions. About 400 persons were aided in FY 77 at an average cost of $1,225 per patient. Benefits are not conditioned on need.

FY 77 Expenditure (est.): **$305,000**

SICKLE CELL AND GENETIC COUNSELING

Department of Human Resources

Members of ethnic groups in which the incidence of sickle cell disease is high and those in need of genetic counseling are provided services including medical and psychological support, screening and PKU testing. Benefits are in kind, funded by grants to participating institutions. About 5,300 persons received benefits in FY 77. Benefits are not conditioned on need.

FY 77 Expenditure (est.): **$811,000**

CRIPPLED CHILDREN

Department of Human Resources

Indigent children with chronic handicaps are provided diagnosis, treatment and follow-up service. Treatment may include medical assistance, prosthesis, appliances, drugs and physical therapy. Benefits are in kind, funded by grants to participating institutions. Approximately 20,000 children were aided in FY 77 at a total average cost of $285 per child. Benefits are conditioned on need.

FY 77 Expenditure (est.): **$3,915,000**

Federal matching funds are added to the above state expenditure.

CRIPPLED CHILDREN'S HOSPITAL

Department of Human Resources

Children under 21 years old with crippling disabilities, deformities and correctable conditions are provided treatment through diagnosis, medical care and hospital services. Services include inpatient and outpatient care, home instruction, special education, therapy and psychological care. Benefits are in kind, funded by grants to two state institutions. Over 600 children were aided in FY 77. Benefits are not directly conditioned on need.

FY 77 Expenditure (est.): **$357,000**

MEDICAL CARE AND TREATMENT—CHILDREN'S MENTAL HEALTH

Department of Human Resources

Children with mental illness are provided diagnosis, treatment, educational programs, therapy, vocational training and counseling in order to restore their health. Benefits are in kind, funded by grants through area agencies to psychiatric hospitals. Over 9,500 children were aided in FY 77. Benefits are not directly conditioned on need.

FY 77 Expenditure (est.): **$2,696,000**

COMMUNITY-BASED SERVICES—CHILDREN'S MENTAL HEALTH

Department of Human Resources

Children under 21 are provided services to complement hospital care like inpatient care, outpatient care, consultation and therapeutic treatment. Benefits are in kind, funded by grants to area programs. Over 80,000 children with mental disorders are aided annually. Benefits are not conditioned on need.

FY 77 Expenditure (est.): **$5,180,000**

COMMUNITY-BASED SERVICES—ADULT MENTAL HEALTH

Department of Human Resources

The adult mentally retarded are provided treatment in community-based mental health centers in order to reduce the need for institutional care. Benefits are in kind, funded by grants to area and local non-profit organizations. Services include mental health care, sheltered workshops, daycare and senior citizens' assistance. Over 64,000 persons received services in FY 77. Benefits are not directly conditioned on need.

FY 77 Expenditure (est.): **$7,915,000**

REHABILITATION SERVICES—ADULT MENTAL HEALTH

Department of Human Resources

Mentally ill persons are provided services to help their rehabilitation and readjustment through therapeutic activities. Benefits are in kind, funded by grants to area centers. Services include occupational and recreational therapy, workshops to develop skills and personal services. Benefits are not conditioned on need.

FY 77 Expenditure (est.): **$2,685,000**

North Carolina

COMMUNITY-BASED SERVICES—ALCOHOL AND DRUG ABUSE

Department of Human Resources

Alcoholics and persons with serious drug problems are provided diagnostic and primary care at local community-based centers. Benefits are in kind and include detoxification services funded by grants to area hospitals and centers. Approximately 3,000 individuals were aided in FY 77. Benefits are not conditioned on need.

FY 77 Expenditure (est.): **$6,640,000**

Of the above amount, $1,631,000 are Federal funds.

REHABILITATION SERVICES—ALCOHOL AND DRUG ABUSE

Department of Human Resources

Alcoholics and drug abusers are provided services so that they may attain a more acceptable psychological and social condition. Benefits are in kind and include job and placement services, art recreation and industrial and educational therapy. Benefits are funded by grants to area centers. Over 300 individuals were aided in FY 77. Benefits are not conditioned on need.

FY 77 Expenditure (est.): **$726,000**

MEDICAL CARE AND TREATMENT—ALCOHOL AND DRUG ABUSE

Department of Human Resources

Alcoholics and drug abusers are provided treatment so that they may readjust to society. Services include medication, treatment, detoxification, psychiatric care, psychological, occupational and recreational therapy. Benefits are in kind, funded by grants to area centers. Over 250 individuals are aided monthly. Benefits are not conditioned on need.

FY 77 Expenditure (est.): **$2,958,000**

COMMUNITY-BASED SERVICES—MENTAL RETARDATION

Department of Human Resources

Mentally retarded persons are provided services to increase their development potential by reducing the physical and psychological separation between them, their families and communities. Benefits are in kind, funded by grants to area mental health programs. Services include childhood intervention and respite care and daycare centers for children and adults. Almost 16,000 persons were aided in FY 77. Benefits are not directly conditioned on need.

FY 77 Expenditure (est.): **$13,975,000**

Of the above amount, $1,160,000 are Federal funds and $3,127,000 are local funds.

SHELTERED WORKSHOPS

Department of Human Resources

Mentally retarded and severely handicapped individuals who are considered "uneducable" and cannot obtain employment in business or industry are provided jobs and care within sheltered facilities. Benefits are in the form of cash compensation for work performed and in kind, consisting mainly of supervision of social services in the shelters. Funding is on a per-client basis directly to private, non-profit workshop facilities. Approximately 50 individuals were aided in FY 77. Benefits are not directly conditioned on need.

FY 77 Expenditure (est.): **$66,000**

MEDICAL EYE CARE

Department of Human Resources

Medically indigent persons who are blind or in danger of becoming blind are provided treatment in order to prevent blindness and to restore sight. Benefits are in the form of cash, funded by payments to participating institutions. Over 41,000 persons received services in FY 77 at an average cost of $11 per case for eyeglasses and prosthetic devices. Benefits are conditioned on need.

FY 77 Expenditure (est.): **$1,660,000**

SCHOLARSHIPS FOR CHILDREN OF CERTAIN DISABLED, DECEASED AND POW/MIA VETERANS

Department of Veterans' Affairs

Children of disabled or deceased veterans are provided financial assistance in four categories to help them complete their higher education while attending public and private colleges within North Carolina. Benefits are in the form of cash paid to the institution for a period not to exceed four academic years. For children of deceased veterans in private colleges the maximum award is $930 per academic year. In state schools the award can cover tuition, fees, or room and board or all of those expenses, depending on the circumstances. About 600 students were aided in FY 77. Benefits are not conditioned on need.

FY 77 Expenditure (est.): **$2,110,000**

TUITION GRANTS—PRIVATE AND NON-STATE SCHOOLS

Department of Education

Residents of the state, enrolled on a full-time basis at private and non-state (community) colleges and universities within the state, are provided tuition subsidies. Benefits are in the form of cash assistance, funded by payments directly to participating institutions. Over 23,000 people took advantage of the program, receiving an average grant of $200. Benefits are conditioned on need.

FY 77 Expenditure (est.): **$4,600,000**

SUPPLEMENTAL EDUCATIONAL OPPORTUNITY GRANTS

Department of Education

College students who are residents of North Carolina are provided supplements to other educational assistance grants, depending on their financial resources. Benefits are in the form of cash, paid directly to the student. About 500 students received benefits in FY 77. Benefits are conditioned on need.

FY 77 Expenditure (est.): **$2,227,000**

STUDENT AID—SCHOLARSHIPS

Department of Education

Undergraduate students are provided financial support for attendance at post-secondary educational institutions, in order to make higher education attainable for those who could not otherwise afford it and to help eliminate racial Inequality in the university system. Benefits are in the form of cash, funded by grants to the schools. About 10,000 students are aided annually at an average cost of almost $1,000 each. Benefits are conditioned on need.

FY 77 Expenditure (est.): **$9,500,000**

SCHOLARSHIPS, LOANS AND GRANTS

Department of Education

Persons wishing to become teachers in the North Carolina public schools are provided financial assistance in the form of loans, scholarships and grants. Benefits are in the form of cash assistance and favorable credit terms. About 1,300 persons received aid in FY 77. The maximum grant, loan or scholarship is $900 per year. Loans need not be repaid if those receiving aid subsequently teach in the state public school system on the basis of one year for each year they receive assistance. Benefits are conditioned on need.

FY 77 Expenditure (est.): **$100,000**

STUDENT AID—LOANS

Department of Education

Undergraduate students are provided low-interest, deferred loans at an average of $1,029 per loan to cover the cost of tuition and books. Over 2,000 students are aided annually. Benefits are in the form of favorable credit terms. Benefits are conditioned on need.

FY 77 Expenditure (est.): **$2,115,000.**

PERSONAL INCOME TAX PROVISIONS

Department of Revenue

Low-Income Exemption. Indirect financial assistance is provided to persons whose annual gross income does not exceed scheduled limits ranging from $1,000 for single persons to $2,000 for married or divorced persons with custody of a child and receiving no support, or for heads of household with a child. Anyone aged 65 or over, blind, deaf or a hemophiliac, may add $1,000 to the limits for each of the scheduled categories. Benefits are in the form of tax relief, funded by allowing the taxpayer a total exemption of his income from personal income taxation. Benefits are conditioned on need.

Exclusion of Public Employees' Pensions. Indirect financial assistance is provided to certain public employees who receive pensions or other retirement income. Benefits are in the form of tax relief, funded by allowing the taxpayer to exclude from his income, subject to personal income taxation, such pension and retirement payments. Benefits are not directly conditioned on need.

Additional Exemption for Hemophiliacs. Indirect financial assistance is provided to taxpayers who are hemophiliacs or who have a hemophiliac dependent. Benefits are in the form of tax relief, funded by allowing the taxpayer an additional $1,000 exemption from his income subject to personal income taxation. Benefits are not directly conditioned on need.

Additional Exemption for Retarded Dependent. Indirect financial assistance is provided to taxpayers who claim mentally retarded dependents. Benefits are in the form of tax relief, funded by allowing the taxpayer an additional $2,000 exemption from his income subject to personal income taxation. Benefits are not directly conditioned on need.

Additional Exemptions for the Disabled. Indirect financial assistance is provided to taxpayers who are blind or deaf. Benefits are in the form of tax relief, funded by allowing the taxpayer an additional $1,000 exemption from his income subject to personal income taxation for each disability. Benefits are not directly conditioned on need.

Deduction for Care of Dependent in Institution. Indirect financial assistance is provided to taxpayers who must pay for the care of a dependent relative institutionalized for mental or physical defects. Benefits are in the form of tax relief, funded by allowing the taxpayer a deduction from his income, subject to personal income taxation, an amount of up to $800. Benefits are not directly conditioned on need.

Deduction for Seeing-Eye Dogs. Indirect financial assistance is provided to taxpayers who use seeing-eye dogs. Benefits are in the form of tax relief, funded by allowing the taxpayer to deduct from his income, subject to personal income taxation, the costs of purchase, maintenance and veterinary care of a seeing-eye dog. Benefits are not directly conditioned on need.

OHIO

Population 10,701,000

Total State and Local Expenditures
for all Purposes:
$11,871,000,000

MAJOR FEDERALLY ENABLED
INCOME TRANSFER PROGRAMS

FY 77 Expenditures (est.)

Program	State	Local
Aid to Families with Dependent Children	$205,650,000	$12,600,000
Medicaid	255,970,000	610,000
Social Services	11,100,000	20,290,000

OPTIONAL STATE SUPPLEMENTATION FOR SSI

Department of Mental Health and Mental Retardation

Mentally retarded and developmentally disabled persons are provided cash supplements to their Federal SSI benefits for basic needs. Basic needs are food, shelter, clothing and daily living necessities. Benefits are provided to eligible individuals living in state-approved institutional settings. Benefits average over $400 monthly per individual and they vary according to the facility in which the individual is housed. Payments and eligibility are determined by the state. Over 1,400 individuals receive benefits monthly. Benefits are conditioned on need.

FY 77 Expenditure (est.): **$6,000,000**

POLICE AND FIREMEN'S DISABILITY AND PENSION FUND

Treasury Department

Police and firefighters who retire at age 52 with at least 25 years of service, or age 62 with 15 years of service, and their dependents are provided with financial assistance to replace income lost through retirement. Benefits are paid directly to the beneficiary in the form of cash without any restriction on its use. Payments average $552 per month. Some 11,562 individuals benefit from this program. Members contribute seven percent of salary while the state contributes between 17.5 and 19 percent. Benefits are not directly conditioned on need.

FY 77 Expenditure (est.): **$54,543,000**

Benefits paid total $53,804,000.
Administrative costs total $639,000.
State contributions total $9,395,000.

HIGHWAY PATROL RETIREMENT SYSTEM

Treasury Department

Members of the Highway Patrol who retire at age 52 with at least 20 years of service and their dependents are provided with financial assistance to replace income lost through retirement. Benefits are paid directly to the beneficiary in the form of cash without any restriction on its use. Payments average $528 per month. Some 345 individuals receive such monthy benefits. Members contribute eight percent of salary while the state contributes 13.25 percent. Benefits are not directly conditioned on need.

FY 77 Expenditure (est.): **$1,631,000**

Benefits paid total $1,627,000.
Administrative costs total $4,000.
State contributions total $17,000.

SCHOOL EMPLOYEES' RETIREMENT SYSTEM

Treasury Department

Full-time school employees (excluding teachers) who retire at age 65 with at least five years of service, or regardless of age with 30 years of service, and their dependents are provided with financial assistance to replace income lost through retirement. Benefits are paid directly to the beneficiary in the form of cash without any restriction on its use. Payments average $146 per month. Some 23,462 individuals benefit from this program. Members contribute eight percent of salary and the state contributes 12.5 percent. Benefits are not directly conditioned on need.

FY 77 Expenditure (est.): **$45,100,000**

Benefits paid total $43,300,000.
Administrative costs total $1,800,000.
State contributions total $1,300,000.

TEACHERS' RETIREMENT SYSTEM

Treasury Department

Full-time teachers in public schools of the state who retire at age 65 with at least five years of service, or regardless of age with 30 years of service, and their dependents are provided with financial assistance to replace income lost through retirement. Benefits are paid directly to the beneficiary in the form of cash without any restriction on its use. Payments average $440 per month. Some 42,790 individuals benefit from this program. Members contribute 8.5 percent of salary while the state contributes 13.5 percent. Benefits are not directly conditioned on need.

FY 77 Expenditure (est.): **$226,400,000**

Benefits paid total $223,700,000.
Administrative costs total $2,700,000.
State contributions total $3,700,000.

PUBLIC EMPLOYEES' RETIREMENT SYSTEM
Treasury Department

Full-time employees of the state and its political subdivisions who retire at age 65 with at least five years of service, or regardless of age with 30 years of service (except sheriffs who may retire at age 52 with 25 years of service), and their dependents are provided with financial assistance to replace income lost through retirement. Benefits are paid directly to the beneficiary in the form of cash without any restriction on its use. Payments average $240 per month. Some 60,393 individuals benefit from this program. Members contribute 8.5 percent of salary while the state contributes 13.7 percent. Benefits are not directly conditioned on need.

FY 77 Expenditure (est.): **$177,600,000**

Benefits paid total $173,400,000.
Administrative costs total $4,200,000.
State contributions total $3,000,000.

PROPERTY TAX RELIEF FOR HOMEOWNERS

Department of Taxation

Indirect financial assistance is provided to all property owners. Benefits are in the form of tax relief, funded by allowing local property tax reductions amounting to ten percent of the tax bill. Local governments are reimbursed by the state for lost revenues. Over two million homeowners received benefits in FY 77. Benefits are not conditioned on need.

FY 77 Expenditure (est.): **$180,000,000**

SENIOR CITIZEN AND DISABLED HOMESTEAD EXEMPTION

Department of Taxation

Indirect financial assistance is provided to disabled persons and to those 65 years or older, with an income of $10,000 or less. Benefits are in the form of tax relief, funded by local property tax exemptions ranging up to 70 percent of assessed value or $5,000, whichever is less, for incomes below $3,000, and up to 40 percent of assessed value or $2,000 for incomes above $7,000. Approximately 330,000 persons were aided in FY 77, at an average of $135 each. Local governments are reimbursed from the state general revenue fund for any loss of revenues. Benefits are conditioned, in part, on need.

FY 77 Expenditure (est.): **$44,614,000**

ELDERLY BUS FARE ASSISTANCE

Department of Transportation

Persons over age 65 are provided transportation assistance to utilize passenger buses, by means of a half-fare program. Benefits are in kind, funded by the state, to both public and private carriers. Over 500,000 riders took advantage of the half-fare programs in FY 77. Benefits are not directly conditioned on need.

FY 77 Expenditure (est.): **$2,000,000**

GENERAL ASSISTANCE PROGRAM

Department of Public Welfare

Maintenance payments, short-term or emergency aid to cover the costs of food, shelter, clothing and other items of daily living are made to individuals, couples, families with children and fathers unemployed due to a strike. Emergency aid is also available to non-resident individuals pending return to their legal place of residence. Benefits are paid directly to the beneficiary in the form of cash without any restrictions on its use or through vendor payments (to the suppliers of goods and services including medical care). Shelter and utility payments to vendors are limited to $72. Employable persons must accept work project assignments. Payments are in amounts varying according to each beneficiary's needs as determined under state law. Benefits are funded by grants to local offices of the state public assistance agency. This program is financed by state and local funds. Each month an average of 50,660 recipients (in some 42,625 cases) are aided. The average monthly benefit per recipient is $76 (per case, the average is $90). Benefits are conditioned on need.

FY 77 Expenditure (est.): **$46,245,000**

WORKERS' COMPENSATION PROGRAM

Bureau of Workers' Compensation

Workers injured or disabled on the job, as well as the surviving dependents of workers who die as a result of such injury, are provided financial assistance both as compensation for lost wages and to pay for the cost of any required medical or rehabilitative care. Benefits are in the form of cash payments, funded by means of a state-administered insurance program to which each covered employer must contribute a percentage of payroll determined by the employer's experience rating and industrial classification. Beneficiaries receive two-thirds of normal wages, up to a maximum weekly compensation benefit of $198. These benefits may be received for the total period of disability and the total amount of benefits one may receive is unlimited. In addition, a funeral allowance of $1,200 is provided for workers who die on the job. Approximately 72,000 workers and survivors were aided weekly in FY 77. Benefits are not directly conditioned on need.

FY 77 Expenditure (est.): **$524,556,000**

Ohio

SOLDIERS' AND SAILORS' ORPHANS' HOME

Department of Human Services

Orphans of Ohio veterans are provided educational, mental, medical and dental treatment. Benefits are in kind, aimed primarily at
emotionally disturbed children. Services also include vocational
classes, psychological appraisals and counseling, and training in
livestock production. About 140 children are aided annually.
Benefits are conditioned, in part, on need.

FY 77 Expenditure (est.): **$3,345,000**

RESIDENTIAL PROGRAMS FOR THE ELDERLY AND MENTAL PATIENTS

Department of Human Services

Needy elderly persons and mental patients are provided services to
promote independent living. Benefits are in kind, funded by grants
to care facilities. Services include needs, health and personal care
and recreational services at state "terrace" facilities at Glendale,
Toledo, Worley and Columbus. About 400 persons received benefits
in FY 77. Benefits are conditioned on need.

FY 77 Expenditure (est.): **$445,000**

HEMOPHILIA STUDY

Department of Health

Hemophiliacs are provided home care therapy, medical services at
centers and drugs. Medical care is aimed at preventing crippling
and prolonged hospitalization. Benefits are in kind, funded by
grants to centers across the state. Almost 600 persons were treated
in FY 77. Benefits are not directly conditioned on need.

FY 77 Expenditure (est.): **$250,000**

TB CONTROL

Department of Health

People with tuberculosis or at risk of having tuberculosis are provided assistance. Benefits are in kind, funded by grants through the counties to participating hospitals and clinics. Over 1,300 people were aided in FY 77, at an average cost of $400 per patient. Benefits are not conditioned on need.

FY 77 Expenditure (est.): **$588,000**

MENTAL HEALTH COMMUNITY SERVICES

Department of Mental Health

Mentally ill persons are provided inpatient and outpatient services including consultation, hospitalization, precare and aftercare services. Benefits are in kind, funded by payments to institutions. About 300,000 persons receive benefits annually. Benefits are not conditioned on need.

FY 77 Expenditure (est.): **$26,067,000**

MENTAL RETARDATION AND DEVELOPMENTAL DISABILITIES SERVICES

Department of Mental Health

Mentally retarded and developmentally disabled persons (i.e., those suffering substantial handicaps resulting from mental retardation, cerebral palsy, epilepsy or other neurological conditions developed in childhood) are provided care so that their capacity to function in the community and avoid institutionalization is improved. Benefits are in kind, funded by grants to participating homemaker training, education and workshop programs. Over 21,000 persons are aided annually. Benefits are not directly conditioned on need.

FY 77 Expenditure (est.): **$16,029,000**

Ohio

MENTAL RETARDATION AND DEVELOPMENTAL DISABILITIES LOCAL DISTRICT SERVICES

Department of Mental Health

Mentally retarded and developmentally disabled persons are provided medical and social services that enable them to function in a community environment. Benefits are in kind, funded by grants to facilities offering services. Over 18,000 persons were aided in FY 77. Benefits are not directly conditioned on need.

FY 77 Expenditure (est.): **$2,943,000**

TRANSPORTATION FOR MENTALLY RETARDED

Department of Mental Health

Mentally retarded individuals are provided transportation to community educational and workshop training programs and to adult sheltered workshops. Benefits are primarily in kind, funded by payments to counties to cover the costs of drivers' salaries and the purchase of gasoline, equipment and related expenses. Almost 14,000 persons are aided annually. Benefits are not directly conditioned on need.

FY 77 Expenditure (est.): **$2,631,000**

PROGRAM FOR MENTALLY DEFICIENT

Department of Mental Health

Mentally retarded adults and children are provided pre-school and school-age education, home training, living skills training and sheltered workshop supervision. Benefits are mainly in kind, funded by payments to county boards of mental retardation, who then contract locally for services. Approximately 8,000 adults and 12,000 children are aided annually at a maximum reimbursement level of $450 per child and $600 per adult. Benefits are not directly conditioned on need.

FY 77 Expenditure (est.): **$11,000,000**

WAR ORPHANS' SCHOLARSHIP PROGRAM

Department of Higher Education

Children of disabled or deceased veterans are provided financial aid to assist them in completing their higher education while attending college within Ohio. Benefits are in the form of cash, paid directly to the students. About 2,130 individuals are aided annually at a rate of almost $800 per year, per person. Benefits are not conditioned on need.

FY 77 Expenditure (est.): **$3,397,000**

INSTRUCTIONAL GRANT PROGRAM

Department of Higher Education

Low- and middle-income undergraduate students, from families with incomes below $17,000, are provided financial aid not to exceed the cost of tuition at state colleges and universities. Benefits are in the form of cash, paid directly to institutions. About 4,000 students were aided in FY 77 at an average of about $470 per year. Benefits are conditioned on need.

FY 77 Expenditure (est.): **$26,700,000**

Of the above amount $2,400,000 are Federal funds.

PERSONAL INCOME TAX PROVISIONS

Department of Taxation

Deduction for Retirement Benefits. Indirect financial assistance is provided to taxpayers who receive retirement income or pensions. Benefits are in the form of tax relief, funded by allowing the taxpayer to deduct up to $4,000 from his adjusted gross income subject to personal income taxation. Benefits are not directly conditioned on need.

PENNSYLVANIA

Population 11,785,000

Total State and Local Expenditures
for all Purposes:
$13,746,000,000

MAJOR FEDERALLY ENABLED
INCOME TRANSFER PROGRAMS
FY 77 Expenditures (est.)

Program	State	Local
Aid to Families with Dependent Children	$365,810,000	$ 10,000
Medicaid	564,870,000	0
Social Services	24,180,000	11,140,000

OPTIONAL STATE SUPPLEMENTATION FOR SSI

Department of Public Welfare

The aged, over 65 years old, the blind and the disabled are provided cash supplements to their SSI benefits for basic and special needs. Basic needs are food, shelter, clothing, utilities and daily living necessities. Special needs are those not provided for through monthly or optional SSI payments and include burial and moving expenses. Benefits are provided to eligible persons living independently, in the household of another, with an essential person, with an essential person in the household of another, or in a domiciliary-care facility. Benefits are $32 monthly for individuals and $48 for couples living independently and vary for other categories. Benefits are in the form of direct cash payments, funded wholly by the state. Payments are administered by the Federal government; eligibility is determined at Social Security district offices. Over 155,000 individuals are aided monthly. Benefits are conditioned on need.

FY 77 Expenditure (est.): **$62,012,400**

POLICE AND FIREFIGHTERS' RETIREMENT SYSTEMS

Locally administered

Police officers and firefighters, through their local districts, are provided with financial assistance to replace income lost through retirement. Qualifications for retirement vary depending upon the size of the locality. Minimum age may be 50 years with 20 to 25 years of service. Benefits are in the form of cash. There are approximately 1,000 police retirement systems and 2,000 firefighters' retirement systems in the state. Benefits are not directly conditioned on need.

FY 77 Expenditure (est.): **$52,188,120**

This figure represents the state contribution to the various police and firefighters' retirement systems.

Pennsylvania

LAW ENFORCEMENT OFFICERS' DEATH BENEFIT

Department of the Treasury

Children and widows of firemen or policemen killed in the line of duty are provided death benefits in the amount of $25,000. Benefits are in the form of cash, paid directly to the families of the victims. Benefits are not conditioned on need.

FY 77 Expenditure (est.): **$500,000**

PUBLIC SCHOOL EMPLOYEES' RETIREMENT SYSTEM

Treasury Department

All employees of Pennsylvania public schools who retire at age 62 with ten years of service, or at age 60 with 30 years of service, and their dependents are provided with financial assistance to replace income lost through retirement. Benefits are paid directly to the beneficiary in the form of cash without any restriction on its use. Payments average over $500 per month. Some 57,000 individuals benefit from this program. Members contribute 5.25 percent of salary (this varies according to class of membership). The state contributes about 6.7 percent. Benefits are not directly conditioned on need.

FY 77 Expenditure (est.): **$366,000,000**

Benefits paid total $366,000,000.
Administrative costs are covered by excess earnings of the fund.

RETIREMENT SYSTEM FOR STATE EMPLOYEES AND OFFICERS

Treasury Department

All state employees (except legislators and certain elected officials who choose not to participate) who retire at age 60 with at least three years of service, or at any age with 25 years of service, and their dependents are provided with financial assistance to replace income lost through retirement. Benefits are paid directly to the beneficiary in the form of cash without any restriction on its use. Payments range from $104 to $1,224 per month depending upon length of service. Some 33,176 retirees and 3,608 other beneficiaries receive such monthly benefits. Members contribute five percent of salary. The state contributes an amount which is actuarily determined. In FY 77 this amount was 13.1 percent of payroll. Benefits are not directly conditioned on need.

FY 77 Expenditure (est.): **$194,333,000**

Benefits paid total $192,713,000.
Administrative costs total $1,620,000.

TAX RELIEF FOR HOMEOWNERS AND RENTERS

Department of Revenue

Indirect financial assistance is provided to lower-income home-owners and renters, 65 years and older, and to widows and widowers, 50 and older. Total household income must be $7,500 or less. Benefits are in the form of tax relief, funded by means of a tax rebate ranging from 100 percent of property taxes (or 20 percent of rent) for incomes less than $3,000 (maximum benefit is $200) to ten percent of tax for incomes greater that $7,000. Approximately 415,000 persons were aided in FY 77, at an average of $142 each. Benefits are conditioned on need.

FY 77 Expenditure (est.): **$58,918,000**

GENERAL ASSISTANCE PROGRAM

Department of Public Welfare

Maintenance payments, short-term or emergency aid to cover the costs of food, shelter, clothing and other items of daily living are made to individuals, couples, families with children and fathers unemployed due to a strike. Emergency aid is also available to non-resident individuals pending return to their legal place of residence. Benefits are paid directly to the beneficiary in the form of cash without any restrictions on its use or through vendor payments (to the suppliers of goods and services). Employable persons must accept work project assignments. Payments are in amounts varying according to each beneficiary's needs as determined under state law. Benefits are funded by grants to local offices of the state public assistance agency. This program is financed by state funds. Medical care is financed under the state's medical assistance program. Each month an average of 162,400 recipients (in some 135,546 cases) are aided. The average monthly benefit per recipient is $137 (per case, the average is $164). Benefits are conditioned on need.

FY 77 Expenditure (est.): **$266,500,000**

WORKERS' COMPENSATION PROGRAM

Department of Labor and Industry

Workers injured or disabled on the job, as well as the surviving dependents of workers who die as a result of such injury, are provided financial assistance both as compensation for lost wages and to pay for the cost of any required medical or rehabilitative care. Benefits are in the form of cash payments, funded by means of state-administered and state-regulated private insurance programs to which each covered employer must contribute a percentage of payroll determined by the employer's experience rating and industrial classification. Beneficiaries receive two-thirds of normal wages, up to a maximum compensation benefit of $199. These benefits may be received for the total period of disability and the total amount of benefits one may receive is unlimited. In addition, a funeral allowance of $1,500 is provided for workers who die on the job. Approximately 42,000 workers and survivors were aided weekly in FY 77. Benefits are not directly conditioned on need.

FY 77 Expenditure (est.): **$306,220,000**

FREE ELDERLY TRANSIT

Department of Transportation

Persons 65 years or older are provided free transportation in order to increase their mobility and enable them to participate more fully in community life. Benefits are in kind and consist of free transit during non-rush hours on weekdays and at all times on holidays and weekends. Funding is derived from the state lottery fund. Over 60 million trips are provided annually. Benefits are not directly conditioned on need.

FY 77 Expenditure (est.): **$13,576,000**

TRANSPORTATION FOR RURAL CITIZENS

Department of Agriculture

Poverty-level rural inhabitants are provided transportation within rural areas where service previously did not exist. Benefits are in kind, funded by subsidies to providers of transportation services. Approximately 850,000 rides were subsidized in FY 77. Benefits are not directly conditioned on need.

FY 77 Expenditure (est.): **$415,000**

TEAM—MANPOWER ASSISTANCE AND TRAINING

Department of Community Affairs

Hard-core unemployed and underemployed individuals with social and economic problems are provided training, education and placement in jobs with advancement potential. Benefits are in kind, funded by state grants to local agencies. About 2,400 people take advantage of this program yearly. Benefits are conditioned, in part, on need.

FY 77 Expenditure (est.): **$1,750,000**

Pennsylvania

VETERANS' ASSISTANCE

Department of Military Affairs

Veterans in need of support are provided temporary financial assistance. Benefits are in the form of cash for food, shelter and clothing for a period not to exceed three months. Over 16,000 persons are assisted annually. Benefits are conditioned on need.

FY 77 Expenditure (est.): **$650,000**

BLIND VETERANS' PENSION

Department of Military Affairs

Honorably discharged blind veterans are provided grants in order to help them meet the costs of living within their handicap. Benefits are in the form of cash, paid directly to the veterans. Over 130 persons receive aid monthly at the rate of $50 each. Benefits are not directly conditioned on need.

FY 77 Expenditure (est.): **$80,000**

SERVICES TO THE BLIND

Department of Public Welfare

Blind people are provided remedial eye care, vocational rehabilitation and other services in order to help them cope with the restrictions of blindness. Benefits are in kind, funded by payments to providers. About 7,000 persons receive aid annually. Benefits are conditioned, in part, on need.

FY 77 Expenditure (est.): **$798,000**

STATE BLIND PENSION

Department of Public Welfare

Blind persons over 21 years of age are provided financial assistance to help compensate for their disability. Benefits are in cash, paid directly to beneficiaries. Over 7,000 persons were aided in FY 77. Benefits are not directly conditioned on need.

FY 77 Expenditure (est.): **$7,094,000**

HOSPITALIZATION AND MEDICAL SERVICES

Department of Public Welfare

People who live in areas where local communities have been unable to assume hospital and medical services are provided those services through state-operated care facilities. Benefits are in kind, funded by grants to service facilities. Over 740 persons were treated monthly in FY 77. Benefits are conditioned, in part, on need.

FY 77 Expenditure (est.): **$7,243,000**

TREATMENT OF DRUG AND ALCOHOL ABUSE

Council on Drug and Alcohol Abuse

Alcoholics and drug users who have reached a dysfunctional level of substance abuse are provided diagnostic and primary care on an inpatient and outpatient basis at clinics and hospitals across the state. Benefits are in kind, funded by payments to area programs. Services include medication, treatment, detoxification, psychiatric care and psychological, occupational and recreational therapy. Over 20,000 persons are treated annually on an inpatient basis, while some 28,000 are treated as outpatients. Benefits are not conditioned on need.

FY 77 Expenditure (est.): **$27,259,000**

Of the above amount, $11,617,000 are Federal funds.

Pennsylvania

HEMOPHILIA PROGRAM

Department of Health

Hemophiliacs are provided outpatient care and other medical services in clinics and hospitals throughout the state. Benefits are in
kind, funded by grants from the state directly to the hospitals and
clinics to pay the cost of services not covered by medical insurance
or other assistance programs. Over 300 people are aided annually.
Benefits are not directly conditioned on need.

FY 77 Expenditure (est.): **$1,190,000**

RENAL DISEASE PROGRAM

Department of Health

Persons requiring long-term hemodialysis due to chronic renal
disease are provided medical care in hospitals and outpatient centers. Benefits are in kind, funded by payments to participating hospitals. Those payments not covered by other programs are covered
by the state up to 55 percent of costs for the first year of treatment.
Thereafter not less than 25 percent is covered. Approximately 1,500
people were aided in FY 77. Benefits are not directly conditioned on
need.

FY 77 Expenditure (est.): **$2,737,000**

COAL WORKERS' PNEUMOCONIOSIS

Department of Health

Miners who are victims of black lung disease are provided comprehensive health care services at hospitals and clinics throughout
Pennsylvania. Benefits are in kind, funded by payments to participating hospitals and care centers. Approximately 2,900 persons
were aided in FY 77. Benefits are not directly conditioned on need.

FY 77 Expenditure (est.): **$341,000**

VICTIMS OF VIOLENT CRIME—COMPENSATION

Treasury Department

Victims of violent crime are provided assistance to compensate for their losses. Benefits are in the form of cash and provide for losses not replaced by insurance or other plans. Victims must have incurred a minimum out-of-pocket loss of $100 or two continuous weeks' earnings or support. The maximum payment is $25,000. Benefits are not conditioned on need. This program is administered by the state Justice Department.

FY 77 Expenditure (est.): **$700,000**

Benefits paid total $500,000
Administrative costs total $200,000.

EDUCATION OF VETERANS' CHILDREN

Department of Military Affairs

Children of disabled or deceased veterans are provided financial assistance to assist them in completing higher education while attending college within Pennsylvania. Benefits are in the form of cash, paid directly to the students. About 160 individuals are aided annually at a rate of $200 per semester. Benefits are not conditioned on need.

FY 77 Expenditure (est.): **$65,000**

VETERANS' EDUCATIONAL ASSISTANCE

Higher Education Assistance Agency

Non-dishonorably discharged veterans, who are academically qualified, are provided financial assistance toward the cost of tuition, books and living expenses to attend college within the state. Benefits are in the form of cash, funded by payments to higher education institutions. Over 11,000 veterans were aided in FY 77. The average award was $810. Benefits are conditioned, in part, on need.

FY 77 Expenditure (est.): **$9,000,000**

Pennsylvania

STUDENT SCHOLARSHIPS

Higher Education Assistance Agency

Academically qualified students from families with an annual income of under $18,000 are provided financial assistance toward the cost of tuition, books and daily living expenses to attend college within the state. Benefits are in the form of cash, funded by payments to the higher education institutions. Almost 112,000 students received assistance in FY 77. The average award was $570. Benefits are conditioned, in part, on need.

FY 77 Expenditure (est.): **$61,400,000**

Of the above amount, $2,000,000 are Federal funds.

GUARANTEED STUDENT LOAN PROGRAM

Higher Education Assistance Agency

Academically and financially qualified students are provided guaranteed loans to help meet the costs of tuition, books and daily living expenses to attend college within the state. Benefits are in the form of favorable credit terms, funded by the state's guarantee of 20 percent of the value of outstanding loans committed by any lending institution. Some 75,000 students were aided in FY 77 and a total loan value of $113,000,000 was committed. Benefits are conditioned, in part, on need.

FY 77 Expenditure (est.): **$4,700,000**

The above amount represents an appropriation to the reserve for losses, administrative costs and required matching funds.

PERSONAL INCOME TAX PROVISIONS

Department of Revenue

Low-Income Exemption. Indirect financial assistance is provided to low-income persons. Benefits are in the form of tax relief, funded by allowing the taxpayer either a credit against, or refund of, his personal income tax liability. Taxpayers with no dependents and a total income not exceeding $3,000 are entitled to a 100 percent tax credit which generates a refund of any monies already paid. Credit is reduced by ten percent for each $100 above $3,000 up to $3,900. Additional income allowances of $1,200 for the first dependent and $750 for each additional dependent are permitted. Therefore the income base varies for individual taxpayers, but the credit is still reduced by ten percent for each $100 above the base. Benefits are conditioned on need.

Exclusion of Public Employees' Pensions. Indirect financial assistance is provided to certain public employees who receive pensions or other retirement income. Benefits are in the form of tax relief, funded by allowing the taxpayer to exclude from his income, subject to personal income taxation, pension or other retirement payments. Benefits are not directly conditioned on need.

SOUTH CAROLINA

Population: 2,876,000

Total State and Local Expenditures
for all Purposes:
$2,814,000,000

MAJOR FEDERALLY ENABLED
INCOME TRANSFER PROGRAMS
FY 77 Expenditures (est.)

Program	State	Local
Aid to Families with Dependent Children	$15,190,000	$400,000
Medicaid	44,300,000	0
Social Services	6,780,000	0

OPTIONAL STATE SUPPLEMENTATION FOR SSI

Department of Public Welfare

The aged, over 65 years old, the blind and the disabled are provided cash supplements to their SSI benefits for basic needs. Basic needs are food, shelter, clothing, utilities and daily living necessities. Benefits are provided to eligible persons living with an ineligible spouse or living in licensed residential-care facilities. Benefits average $89 monthly for individuals. Benefits vary for other categories. Benefits are in the form of direct cash payments, funded wholly by the state. Payments are administered by the state; eligibility is determined at county offices of the Department of Social Services. Over 1,000 individuals are aided monthly. Benefits are conditioned on need.

FY 77 Expenditure (est.): **$1,320,000**

GENERAL DISABILITY ASSISTANCE PROGRAM

Department of Social Services

People 18 to 65 years of age who are temporarily and totally disabled and in need are provided financial assistance for a period up to six months. Benefits are in the form of direct cash payments, generally for several months. Approximately 750 persons received this aid while waiting for their Federal Supplementary Security Income payments to be processed. Benefits are conditioned on need.

FY 77 Expenditure (est.): **$5,100,000**

South Carolina

POLICE OFFICERS' RETIREMENT SYSTEM

Treasury Department

Police officers and firefighters who retire at age 55 with at least five years of service, or regardless of age with 30 years of service, and their dependents are provided with financial assistance to replace income lost through retirement. Benefits are paid directly to the beneficiary in the form of cash without any restriction on its use. Payments average $238 per month. Some 1,142 individuals benefit from this program. Members contribute five percent while the state contributes ten percent. Benefits are not directly conditioned on need.

FY 77 Expenditure (est.): **$3,344,000**

Benefits paid total $3,197,000.
Administrative costs total $147,000.

GENERAL ASSEMBLY RETIREMENT SYSTEM

Treasury Department

Members of the General Assembly who retire at age 60, or regardless of age with 30 years of service, and their dependents are provided with financial assistance to replace income lost through retirement. Benefits are paid directly to the beneficiary in the form of cash without any restriction on its use. Payments average $405 per month. Some 43 individuals benefit from this program. Members contribute ten percent of salary while the state contributes an amount which is actuarily determined. Benefits are not directly conditioned on need.

FY 77 Expenditure (est.): **$214,000**

Benefits paid total $210,000.
Administrative costs total $4,000.

PUBLIC EMPLOYEES' RETIREMENT SYSTEM

Treasury Department

Full-time employees of the state and its political subdivisions (including teachers) who retire at age 65, or regardless of age with 30 years of service, and their dependents are provided with financial assistance to replace income lost through retirement. Benefits are paid directly to the beneficiary in the form of cash without any restriction on its use. Payments average $231 per month. Some 19,946 individuals benefit from this program. Members contribute four percent of the first $4,800 of salary plus six percent of any additional amount. The state contributes 6.8 percent. Benefits are not directly conditioned on need.

FY 77 Expenditure (est.): **$56,586,000**

Benefits paid total $55,334,000.
Administrative costs total $950,000.

SENIOR CITIZEN PROPERTY TAX EXEMPTION

Tax Commission

Indirect financial assistance is provided to homeowners 65 years and over. Benefits are in the form of tax relief, funded by allowing the senior citizen homeowner to exempt from property taxes $10,000 of assessed value of his homestead property. Approximately 80,000 persons benefit yearly. Benefits are not directly conditioned on need.

FY 77 Expenditure (est.): **$4,000,000**

WORKERS' COMPENSATION PROGRAM

Workmen's Compensation Fund

Workers injured or disabled on the job, as well as the surviving dependents of workers who die as a result of such injury, are provided financial assistance both as compensation for lost wages and to pay for the cost of any required medical or rehabilitative care. Benefits are in the form of cash payments, funded by means of a state-regulated private insurance program to which each covered employer must contribute a percentage of payroll determined by the employer's experience rating and industrial classification. Beneficiaries receive two-thirds of normal wages, up to a maximum weekly compensation benefit of $160. These benefits may be received for no more than 500 weeks and the total amount of benefits one may receive is $40,000. In addition, a funeral allowance of $2,000 is provided for workers who die on the job. Approximately 7,000 workers and survivors were aided weekly in FY 77. Benefits are not directly conditioned on need.

FY 77 Expenditure (est.): **$40,597,000**

GENERAL ASSISTANCE PROGRAM

Department of Social Services

Maintenance payments to cover the costs of food, shelter, clothing and other items of daily living are made to resident individuals, couples (if the spouse is in the home and not an AFDC or SSI recipient) and families without an employable member. Benefits are paid directly to the beneficiary in the form of vendor payments (including medical). Payments are in amounts varying according to each beneficiary's needs as determined under state law. Benefits are funded by grants to the administering local welfare agencies. Separate county programs, using local funds are used for emergency assistance. This program is financed by state funds. Each month some 895 recipients in some 819 cases are aided. The average monthly benefit per recipient is $51; per case, the average is $56. Benefits are conditioned on need.

FY 77 Expenditure (est.): **$546,000**

HEART DISEASE CONTROL

Department of Health and Environmental Control

Medically indigent individuals are provided diagnosis, treatment and prophylaxis for cardiovascular disease. Benefits are in kind, funded by payments to participating programs and institutions. About 2,200 persons were aided in FY 77. Benefits are conditioned on need.

FY 77 Expenditure (est.): **$125,000**

END-STAGE RENAL DISEASE PROGRAM

Department of Health and Environmental Control

Individuals with end-stage renal disease who are indigent and who are not receiving aid from other sources are provided medical services including kidney transplantation, dialysis, hospital care, home care and drugs. Benefits are in kind, funded by payments to hospitals. About 170 persons are aided annually. Benefits are conditioned on need.

FY 77 Expenditure (est.): **$149,000**

CRIPPLED CHILDREN'S CARE PROGRAM AND HEMOPHILIA

Department of Health and Environmental Control

Children under 21 years old with crippling disabilities, deformities, or convertible conditions, and hemophiliacs are provided treatment through diagnosis, medical care, drugs and hospital services. Services include inpatient and outpatient care, home instruction, special education, therapy and psychological care. Benefits are in kind, funded by payments to institutions where service is provided. Over 8,000 children and 90 hemophiliacs are aided annually. Benefits are not directly conditioned on need.

FY 77 Expenditure (est.): **$2,455,000**

South Carolina

ADULT HEALTH—TUBERCULOSIS CONTROL

Department of Health and Environmental Control

Persons with tuberculosis and those at risk of contracting tuberculosis are provided care in community hospitals and treatment facilities. Benefits are in kind, funded partly by payments to participating facilities. Services include testing, drugs and diagnosis. Over 900 persons received treatment and over 1,000 received screening services in FY 77. Benefits are conditioned on need.

FY 77 Expenditure (est.): **$170,000**

PRECARE, SCREENING AND PERSONAL SERVICES

Department of Mental Health

Persons in need who are mentally ill and can be treated outside hospitals are provided services to help reduce the number of admissions to state mental hospitals and to provide treatment alternatives. Services include precare screening, personal medical attention, drugs and group therapy. Benefits are in kind, funded by payments to treatment facilities. Approximately 7,300 persons are aided annually. Benefits are conditioned on need.

FY 77 Expenditure (est.): **$499,000**

COMMUNITY TREATMENT SERVICES

Commission on Alcohol and Drug Abuse

Alcoholics and persons with serious drug problems are provided diagnostic and primary care at local community-based centers. Benefits are in kind and include detoxification services, funded by payments to area hospitals and centers. Approximately 19,000 patient contacts occur annually. Benefits are not conditioned on need.

FY 77 Expenditure (est.): **$227,000**

TUITION GRANTS

Department of Higher Education

Residents of the state, enrolled on a full-time basis at certain independent colleges and universities within the state are provided tuition subsidies in order for them to pursue a college education. Benefits are in the form of cash, funded by payments directly to participating institutions. The maximum grant is $1,600 per year. Approximately 6,700 students received aid in FY 77. Benefits are conditioned on need.

FY 77 Expenditure (est.): **$7,217,000**

PERSONAL INCOME TAX PROVISIONS

Tax Commission

Low-Income Exemption. Indirect financial assistance is provided to persons whose annual gross income is less than $800. Benefits are in the form of tax relief, funded by allowing the individual total exemption of his income from personal income taxation. Benefits are conditioned on need.

Senior Citizen Low-Income Exemption. Indirect financial assistance is provided to persons aged 65 and older whose annual income is less than $2,800 for a single person and $4,000 for a married couple. Benefits are in the form of tax relief, funded by allowing the individual a total exemption of his income from personal income taxation. Benefits are conditioned on need.

Public Employees' Retirement Income Exemption. Indirect financial assistance is provided to certain public employees who receive pensions or other retirement income. Benefits are in the form of tax relief, funded by allowing the taxpayer to exempt from personal income taxation the income received from teachers', city employees' or state employees' retirement funds. Benefits are not directly conditioned on need.

Disability Exemption. Indirect financial assistance is provided to taxpayers with mentally or physically disabled dependents. Benefits are in the form of tax relief, funded by allowing the taxpayer an additional $800 exemption from his income subject to personal income taxation. Benefits are not directly conditioned on need.

TENNESSEE

Population: 4,299,000

Total State and Local Expenditures
for all Purposes:
$4,266,000,000

MAJOR FEDERALLY ENABLED
INCOME TRANSFER PROGRAMS
FY 77 Expenditures (est.)

Program	State	Local
Aid to Families with Dependent Children	$31,890,000	$ 0
Medicaid	69,860,000	0
Social Services	10,020,000	0

AGED TEACHERS' PENSIONS

Department of Education

Aged teachers who are not covered by the teachers' retirement system are provided monthly cash payments to replace earnings lost through retirement. Benefits are paid directly to the beneficiary in the form of cash, without any restriction on its use. Benefits are not directly conditioned on need.

FY 77 Expenditure (est.): **$2,764,000**

CONSOLIDATED RETIREMENT SYSTEM

Treasury Department

Employees of the state and its political subdivisions (including teachers and elected or appointed officials) who retire at age 60 with at least four years of service, or regardless of age with 30 years of service, and their dependents are provided with financial assistance to replace income lost through retirement. Benefits are paid directly to the beneficiary in the form of cash without any restriction on its use. Payments average $251 per month. Some 26,668 individuals benefit from this program. Members contribute five percent of salary on which Social Security is also deducted plus 5.5 percent of any additional amount. The state contributes 7.9 percent (17 percent for teachers). Benefits are not directly conditioned on need.

FY 77 Expenditure (est.): **$82,454,000**

Benefits paid total $80,400,000.
Administrative costs total $2,054,000.
State contributions total $116,306,000.

HOMEOWNERSHIP MORTGAGE LOAN PROGRAM

Tennessee Housing Development Agency

Low and moderate income persons are provided loans for the purchase of homes. Benefits are in the form of favorable credit terms for persons with annual family incomes of $12,000-$16,000 from all sources. About 1,000 households were aided in FY 77. Benefits are conditioned on need.

FY 77 Expenditure (est.): **$20,897,000**

This amount includes administrative costs and loan funding.

PROPERTY TAX RELIEF FOR THE ELDERLY AND DISABLED HOMEOWNERS

Department of Revenue

Indirect financial assistance is provided to taxpayers, 65 years and older, and to those permanently and totally disabled, whose annual income does not exceed $4,800. Benefits are in the form of tax relief, funded by means of a tax rebate equal to the state and local property taxes paid on the first $5,000 of assessed value of the taxpayer's residence. About 100,000 elderly and disabled homeowners benefit yearly. Benefits are conditioned on need.

FY 77 Expenditure (est.): **$4,000,000**

PROPERTY TAX RELIEF FOR DISABLED VETERANS

Department of Revenue

Indirect financial assistance is provided to veterans with severe service-related disabilities such as paraplegia or total blindness, or to their surviving spouses. Benefits are in the form of tax relief, funded by means of an exemption allowed from local property taxes on the first $25,000 of assessed value of the taxpayer's residence. The state reimburses localities for lost tax revenues. Only a few hundred veterans benefit yearly. Benefits are not directly conditioned on need.

FY 77 Expenditure (est.): **$60,000**

WORKERS' COMPENSATION PROGRAM

Department of Labor

Workers injured or disabled on the job, as well as the surviving dependents of workers who die as a result of such injury, are provided financial assistance both as compensation for lost wages and to pay for the cost of any required medical or rehabilitative care. Benefits are in the form of cash payments, funded by means of a state-regulated private insurance program to which each covered employer must contribute a percentage of payroll determined by the employer's experience rating and industrial classification. Beneficiaries received two-thirds of normal wages, up to a maximum weekly compensation benefit of $100. These benefits may be received for the total period of disability and the total amount of benefits one may receive is $40,000. In addition, a funeral allowance of $750 is provided for workers who die on the job. Approximately 22,000 workers and survivors were aided weekly in FY 77. Benefits are not directly conditioned on need.

FY 77 Expenditure (est.): **$81,397,000**

GENERAL ASSISTANCE PROGRAM

Department of Human Resources

Maintenance payments, short-term or emergency aid to cover the costs of food, shelter, clothing and other items of daily living are to be made to resident individuals, if unemployable and to couples and families with children without an employable member. (Emergency assistance is also available to nonresident individuals.) Benefits accrue to the beneficiary through vendor payments to the supplier of goods and services (including medical care). Payments are in amounts varying according to each beneficiary's needs. Benefits are funded by appropriations to the administering local welfare agencies from local revenues. A monthly average of over 5,000 recipients (in some 2,500 cases) are aided. The average benefit is $25 per individual. Benefits are conditioned on need.

FY 77 Expenditure (est.): **$1,800,000**

BOARD AND CARE CONTRIBUTIONS

Department of Human Services

Children not receiving Federal public assistance, who cannot remain in their homes because of abuse or neglect, are provided placement and care at homes or home care facilities within the state. Benefits are in kind, funded by grants to placement areas. Over 2,400 children are aided monthly. Benefits are not conditioned on need.

FY 77 Expenditure (est.): **$7,459,000**

Of the above amount, $2,323,000 are Federal funds.

DISEASE CONTROL AND ADMINISTRATION

Department of Public Health

Those who suffer from communicable diseases, tuberculosis or chronic diseases are provided screening services and treatment. Benefits are in kind, funded by grants to the various programs. Services include immunization, venereal disease control, rabies control and screening services. Over 120,000 persons were screened and 4,900 patients treated in FY 77. Benefits are conditioned on need.

FY 77 Expenditure (est.): **$3,287,000**

CHRONIC RENAL DISEASE

Department of Public Health

Victims of chronic renal disease are provided treatment, preventive services and financial assistance to help combat the effects of the disease. Benefits are in kind and in cash, paid directly to participating hospitals. Approximately 325 persons received dialysis treatment and 25 obtained kidney transplants in FY 77. Benefits are not directly conditioned on need.

FY 77 Expenditure (est.): **$652,000**

DEVELOPMENTAL CENTERS—MENTAL RETARDATION

Department of Social and Health Services

Mentally retarded persons are provided developmental services including personal care and housing so that they might adapt to society. Emphasized services are those that develop physical, emotional, intellectual and social skills. Benefits are in kind, funded by state grants to three centers at Arlington, Clover and Greece Valley. About 2,200 persons are aided annually. Benefits are not directly conditioned on need.

FY 77 Expenditure (est.): **$6,200,000**

COMMUNITY MENTAL RETARDATION PROGRAM

Department of Mental Health

Mentally retarded people are provided care and self-help training, on an outpatient basis, in order to prevent institutionalization. Benefits are in kind, funded by state grants to non-profit organizations. About 700 persons were aided in FY 77. Benefits are not directly conditioned on need.

FY 77 Expenditure (est.): **$3,750,000**

SERVICES FOR THE BLIND

Department of Human Services

Blind people are provided rehabilitation, employment and medical aid, in order to alleviate and improve their condition. Benefits are in the form of cash compensation for work performed and in kind, funded by grants to workshops and clinics. Over 2,600 blind persons received vocational rehabilitation services in FY 77, while about 8,900 obtained preventive treatment. Benefits are not conditioned on need.

FY 77 Expenditure (est.): **$1,293,000**

STUDENT AID

Student Assistance Corporation

Students attending higher education institutions are provided financial assistance to cover the cost of tuition, books and daily living expenses at college. Benefits are in the form of scholarships, grants and loans, funded by payments to the higher education institution. Almost 3,000 students were aided in FY 77. Benefits are conditioned, in part, on need.

FY 77 Expenditure (est.): **$2,740,000**

Of the above amount, $990,000 are Federal funds.

PERSONAL INCOME TAX PROVISIONS

Department of Revenue

Low-income Exemption. Indirect financial assistance is provided to persons whose total stock and bond dividend income does not exceed $25. Benefits are in the form of tax relief, funded by allowing the individual a total exemption of such dividends from state taxation of stock and bond income. Benefits are not conditioned on need.

Senior Citizen Exemption. Indirect financial assistance is provided to senior citizens, aged 65 and older, whose total annual income, including disability pensions, Social Security payments, Railroad Retirement benefits, etc., is under $4,800 for single persons and under $6,000 for a married couple. Benefits are in the form of tax relief, funded by allowing the individual a total exemption of stock and bond income from state taxation of stock and bond dividends. Benefits are conditioned on need.

Exemption for Blind Taxpayers. Indirect financial assistance is provided to blind persons. Benefits are in the form of tax relief, funded by allowing the individual a total exemption of his stock and bond income from state taxation of stock and bond dividends. Benefits are not directly conditioned on need.

TEXAS

Population: 12,830,000

Total State and Local Expenditures
for all Purposes:
$12,873,000,000

MAJOR FEDERALLY ENABLED
INCOME TRANSFER PROGRAMS
FY 77 Expenditures (est.)

Program	State	Local
Aid to Families with Dependent Children	$ 46,750,000	$ 0
Medicaid	284,610,000	0
Social Services	33,020,000	2,560,000

TEACHERS' RETIREMENT SYSTEM

Employees' Retirement System Administration

Full-time teachers of the state's public schools and universities (who do not participate in another retirement system) who retire at age 65 with at least ten years of service, or at age 60 with 20 years of service, and their dependents are provided with financial assistance to replace income lost through retirement. Benefits are paid directly to the beneficiary in the form of cash without any restriction on its use. Payments average $289 per month. Some 60,741 individuals benefit from this program. Members contribute six percent of salary while the state matches this with six percent. Benefits are not directly conditioned on need.

FY 77 Expenditure (est.): **$215,043,000**

Benefits paid total $210,503,000.
Administrative costs total $4,540,000.
State contributions total $189,742,000.

JUDICIAL RETIREMENT SYSTEM

Employees' Retirement System Administration

Judges of the state courts who retire at age 65 with at least ten years of service, or regardless of age with 24 years of service, and their dependents are provided with financial assistance to replace income lost through retirement. Benefits are paid directly to the beneficiary in the form of cash without any restriction on its use. Payments average $1,324 per month. Some 140 individuals benefit from this program. Members contribute six percent of salary, while the state contributes an amount appropriated out of the state's general revenue fund.

FY 77 Expenditure (est.): **$2,409,500**

Benefits paid total $2,394,000.
Administrative costs total $15,500.

STATE EMPLOYEES' RETIREMENT SYSTEM

Employees' Retirement System Administration

Full-time employees of the state and elected officials who retire at age 60 with at least ten years of service and their dependents are provided with financial assistance to replace income lost through retirement. Benefits are paid directly to the beneficiary in the form of cash without any restriction on its use. Payments average $200 per month. Some 12,701 individuals benefit from this program. Members contribute six percent of compensation (salary plus benefits) while the state contributes eight percent. Benefits are not directly conditioned on need.

FY 77 Expenditure (est.): **$39,788,000**

Benefits paid total $38,397,000.
Administrative costs total $1,391,000.
State contributions total $75,321,000.

HOMESTEAD EXEMPTION

Office of the Comptroller

Indirect financial assistance is provided to residents whose property value does not exceed $10,000 and who use the property as a residence, or whose rural property does not exceed 200 acres (100 acres for a single person). Benefits are in the form of tax relief, funded by means of an exemption from county property taxation allowed on the first $3,000 of assessed value. Over two million homeowners benefit yearly. Benefits are not conditioned on need.

FY 77 Expenditure (est.): **$3,000,000**

ADDITIONAL HOMESTEAD EXEMPTION FOR SENIOR CITIZENS

Office of the Comptroller

Indirect financial assistance is provided to persons 65 years and older owning a residence homestead. Benefits are in the form of tax relief, funded by either an exemption from local property taxes allowed on at least an additional $3,000 of assessed value of the taxpayer's residence or by the option to defer tax payments until the property is sold or the owner dies. This program is adopted by local jurisdictions and administered by the local tax assessor who shall determine eligibility. Over 400,000 persons receive benefits yearly. Benefits are not directly conditioned on need.

FY 77 Expenditure (est.): **$50,000,000**

PROPERTY TAX EXEMPTIONS FOR SURVIVING SPOUSE OR CHILD OF THOSE DECEASED ON ACTIVE DUTY

Office of the Comptroller

Indirect financial assistance is provided to surviving spouses or children of persons who died while on active duty in the Armed Forces. Benefits are in the form of tax relief, funded by means of an exemption from all property taxation allowed on $2,500 of the assessed value of the spouse's or child's property. Some 5,000 survivors benefit yearly. Benefits are not directly conditioned on need.

FY 77 Expenditure (est.): **$500,000**

PROPERTY TAX EXEMPTIONS FOR DISABLED VETERANS

Office of the Comptroller

Indirect financial assistance is provided to veterans with service-related disabilities and to their surviving spouses or children. Benefits are in the form of tax relief, funded by means of an exemption from all property taxation allowed on the assessed value of the taxpayer's property. The amount of the exemption is based on the extent of the disability (10-100 percent) and ranges from $1,500 to $3,000 of assessed value. Veterans 65 years or older with at least a ten percent disability are entitled to the maximum exemption. Over 25,000 veterans and their survivors benefit yearly. Benefits are not directly conditioned on need.

FY 77 Expenditure (est.): **$10,000,000**

WORKERS' COMPENSATION PROGRAM

Attorney General's Office

Workers injured or disabled on the job, as well as the surviving dependents of workers who die as a result of such injury, are provided financial assistance both as compensation for lost wages and to pay for the cost of any required medical or rehabilitative care. Benefits are in the form of cash payments funded by means of a state-regulated private insurance program to which each covered employer must contribute a percentage of payroll determined by the employer's experience rating and industrial classification. Beneficiaries receive two-thirds of normal wages, up to a maximum weekly compensation benefit of $91. These benefits may be received for no more than 401 weeks and the total amount of benefits one may receive is unlimited. In addition, a funeral allowance of $1,250 is provided for workers who die on the job. Approximately 132,000 workers and survivors were aided weekly in FY 77. Benefits are not directly conditioned on need.

FY 77 Expenditure (est.): **$434,655,000**

GENERAL ASSISTANCE PROGRAM

Department of Public Welfare

Maintenance payments, short-term or emergency aid to cover the costs of food, shelter, clothing and other items of daily living are made to resident individuals, if unemployable, and to couples and families with children without an employable member. (Emergency assistance is also available to nonresident individuals). Benefits are made to the beneficiary through vendor payments to the supplier of goods and services (including medical care). Payments are in amounts varying according to each beneficiary's needs. Benefits are funded by appropriations to the administering local welfare agencies from local revenues. A monthly average of 15,000 recipients (in some 7,000 cases) are aided. The average benefit is $25 per individual. Benefits are conditioned on need.

FY 77 Expenditure (est.): **$5,000,000**

PERSONAL HEALTH SERVICES

Department of Health Resources

Personal health services include health care diagnosis and treatment for low-income women, infants and children, health services for crippled children and diagnosis and treatment for persons with chronic kidney disease. Benefits are in kind, funded by state grants to the various service-related programs. Over 13,000 crippled children and 1,855 kidney patients received services in FY 77. The average benefit for all categories was $830. Benefits are conditioned, in part, on need.

FY 77 Expenditure (est.): **$20,500,000**

Of the above amount, $5,500,000 went to the kidney program. Federal Funds are included at varying percentages for some programs.

COMMUNICABLE DISEASE CONTROL

Department of Health Resources

Persons with venereal disease, rabies, Hansen's disease or other communicable diseases are provided medical services in order to prevent the spread of these diseases. Benefits are in kind, funded by payments to local health departments or clinics. Approximately 200,000 persons received services in FY 77. Benefits are not conditioned on need.

FY 77 Expenditure (est.): **$5,310,000**

Of the above amount, $1,500,000 are Federal funds.

CHEST HOSPITALS

Department of Health Resources

Persons with tuberculosis and chronic respiratory disease are provided inpatient and outpatient treatment at three chest hospitals: East Texas, San Antonio and Harlingen State. Benefits are in kind, funded by grants directly to the hospitals. Over 400 persons were aided daily in FY 77, at an average cost of $85 per patient per day. Benefits are not conditioned on need.

FY 77 Expenditure (est.): **$15,600,000**

CHRONIC HOME DIALYSIS CENTER

Public Education Agency

To ensure that persons with serious kidney disease receive life-sustaining treatment at the lowest possible cost, this program pays the renal disease facility at the University of Texas Medical Branch at Galveston for medical and surgical services. Benefits are in kind and are aimed at procedures such as home dialysis and transplantation. Approximately 2,400 persons received benefits under this program in FY 77. Benefits are not directly conditioned on need.

FY 77 Expenditure (est.): **$1,087,000**

TUBERCULOSIS CONTROL

Department of Health Resources

People with tuberculosis, or at risk of contracting the disease, are provided treatment, drugs and diagnosis at outpatient clinics and health departments. Benefits are in kind, funded by state payments to participating hospitals. Over 2,300 persons were aided in FY 77. Benefits are not conditioned on need.

FY 77 Expenditure (est.): **$7,098,000**

VISUALLY HANDICAPPED CHILDREN'S SERVICES

Department of Health, Welfare and Rehabilitation

Blind children are provided family and individual counseling and sight restoration services. Benefits are in kind, funded by grants to families. Almost 6,600 visually handicapped children were aided in FY 77. Benefits are not directly conditioned on need.

FY 77 Expenditure (est.): **$1,061,000**

Of the above amount, $384,000 are Federal funds.

CLIENT SERVICES FOR THE HEARING-IMPAIRED

Texas Rehabilitation Commission

Persons with hearing impairment are provided services such as job placement, counseling, medical care, prescription drugs and education. Benefits are in kind, funded by grants to various service programs. Over 700 persons were aided in FY 77 at an average cost of over $800 per person. Benefits are not conditioned on need.

FY 77 Expenditure (est.): **$626,000**

HOSPITALS FOR THE MENTALLY ILL

Department of Mental Health and Mental Retardation

Mentally ill persons are provided nonresidential treatment, education and rehabilitation services at institutions for the mentally ill. Benefits are in kind, funded by grants to participating hospitals sponsoring programs. Over 6,100 individuals were aided at an average daily cost of $45 per person. Benefits are not directly conditioned on need.

FY 77 Expenditure (est.): **$4,152,000**

ALCOHOL AND DRUG ABUSE

Department of Community Affairs

Alcoholics and drug abusers are provided outpatient and other services including detoxification, counseling and rehabilitation. Benefits are in kind, funded by grants to contractors, private or public, who provide services. Over 10,000 persons were aided in FY 77. Benefits are not conditioned on need.

FY 77 Expenditure (est.): **$6,822,000**

STATE CENTERS FOR HUMAN DEVELOPMENT

Department of Mental Health and Mental Retardation

Mentally retarded persons are provided nonresidential treatment, education and rehabilitation at three state centers for human development. Benefits are in kind, funded by grants to these centers. Approximately 350 persons were aided in FY 77. Benefits are not directly conditioned on need.

FY 77 Expenditure (est.): **$5,081,000**

SCHOOLS FOR THE MENTALLY RETARDED

Department of Mental Health and Mental Retardation

Mentally retarded persons are provided nonresidential treatment, education and rehabilitation services at 14 state schools. Benefits are in kind, funded by grants to these schools. Over 10,600 person were aided in FY 77 at an average cost of $37 per person daily. Benefits are not directly conditioned on need.

FY 77 Expenditure (est.): **$3,819,000**

TUITION EQUALIZATION GRANT

Department of Education

Undergraduate residents, in need, enrolled at private colleges within the state are provided financial assistance in order to make up the difference in tuition costs between private and state institutions. Benefits are in the form of cash, paid directly to institutions. Almost 20,000 students received aid in FY 77 at an average cost of $533 per student. The maximum award is $600. Benefits are conditioned on need.

FY 77 Expenditure (est.): **$9,000,000**

HINSON—HAZLEWOOD STUDENT LOAN

Department of Education

Residents with demonstrable need are provided long-term low-interest loans for tuition and other college expenses to permit them to pursue a higher education. Benefits are in the form of favorable credit terms, repaid at seven percent interest. About 12,000 students are aided annually at an average of about $500 per loan. Benefits are conditioned on need.

FY 77 Expenditure (est.): **$12,044,000**

VIRGINIA

Population: 5,135,000

Total State and Local Expenditures
for all Purposes:
$5,672,000,000

MAJOR FEDERALLY ENABLED
INCOME TRANSFER PROGRAMS
FY 77 Expenditures (est.)

Program	State	Local
Aid to Families with Dependent Children	$ 62,290,000	$3,510,000
Medicaid	103,930,000	0
Social Services	5,080,000	8,370,000

OPTIONAL STATE SUPPLEMENTATION FOR SSI

Department of Welfare

The aged, over 65 years old, the blind and the disabled are provided cash supplements to their SSI benefits for basic needs. Basic needs are food, shelter, clothing, utilities and daily living necessities. Benefits are provided to eligible persons living in licensed homes for the aged or domiciliary institutions. Benefits average $72 monthly for individuals and vary for other categories and may be lower depending on the cost of the facility. Benefits are in the form of direct cash payments, funded 62.5 percent by the state and 37.5 percent by localities. Payments are administered by the state; eligibility is determined at local offices of the state Department of Welfare. Over 2,000 individuals are aided monthly. Benefits are conditioned on need.

FY 77 Expenditure (est.): **$1,680,000**

PUBLIC EMPLOYEES' RETIREMENT SYSTEM

Treasury Department

Full-time employees of the state and its political subdivisions who retire at age 65, or at age 60 with 30 years of service, and their dependents are provided with financial assistance to replace income lost through retirement. Benefits are paid directly to the beneficiary in the form of cash without any restriction on its use. Payments range from $420 to $1,250 per month. Some 27,000 individuals benefit from this program. Members contribute five percent of salary while the state's contribution is actuarily determined. Benefits are not directly conditioned on need.

FY 77 Expenditure (est.): **$101,000,000**

Benefits paid total $99,000,000.
Administrative costs total $2,000,000.
State contributions total $76,500,000.

PROPERTY TAX EXEMPTION OR DEFERRAL

Department of Taxation

Indirect financial assistance is provided to persons 65 years and older and to permanently and totally disabled persons. Counties, cities and towns have the option of providing either deferrals or exemptions on local property taxes. Each locality must decide the eligibility criteria for applicants; the maximums set by the state are $11,000 combined annual income and a net worth of $35,000 or less. Approximately 25,000 persons were aided in FY 76 (the last year for which data are available) at an average of $140 each. Benefits are conditioned, in part, on need.

FY 77 Expenditure (est.): **$3,300,000**

WORKERS' COMPENSATION PROGRAM

Industrial Commission

Workers injured or disabled on the job, as well as the surviving dependents of workers who die as a result of such injury, are provided financial assistance both as compensation for lost wages and to pay for the cost of any required medical or rehabilitative care. Benefits are in the form of cash payments, funded by means of a state-regulated private insurance program to which each covered employer must contribute a percentage of payroll determined by the employer's experience rating and industrial classification. Beneficiaries receive two-thirds of normal wages, up to a maximum weekly compensation benefit of $175. These benefits may be received for no more than 500 weeks and the total amount of benefits one may receive is unlimited. In addition, a funeral allowance of $1,000 is provided for workers who die on the job. Approximately 14,000 workers and survivors were aided in FY 77. Benefits are not directly conditioned on need.

FY 77 Expenditure (est.): **$88,323,000**

GENERAL ASSISTANCE PROGRAM

Department of Welfare

Short-term assistance or emergency aid to cover the costs of food, shelter, clothing and other items of daily living are made to unemployable or temporarily unemployable individuals, couples, families with children and widows of Confederate veterans (in the form of pensions). Benefits are paid directly to the beneficiary in the form of cash without any restrictions on its use or through vendor payments (to the suppliers of goods and services including medical care). Employable persons must register for work. Payments are in amounts varying according to each beneficiary's needs as determined under state law. Benefits are funded by grants to the administering local welfare agencies. This program is financed by state and local funds. Each month an average of some 11,567 recipients (in some 7,769 cases) are aided. The average monthly benefit per recipient is $76 (per case, the average is $113). Benefits are conditioned on need.

FY 77 Expenditure (est.): **$10,470,000**

TUBERCULOSIS PREVENTION AND CONTROL

Department of Health

Persons with tuberculosis or at risk of having tuberculosis are provided medical treatment, drugs and x-ray testing at chest clinics and hospitals across the state. Benefits are in kind, funded by payments to regional clinics and facilities. About 700 persons received treatment in FY 77. Benefits are not directly conditioned on need.

FY 77 Expenditure (est.): **$790,000**

MENTAL RETARDATION—COMMUNITY SERVICES

Department of Mental Health and Mental Retardation

Mentally retarded persons are provided various community services in order to help them function within society. Benefits are primarily in kind, funded by payments to community centers. Services include adult activity centers, recreational and residential facilities, mental training and an infant stimulation program. About 6,000 persons can utilize these services at capacity, but the actual number varies during the year. Benefits are not directly conditioned on need.

FY 77 Expenditure (est.): **$3,951,000**

CARE AND TRAINING OF THE MENTALLY RETARDED

Department of Human Resources

Mentally retarded children and adults are provided short-term training, education and health care at the Northern Virginia Training Center. Benefits are primarily in kind, funded by payments to the center. Services include sheltered workshops, feeding programs and related activities. About 280 persons are treated annually, almost 90 of them on an outpatient basis. About 50 percent of all persons treated are severely retarded. Benefits are not directly conditioned on need.

FY 77 Expenditure (est.): **$2,403,000**

CARE AND TRAINING OF THE MENTALLY RETARDED

Department of Human Resources

Mentally retarded children and adults are provided short-term training, education and health care at the South Eastern Virginia Training Center. Benefits are primarily in kind, funded by payments to the center. Services include sheltered workshops, feeding programs and related activities. About 220 persons are aided annually, almost 60 of them on an outpatient basis. Benefits are not directly conditioned on need.

FY 77 Expenditure (est.): **$1,949,000**

TUITION ASSISTANCE GRANT AND LOAN PROGRAM

Department of Higher Education

Undergraduate students, attending Virginia's private institutions of higher education, are provided financial assistance in order to reduce the tuition gap between public and private institutions. Benefits are in the form of cash (all students received $400) and favorable credit terms, funded through the institutions. Over 8,500 students received benefits in FY 77. Benefits are not conditioned on need.

FY 77 Expenditure (est.): **$3,422,000**

COLLEGE SCHOLARSHIP ASSISTANCE PROGRAM

Department of Higher Education

Undergraduate students who can demonstrate financial need are provided financial assistance to cover the costs of attendance at Virginia's public and private institutions of higher education. Benefits are in the form of cash, paid directly to institutions. Over 7,000 students were aided in FY 77. The average award was $260. Benefits are determined from the submission of a Virginia Financial Aid Form and therefore are conditioned on need.

FY 77 Expenditure (est.): **$1,835,000**

NURSING SCHOLARSHIPS AND LOANS

Department of Health

Resident undergraduate students, as well as registered nurses seeking postgraduate degrees in nursing, are provided scholarships and loans at institutions of higher education in Virginia. Benefits are in the form of cash and favorable credit terms, funded through the institutions. Loans can be repaid through service in Virginia's hospitals. Some 150 individuals received benefits in FY 77 at a maximum of $4,000 annually for graduate students and $2,000 for undergraduates. This program also funds 12 scholarships at $500 per year for dental hygienists. Benefits are conditioned on need, residency and merit.

FY 77 Expenditure (est.): **$105,000**

AFFIRMATIVE ACTION

Department of Higher Education

Undergraduate minority students, in their junior year of college, who are interested in pursuing a doctoral degree, are provided financial support in order to attend one of Virginia's comprehensive, state-supported, doctoral level institutions. Benefits are in the form of cash, paid to students in the form of a $90 per week stipend during the summer months. About 20 individuals received this award in FY 77 at an average of $1,050 per person. Benefits are not conditioned on need.

FY 77 Expenditure (est.): **$46,000**

Virginia

PERSONAL INCOME TAX PROVISIONS

Department of Taxation

Low-Income Exemption. Indirect financial assistance is provided to persons whose annual gross income does not exceed scheduled limits ranging from $1,900 for single persons under age 65 ($2,900 if 65 or over) to $4,500 for a married couple in which both members are aged 65 or older. Benefits are in the form of tax relief, funded by allowing the individual a total exemption of his income from personal income taxation. Benefits are conditioned on need.

Deduction of Public Employees' Pensions. Indirect financial assistance is provided to certain public employees who receive pensions or other retirement income. Benefits are in the form of tax relief, funded by allowing the taxpayer to deduct from his adjusted gross income, subject to personal income taxation, the payments received from such pensions. Benefits are not directly conditioned on need.

WASHINGTON

Population: 3,658,000

Total State and Local Expenditures
for all Purposes:
$5,672,000,000

MAJOR FEDERALLY ENABLED
INCOME TRANSFER PROGRAMS
FY 77 Expenditures (est.)

Program	State	Local
Aid to Families with Dependent Children	$ 87,790,000	$ 0
Medicaid	128,190,000	0
Social Services	10,620,000	0

OPTIONAL STATE SUPPLEMENTATION FOR SSI

Department of Social and Health Services

The aged, over 65 years old, the blind and the disabled are provided cash supplements to their SSI benefits for basic and special needs. Basic needs are food, shelter, clothing, utilities and daily living necessities. Special needs are those not provided for through monthly or optional SSI payments and include food for seeing-eye dogs, utility charges, meals and board. Benefits are provided to eligible persons according to the geographic areas in which they live, who are living independently, in the household of another, with ineligible spouse or essential person, and with ineligible spouse or essential person in the household of another. Benefits are $40 for individuals and $45 for couples living independently and vary for other categories. Benefits are in the form of direct cash payments, funded wholly by the state. Payments are administered by the Federal government; eligibility Is determined at Social Security district offices. Over 43,000 individuals are aided monthly. Benefits are conditioned on need.

FY 77 Expenditure (est.): **$17,028,000**

VOLUNTEER FIREMEN'S RELIEF AND PENSION FUND

Board for Volunteer Firemen

Volunteer firefighters who retire between the ages of 60 and 65 with 25 years of service are provided with financial assistance to replace income lost through retirement. Benefits are paid directly to the beneficiary in the form of cash without any restriction on its use. Payments, depending upon length of service, average $65 per month. Some 573 individuals benefit from this program. Members contribute $20 per year. The state contributes 40 percent of the state tax on fire insurance premiums. Benefits are not directly conditioned on need.

FY 77 Expenditure (est.): **$625,800**

An additional amount not in excess of $50,000 is used to
    pay medical expenses of retirees.
Administrative costs total $41,800.
State contributions are used for pensions, survivors'
    benefits and medical coverage.

LAW ENFORCEMENT OFFICERS' AND FIREFIGHTERS' RETIREMENT SYSTEM

Division of Retirement Systems

Law enforcement officers and firefighters of the state who retire at age 50 with at least five years of service and their dependents are provided with financial assistance to replace income lost through retirement. Benefits are paid directly to the beneficiary in the form of cash without any restriction on its use. Payments average $663 for police and $868 for firefighters per month. Some 2,145 individuals benefit from this program. Members contribute six percent of salary while the state contributes six percent plus an additional .1 percent for administrative cost. Benefits are not directly conditioned on need.

FY 77 Expenditure (est.): **$30,189,500**

Benefits paid total $29,812,500.
Administrative costs total $377,000.

STATE PATROL RETIREMENT SYSTEM

Division of Retirement Systems

Members of the state patrol who retire at age 55 with five years of service and their dependents are provided with financial assistance to replace income lost through retirement. Benefits are paid directly to the beneficiary in the form of cash without any restriction on its use. Payments average $650 per month. Some 182 individuals benefit from this program. Members contribute 7.4 percent of salary while the state makes yearly contributions by appropriation. Benefits are not directly conditioned on need.

FY 77 Expenditure (est.): **$1,400,000**

Benefits paid total $1,400,000.

TEACHERS' RETIREMENT SYSTEM

Division of Retirement Systems

Teachers of the public schools who retire at age 60 with at least five years of service, at age 55 with 25 years of service, or regardless of age with 30 years of service, and their dependents are provided with financial assistance to replace income lost through retirement. Benefits are paid directly to the beneficiary in the form of cash without any restriction on its use. Payments average $390 per month. Some 15,000 individuals benefit from this program. Members contribute six percent of salary. The state contributes an amount which is actuarily determined. Benefits are not directly conditioned on need.

FY 77 Expenditure (est.): **$46,370,000**

Benefits paid total $45,008,000.
Administrative costs total $1,362,000.
State contributions total $37,037,000.

JUDGES' RETIREMENT SYSTEM

Division of Retirement Systems

Judges who retire at age 62 with at least 12 years of service and their dependents are provided with financial assistance to replace income lost through retirement. Benefits are paid directly to the beneficiary in the form of cash without any restriction on its use. Payments average $720 per month. Some 37 individuals benefit from this program. Members contribute about 7.5 percent of salary and the state matches this contribution with 7.5 percent. Benefits are not directly conditioned on need.

FY 77 Expenditure (est.): **$320,000**

Benefits paid total $319,000.
Administrative costs total $1,000.
State contributions total $584,000.

JUDICIAL RETIREMENT SYSTEM

Division of Retirement Systems

Judges who retire at age 60 with at least ten years of service and their dependents are provided with financial assistance to replace income lost through retirement. Benefits are paid directly to the beneficiary in the form of cash without any restriction on its use. Payments average $1,800 per month. Some 38 individuals benefit from this program. Members contribute about 7.5 percent of salary while the state matches this with 7.5 percent. Benefits are not directly conditioned on need.

FY 77 Expenditure (est.): **$829,800**

Benefits paid total $820,800.
Administrative costs total $9,000.

PUBLIC EMPLOYEES' RETIREMENT SYSTEM

Division of Retirement Systems

Full-time state employees who retire at age 60 with at least five years of service, at age 55 with 25 years of service, or regardless of age with 30 years of service, and their dependents are provided with financial assistance to replace income lost through retirement. Benefits are paid directly to the beneficiary in the form of cash without any restriction on its use. Payments average $257 per month. Some 28,590 individuals benefit from this program. Members contribute five percent of salary (after July this percentage varies.) The state contributes about six percent. Benefits are not directly conditioned on need.

FY 77 Expenditure (est.): **$88,172,000**

Benefits paid total $87,290,000.
Administrative costs total $882,000.

SENIOR CITIZEN PROPERTY TAX RELIEF

Department of Revenue

Indirect financial assistance is provided to senior citizens 62 years and older and to persons disabled and retired by reason of their disability with incomes under $8,000. Benefits are in the form of tax relief, funded by allowing eligible persons a range of exemptions on their local property taxes, depending on total household income. Approximately 77,560 persons were aided in FY 77 at an average of $130 per person. Benefits are conditioned, in part, on need.

FY 77 Expenditure (est.): **$10,500,000**

WORKERS' COMPENSATION PROGRAM

Department of Labor and Industries

Workers injured or disabled on the job, as well as the surviving dependents of workers who die as a result of such injury, are provided financial assistance both as compensation for lost wages and to pay for the cost of any required medical or rehabilitative care. Benefits are in the form of cash payments, funded by means of a state-administered insurance program to which each covered employer must contribute a percentage of payroll determined by the employer's experience rating and industrial classification. Beneficiaries receive 60 to 75 percent of normal wages, according to the number of dependents, up to a maximum weekly compensation benefit of $163. These benefits may be received for the total period of disability and the total amount of benefits one may receive is unlimited. In addition, a funeral allowance of $1,000 is provided for workers who die on the job. Approximately 33,000 workers and survivors were aided weekly in FY 77. Benefits are not directly conditioned on need.

FY 77 Expenditure (est.): **$196,411,000**

GENERAL ASSISTANCE PROGRAM

Department of Social and Health Services

Maintenance payments, short-term or emergency aid to cover the costs of food, shelter, clothing and other items of daily living are made to resident individuals, couples, families with children and fathers unemployed due to a strike. Emergency aid is also available to nonresident individuals pending return to their legal place of residence. Benefits are paid directly to the beneficiary in the form of cash without any restrictions on its use. Employable persons must register with the state employment service. Payments are in amounts varying according to each beneficiary's needs as determined under state law. Benefits are funded by grants to the local offices of the state public assistance agency. This program is financed by state funds. Medical care is provided under a state medical assistance program and is not paid from general assistance. Each month some 10,280 recipients (in some 9,234 cases) are aided. The average monthly benefit per recipient is $116; per case, the average is $129. Benefits are conditioned on need.

FY 77 Expenditure (est.): **$14,260,000**

VICTIMS OF CRIME

Department of Social and Health Services

Victims of violent crime are provided financial assistance to compensate for their losses. Benefits are in the form of cash and are determined by the Industrial Insurance Determination Board. Over 2,100 persons received some benefit in FY 77. Benefits are not conditioned on need.

FY 77 Expenditure (est.): **$859,000**

CHILDREN'S PATIENT CARE

Department of Social and Health Services

Children with severe, physically handicapping conditions and those in need of appropriate dental care are provided high quality, comprehensive care, including diagnosis, treatment and therapy. Benefits are in kind, funded by grants to participating hospitals and two state-run dental clinics. Approximately 4,500 crippled children were aided in FY 77, and 1,500 children received dental care. Benefits are conditioned, in part, on need.

FY 77 Expenditure (est.): **$2,700,000**

Of the above amount, $900,000 are Federal funds.

KIDNEY CENTERS

Department of Social and Health Services

Individuals with chronic renal disease are provided medical services including diagnosis, dialysis, hospital care in special centers, and drugs. Benefits are in kind, funded by payments to approved kidney centers. Approximately 120 persons were aided in FY 77 Benefits are conditioned, in part, on need.

FY 77 Expenditure (est.): **$345,000**

Of the above amount, $100,000 are Federal funds

DEVELOPMENTAL DISABILITIES—COMMUNITY SERVICES

Department of Social and Health Services

Physically and mentally handicapped persons are provided comprehensive treatment, rehabilitation and training services at group homes and community clinics. Benefits are in kind, funded by the purchase of services from contracted group homes and clinics. About 3,000 people were treated daily in FY 77. Benefits are not directly conditioned on need.

FY 77 Expenditure (est.): **$4,688,000**

MENTAL HEALTH—COMMUNITY SERVICES

Department of Social and Health Services

Mentally ill and severely disturbed individuals, as well as drug abusers, are provided services on an inpatient and outpatient basis. Benefits are in kind, funded by state grants to various clinics. Over 80,000 cases were treated in FY 77. Benefits are not conditioned on need.

FY 77 Expenditure (est.): **$9,523,000**

ALCOHOLISM PROGRAM

Department of Social and Health Services

Alcoholics are provided services at various centers throughout the state. Benefits are in kind, funded on a contract basis by the state. Services include detoxification, client evaluation, referral and outpatient treatment. Over 11,400 persons are treated annually. Benefits are not conditioned on need.

FY 77 Expenditure (est.): **$4,033,000**

REHABILITATION OF INDUSTRIALLY DISABLED WORKERS

Department of Social and Health Services

Disabled workers are provided restorative treatment at the rehabilitation center for the industrially disabled. Benefits are in kind, in the form of services provided to persons receiving treatment. Services include occupational and manual acts therapy, group therapy and vocational guidance. About 685 persons were totally restored in FY 77. Benefits are not conditioned on need.

FY 77 Expenditure (est.): **$2,042,000**

INSTITUTIONAL REHABILITATION SERVICES

Department of Veterans' Affairs

Indigent aged veterans and their wives or widows are provided rehabilitation services at two veterans' homes. Benefits include medical care, nursing care, counseling and clothing allowances. Over 500 persons received services annually. Benefits are funded by state grants to the homes. Benefits are conditioned on need.

FY 77 Expenditure (est.): **$2,341,000**

STUDENT FINANCIAL AID

Department of Education

College students in need, children of veterans, and blind and disabled students are provided financial aid in order to attend college. Benefits are in the form of cash, funded by grants directly to the institutions. Programs include the State Need Program, Tuition and Fee Waiver, Aid to Blind Students and Aid to Children of Veterans. Over 7,000 students were aided in FY 77. Benefits are conditioned on need.

FY 77 Expenditure (est.): **$3,250,000**

WISCONSIN

Population: 4,651,000

Total State and Local Expenditures
for all Purposes:
$6,147,000,000

MAJOR FEDERALLY ENABLED
INCOME TRANSFER PROGRAMS
FY 77 Expenditures (est.)

Program	State	Local
Aid to Families with Dependent Children	$103,960,000	$ 0
Medicaid	207,860,000	0
Social Services	13,810,000	0

OPTIONAL STATE SUPPLEMENTATION FOR SSI

Department of Health and Social Services

The aged, over 65 years old, the blind and the disabled are provided cash supplements to their SSI benefits for basic and special needs. Basic needs are food, shelter, clothing, utilities and daily living necessities. Special needs are those not provided for through monthly or optional SSI payments and include aid for the developmentally disabled. Benefits are provided to eligible persons living independently, in the household of another, in private medical facilities and in private nonmedical facilities for the mentally retarded. Benefits are $76 for individuals and $109 for couples living independently and vary for other categories. Benefits are in the form of direct cash payments, funded wholly by the state. Payments are administered by the Federal government; eligibility is determined at Social Security district offices. Over 58,500 individuals are aided monthly. Benefits are conditioned on need.

FY 77 Expenditure (est.): **$49,140,000**

TEACHERS' RETIREMENT SYSTEM

Department of Employee Trust Funds

Teachers in the state public schools and universities (except in the city of Milwaukee) who retire at age 65 and their dependents are provided with financial assistance to replace income lost through retirement. Benefits are paid directly to the beneficiary in the form of cash without any restriction on its use. Payments average $170 per month. Some 16,800 individuals benefit from this program. Members contribute five percent of salary while the state contributes 6.9 percent. Benefits are not directly conditioned on need.

FY 77 Expenditure (est.): **$46,263,900**

Benefits paid total $45,130,000.
Administrative costs total $1,133,900.
State contributions total $27,093,000.
A supplemental benefit is paid to members who retired
    before 1974 totaling $5,409,000.

PUBLIC EMPLOYEES' BENEFIT FUND

Department of Employee Trust Funds

Employees of the state and its political subdivisions (except employees of the city and county of Milwaukee) who retire at age 65 (police and firefighters can retire at age 55) and their dependents are provided with financial assistance to replace income lost through retirement. Benefits are paid directly to the beneficiary in the form of cash without any restriction on its use. Payments range from $10 to about $390 per month (average payment is $122). Some 24,691 individuals benefit from this program. Members contribute five percent of salary (except police who contribute six percent and firefighters, eight percent—with no Social Security coverage). An additional ten percent of salary may be contributed but is not matched by the state funds. The state contributes about 6.3 percent (15.2 percent for police and firefighters). Benefits are not directly conditioned on need.

FY 77 Expenditure (est.): **$37,102,300**

Benefits paid total $36,272,000.
Administrative costs total $830,300.
State contributions total $27,093,400.

HOMESTEAD CREDIT

Department of Revenue

Indirect financial assistance is provided to homeowners and renters whose annual household income is less than $9,300. Benefits are in the form of tax relief, funded by means of a credit against state income taxes. For taxpayers whose household income is less than $4,000, the credit equals 80 percent of total property tax (25 percent of rent is set as the tax equivalent). For taxpayers whose household income is more than $4,000, the credit equals 80 percent of the property tax in excess of 15 percent of the income over $4,000. The maximum benefit is $640. Approximately 234,000 persons were aided in FY 77, at an average of $205 each. Benefits are conditioned, in part, on need.

FY 77 Expenditure (est.): **$48,139,000**

Wisconsin

WORKERS' COMPENSATION PROGRAM

Department of Industry, Labor and Human Relations

Workers injured or disabled on the job, as well as the surviving dependents of workers who die as a result of such injury, are provided financial assistance both as compensation for lost wages and to pay for the cost of any required medical or rehabilitative care. Benefits are in the form of cash payments, funded by means of a state-regulated private insurance program to which each covered employer must contribute a percentage of payroll determined by the employer's experience rating and industrial classification. Beneficiaries receive two-thirds of normal wages, up to a maximum weekly compensation benefit of $189. These benefits may be received for the total period of disability and the total amount of benefits one may receive is unlimited. In addition, a funeral allowance of $750 is provided for workers who die on the job. Approximately 13,000 workers and survivors were aided weekly in FY 77. Benefits are not directly conditioned on need.

FY 77 Expenditure (est.): **$91,192,000**

GENERAL ASSISTANCE PROGRAM

Department of Health and Social Services

Maintenance payments, short-term or emergency aid to cover the costs of food, shelter, clothing and other items of daily living are made to individuals, couples, families with children and needy veterans and their families. Benefits are paid directly to the beneficiary in the form of cash without any restrictions on its use. Employable persons must accept work project assignments. Payments are in amounts varying according to each beneficiary's needs as determined under state law. Benefits are funded by grants to local administrating welfare agencies. This program is financed by state and local funds. State funds are restricted to specific purposes. Each month some 9,419 recipients (in some 6,879 cases) are aided. The average monthly benefit per recipient is $93 (per case, the average is $127). Benefits are conditioned on need.

FY 77 Expenditure (est.): **$10,470,000**

EMERGENCY FUEL LOAN PROGRAM

Department of Health and Social Services

Low-income persons with fuel or utility emergencies are provided loans to help meet outstanding bills. Benefits are in the form of credit, funded 75 percent by the state and matched 25 percent by the counties. The maximum loan may not exceed $150 per household per winter. Benefits are conditioned on need. This program is unrelated to the Federal Emergency Energy Program.

FY 77 Expenditure (est.): **$600,000**

KIDNEY DISEASE TRANSFER PROGRAM

Department of Health and Social Services

To ensure that persons with chronic kidney disease receive proper treatment at the lowest possible cost, this program pays participating renal disease facilities the cost of dialysis or kidney transplantation not paid for by other sources (i.e. Medicare, Medicaid and private insurance). Benefits are in kind. Approximately 1,100 persons received benefits in FY 77. Benefits are not conditioned on need.

FY 77 Expenditure (est.): **$1,200,000**

VOCATIONAL REHABILITATION SERVICES

Department of Health and Social Services

Physically or mentally handicapped persons who would benefit from vocational rehabilitation are provided services directed toward increasing their employability. Benefits are in kind, funded by payments to participating service organizations. Over 5,000 persons were aided in FY 77. Benefits are not directly conditioned on need.

FY 77 Expenditure (est.): **$5,479,000**

SUBSIDIZED LOANS TO VIETNAM VETS

Department of Veterans' Affairs

Vietnam-era veterans and their families are provided low-cost loans and mortgages, usually at three percent annual interest. Benefits are in the form of favorable credit terms. Over 4,400 veterans received subsidized loans in FY 77. Benefits are conditioned on need.

FY 77 Expenditure (est.): **$9,805,000**

The above amount represents the value of loans made and administrative costs.

SELF-AMORTIZING LOANS TO VIETNAM VETS

Department of Veterans' Affairs

Vietnam-era veterans and their families are provided loans for housing. Benefits are in the form of favorable credit terms. Approximately 8,200 veterans received loans in FY 77. The average loan was $28,900 for the first mortgage on a veteran's home. Benefits are not conditioned on need.

FY 77 Expenditure (est.): **$207,890,000**

The above amount represents the value of loans made and administrative costs.

MEDICAL AND SUBSISTENCE GRANTS

Department of Veterans' Affairs

Vietnam-era veterans and their dependents are provided emergency medical and subsistence grants, including coverage for medical treatment and/or hospitalization. Benefits are in the form of cash and in kind, paid directly to veterans or to participating hospitals. Approximately 1,000 people receive aid annually. The maximum benefit period is 90 days. Benefits are conditioned on need.

FY 77 Expenditure (est.): **$642,000**

HOME FOR VETERANS

Department of Veterans' Affairs

Non-dishonorably discharged veterans with service-connected disabilities and no adequate means of support, veterans suffering from permanent disabilities and in receipt of disability compensation and certain other such veterans unable to defray the costs of domiciliary care, are provided medical assistance, rehabilitation services and personal maintenance care in the home for veterans. Benefits are in kind, funded principally by payments of salaries and expenses to the personnel assigned to the facility. Over 700 veterans and their families are assisted annually. Benefits are conditioned, in part, on need.

FY 77 Expenditure (est.): **$7,482,000**

EDUCATION GRANTS—VIETNAM VETERANS

Department of Veterans' Affairs

Vietnam-era veterans and their families are given grants for college study on a part-time or full-time basis. Benefits are in the form of cash for tuition, books and living expenses. Approximately 9,000 veterans received benefits in FY 77. The maximum benefit for a married person is $400; for a single person, $200. Grants are renewable for up to four years. Benefits are conditioned on need and satisfactory continuance of studies.

FY 77 Expenditure (est.): **$1,300,000**

286

EDUCATIONAL OPPORTUNITY

Higher Education Aid Board

Members of disadvantaged and minority groups, in order to promote interest in higher education and to increase their enrollment
in postsecondary institutions, are provided financial aid. Benefits
are in the form of cash and in kind, in the form of counseling services. Approximately 7,500 students received aid in FY 77. Benefits
are conditioned on need.

FY 77 Expenditure (est.): **$191,000**

FINANCIAL SUPPORT—HIGHER EDUCATION

Higher Education Aid Board

Students in need of financial aid are provided assistance to pursue
a higher education commensurate with their abilities. Benefits are
in the form of cash, paid directly to institutions. Approximately
8,000 students were aided in FY 77. The maximum grant for tuition
was $1,500. Benefits are conditioned on need.

FY 77 Expenditure (est.): **$8,000,000**

SPECIAL ACADEMIC SUPPORT PROJECTS FOR MINORITY AND DISADVANTAGED STUDENTS

Higher Education Aid Board

In order to support their opportunities for academic success, university students are provided academic aid at the University of Wisconsin. Benefits are in kind and consist of pre-collegiate summer
programs for minority students, as well as information and guidance after they matriculate. Over 6,000 students are aided annually.
Benefits are conditioned on need.

FY 77 Expenditure (est.): **$1,182,000**

PERSONAL INCOME TAX PROVISIONS

Department of Revenue

Low-Income Exemption. Indirect financial assistance is provided to persons whose annual gross income does not exceed scheduled limits ranging from $3,200 for single persons under age 65 and $4,200 for those 65 and older, to $7,200 for married couples in which both members are 65 or older. Benefits are in the form of tax relief, funded by allowing the taxpayer a total exemption of his income from personal income taxation. Benefits are conditioned on need.

Low-Income Allowance. Indirect financial assistance is provided to persons with a total income less than $8,667 (or $9,670 if married and both spouses are aged 65 or older) who do not itemize deductions. Benefits are in the form of tax relief, funded by allowing the taxpayer to deduct, for income tax purposes, a specified amount of income, depending upon total income and the number of dependents. Benefits are conditioned, in part, on need.

Federal Pension Exclusion. Indirect financial assistance is provided to taxpayers aged 62 and older. Benefits are in the form of tax relief, funded by allowing the taxpayer to exclude from income, subject to personal income taxation, the first $1,680 of Federal civil service annuities. However, persons having earned income totaling more than $600 must reduce this exemption on a dollar-for-dollar basis by the amount of such excess over $600. Benefits are not directly conditioned on need.

Public Employees' Retirement Income Exemption. Indirect financial assistance is provided to certain public employees who receive pensions or other retirement income. Benefits are in the form of tax relief, funded by allowing the taxpayer to exempt from his income, subject to personal income taxation, the income received from state pensions or retirement funds. Benefits are not directly conditioned on need.

Head of Household Exemption Credit. Indirect financial assistance is provided to taxpayers who are single and maintain a household with one or more dependents. Benefits are in the form of tax relief, funded by allowing the taxpayer an additional $20 exemption credit against his personal income tax liability. Benefits are not conditioned on need.

INDEX

Index

Health
Alcoholism and Drug Abuse
Cancer
Chronic Disease Control

Index

Index

Index

Index